REPOLITICIZING MANAGEMENT

T0347534

Corporate Social Responsibility Series

Series Editor:
Professor David Crowther, London Metropolitan University, UK

This series aims to provide high quality research books on all aspects of corporate social responsibility including: business ethics, corporate governance and accountability, globalization, civil protests, regulation, responsible marketing and social reporting.

The series is interdisciplinary in scope and global in application and is an essential forum for everyone with an interest in this area.

Also in the series

Repoliticizing Management

A Theory of Corporate Legitimacy

CONOR CRADDEN

Routledge
Taylor & Francis Group

LONDON AND NEW YORK

First published 2005 by Ashgate Publishing

Reissued 2018 by Routledge
2 Park Square, Milton Park, Abingdon, Oxon, OX14 4RN
711 Third Avenue, New York, NY 10017, USA

Routledge is an imprint of the Taylor & Francis Group, an informa business

First issued in paperback 2018

ISBN 13: 978-0-815-39146-3 (hbk)
ISBN 13: 978-1-138-62037-7 (pbk)
ISBN 13: 978-1-351-15028-6 (ebk)

Contents

For Charlotte

Preface

I started thinking about the subjects dealt with in this book more than a dozen years ago, when I was working in the voluntary sector in Britain. The organization where I worked was not a happy one. Despite its having entirely admirable aims and principles, and despite providing services to its users that were in many cases truly impressive, there was a malaise about the central administration that left most of us who worked there feeling angry and demotivated. Certainly, there were some thorny financial and administrative problems that needed to be sorted out, but there was nothing fundamentally wrong with the organization. So why the depression in head office? There were two clues. First of all, the head of the department where I worked would always signal that he was about to give some direction with which we the staff were unlikely to agree by prefacing it with the word 'management': it would be his 'management opinion' that certain changes were necessary; or, he would report that the directors of the organization had made a 'management judgement' on some issue. It was as if he was recognizing that the logic of organizational decision-making was not founded on anything we would accept as valid. The second clue was the way in which the senior staff of the organization would talk about each other. The standard response to any kind of criticism of a manager was 'ah, but he knows the organization in great detail'. This meant that although it may have appeared to us that the person in question was doing something stupid, they were acting according to some esoteric organizational rationality that we, the rank and file, did not understand.

These kinds of statements struck me as symptomatic of a kind of 'closed system' thinking about management. The cause of the malaise seemed to be the fact that arguments founded on common sense and decency had absolutely no impact on the managers of the organization. The sheer frustration of trying to work with managers who insisted that their doors were always open, but who were unable or unwilling to engage with arguments that seemed to be perfectly reasonable, led inevitably to depression, disillusion and anger. On the other hand, those who had accepted the peculiar rationality of the organization appeared to be unable to understand why staff were unhappy. Although it almost defies credibility, the directors were genuinely surprised to find that staff were upset by their decision to impose a pay freeze on all of the organization's employees except themselves. Having promised to engage in consultation on the issue, they were further surprised to discover that there were staff who doubted their sincere intention to listen simply because letters confirming the pay freeze were prepared and sent out in the internal post *during* the principal consultation meeting. Attempts to have them understand the staff perspective were in vain. From the managerial point of view, the reaction of their internal opponents was neither comprehensible nor legitimate. Rather, they were irresponsibly threatening the achievement of the organization's goals.

The experience of attempting to organize staff in opposition to these various (as I saw them) idiocies of management led on to a more academic interest in the employment relationship. Having returned to university part-time to study industrial relations, I was struck by how frequently the idea recurred that relationships within organizations could be conceived in several different, mutually incompatible ways at once. Perhaps even more interesting was the discovery that this idea had less often been framed as a disinterested observation than as an opposition between 'right' and 'wrong' or 'correct' and 'incorrect' ways of thinking about relationships at work. From Frederick Taylor's argument that harmonious relationships in the workplace require a 'mental revolution', to the controversy between Elton Mayo and Clark Kerr about the essential nature of industrial man; from Allan Flanders' insistence that management and unions need to ensure that they properly understand their 'social purpose', to the worker 'commitment' to the managerial worldview claimed by the corporate partisans of human resource management;[1] the historic pattern in the study of work and employment strongly suggested that there was something about organizational contexts that lent itself to the creation of closed systems or circles of inference that, once entered into, gave a meaning and direction to action that was both incomprehensible and unassailable from outside the circle.

I had this half-formed thought in my head as I started to look for theoretical resources to inform some research about the transformation of British industrial relations since the 1960s. Via Terry Eagleton's lucid introduction to the subject of ideology (1991) I came across the work of Jürgen Habermas, and in particular, the idea that in certain circumstances communication can be subject to systematic distortion or restriction. As Eagleton put it,

> If a communicative structure is systematically distorted, then it will tend to present the appearance of normativity and justness. A distortion which is so pervasive tends to cancel all the way through and disappear from sight... A systematically deformed network of communication thus tends to conceal or eradicate the very norms by which it might be judged to be deformed, and so becomes peculiarly invulnerable to critique. In this situation, it becomes impossible to raise within the network the question of its own workings or conditions of possibility, since it has, so to speak, confiscated these inquiries from the outset (1991, p.129).

Two further aspects of Habermas's work made it even more attractive. First, unlike either his Frankfurt School predecessors or poststructuralist contemporaries, Habermas arguably left open the possibility that these distorted systems could be 'straightened out' via radical forms of democracy. Second, language and rational argument were central parts of his analytic scheme. At the time, in the mid-1990s,

---

[1] For useful summaries of the work of these and other writers on organizations see Pugh and Hickson, 1989, Rose, 1975, Kerr, 1964 and Flanders, 1975.

the highest-profile critical approaches to the study of management and organization had followed the 'linguistic turn' in the social sciences, but the exponents of Foucault et al. had been accused of having produced critiques that had little to contribute to the practical project of workers' emancipation. In this light, adopting Habermas's theoretical perspective looked like a good bet.

It quickly became clear, however, that it would not be a simple matter to apply Habermas's theories to the employment relationship. For one thing, this was a social context to which he himself had never given any sustained attention. Aside from a few isolated paragraphs here and there, he had little to say about social action as it occurs within business organizations. Another more serious difficulty was that it was not immediately obvious that the binary oppositions of 'system' and 'lifeworld', and 'strategic' and 'communicative' action could adequately capture the nature of the organizational setting, a theoretical grey area if ever one existed. Nevertheless, I remained convinced that Habermas's analysis was too significant to ignore and set about trying to adapt it for my own purposes.

What I wanted to do was to explain how the trade union movement in the UK had suffered such a precipitate decline between the 1970s and the 1990s. It seemed to me that the principal empirical variables – government hostility to labour, including restrictive legislation, the drift from manufacturing to services and high levels of unemployment – could account only for some of the fall in union membership and influence. I took the view that although these factors were undoubtedly significant, their effect had been strongly reinforced by the unions simply losing the argument. They were, quite straightforwardly, failing to convince employees that union membership and union action were worthwhile. Anecdotal evidence arising from my own experience of union organizing and of talking with union activists and officers suggested that it had indeed become much more difficult to convince employees to join unions, despite the existence of very good empirical reasons to believe that the protection of union organization was more important than ever. To union activists and officers, the case for membership was as strong if not stronger than it had been had been in the 1970s, when workers had taken up membership in unprecedented numbers. However, to an increasing proportion of the workforce, that case was unconvincing. Despite this, trade unionists were remarkably reluctant to move away from traditional types of justification for membership and established forms of union action in- and outside the workplace. My inquiries into union policy development showed that aside from the abandoning of plans to introduce a complex structure of economic planning and industrial democracy – plans that were in any case a radical departure from the traditional aims of labour in Britain – the 1980s and 1990s did not see any fundamental change in the unions' approach.

In fact, there appeared to be another 'closed system' effect in operation, although this time on a much wider scale. On the one hand, the unions' way of thinking about the employment relationship no longer made any sense to government, employers and many workers, even though for most of the post-war period this way of thinking had dominated public policy on industrial relations. Those who were committed to the new policy consensus were unmoved by the constructive and conciliatory attitude adopted by the Trades Union Congress, and refused to engage with its arguments, no matter how well-researched and non-partisan. Indeed, opposition to the view of government and employers was treated as at best suspect and at worst seditious – 'the enemy within' in Mrs Thatcher's phrase. On the other hand, the unions seemed unable to accept that their traditional way of thinking could be, if not wrong, then at least no longer appropriate. What is more, many trade unionists took the view that changing their approach would be tantamount to abandoning the labour movement's most cherished aims and values.

I drew three conclusions from these observations. First, there was an historical dimension to these closed ways of thinking about organization and employment. It was obvious that even the longest-established consensuses could break down under the weight of events. Second, there was also a normative dimension to these systems of thought. The adoption of such a system frequently seemed to represent a commitment to certain political or ethical values as much as, if not more than, to an objective mode of explanation and analysis. Finally, the systems were self-supporting, in the sense that if their adherents so chose, opposing arguments and contradictory evidence could be explained away without damaging the integrity of the worldview.

Put together, these conclusions suggested that there was a significant element of normative choice in the interpretation of social action in the organizational context. While empirical evidence could clearly have an impact on systems of thought, that impact was conditioned by the attitudes and value orientations of actors. My problem now, however, was how to avoid falling into relativism. This was where the application of Habermas's general approach to social theory was most crucially important. Uniquely, Habermas combines a recognition of the futility of searching for the indubitable foundations of knowledge with a determined anti-relativism. For him, objective truth and its social analogue, legitimacy, are concepts that are anything but illusory as long as they are defined epistemologically: in terms of a procedure for establishing validity rather than as a finite list of objects or categories that are valid in some absolute sense. The empirical fact of contradiction between different systems of thought has no bearing on whether consensus is possible in principle. From my perspective as a confirmed supporter of employee participation in the management of corporations, this meant that the first step towards the enfranchisement of workers was to find some way to break down the various closed systems of thought that co-existed within businesses, in order to settle on a consensual definition of the corporate situation; one that gave direction and meaning to action while remaining responsive to any type of critique.

Ironically, the possibility of a genuine, unforced and unmanipulated consensus within business organizations was the issue over which I was obliged to part company with Habermas. For all that his discussion of organizational action settings is limited, he makes it clear that what matters in corporations is the capacity of managers to establish their legal right to command. He dismisses the idea that it is possible to establish the legitimacy of a managerial instruction in anything other than this formal sense because the procedural conditions for a valid consensus simply cannot be met within organizations. The absence of valid consensuses implies the absence of legitimizable relationships, and points to the conclusion that only a strategic attitude to action within corporations makes any sense. Arguments about morality and about values will have no purchase.

To my mind, although Habermas's conception of corporations was not implausible, it had to be a mistake to argue that all were *necessarily* like this. The conclusion that there was no hope of democratization across such a huge swathe of social life was entirely contrary to my understanding of the thrust of Habermas's work. For this reason I set about trying to produce a critique and reconstruction of his work that would allow for the conceptualization of legitimate corporate relationships and, hence, legitimate corporate action. After much fumbling, the result is this book. My main criticism of Habermas is that he underestimates the capacity of individuals to make sense of social structures and institutions. My main theoretical proposal is that this sense-making is accomplished via what I will call 'systemic worldviews'. While there is an important sense in which these worldviews are closed intellectual systems, I argue that it remains possible to make a rational – objectively and normatively valid – choice between them. Just as in other spheres of life, the validity of social relationships and forms of action within organizations is a question of how decisions are made: in Habermas's terms, a question of opinion- and will-formation. The appropriate procedural specification for a legitimate practice of corporate life centres on the fairness of markets and on the effectiveness of forms of organization. As we will see, fairness and effectiveness depend above all on the application of radical forms of democracy in the workplace.

As I find the forms 's/he' and 'he or she' as awkward as each other, I have used the female form to refer to the abstract actor in the odd-numbered chapters and the male form in the even-numbered chapters. The only exception to this rule is where I am recounting an imagined dialogue, in which case I have deemed one actor to be male and the other female. This has the added advantage of aiding comprehension.

I want to acknowledge the help and support of two people in particular: my father, Dr Terry Cradden, who provided enthusiastic support and incisive editorial comment, and my wife, Charlotte Beauchamp, the peace of whose maternity leave has been interrupted by a tedious stream of questions about style and referencing. Any remaining misplaced commas, infelicities of usage or errors of fact are, of course, my own responsibility.

C.C.
Gex, France

Chapter 1

Introduction: The Corporate Theory of Society and the Search for Legitimacy

In his monograph *Between Facts and Norms*, the German philosopher and sociologist Jürgen Habermas attempts 'to demonstrate that there is a conceptual or internal relation, and not simply an historically contingent association, between the rule of law and democracy' (Habermas, 1996, p.449). In this book, we want to try to extend this argument to the business context, arguing that there is a similar conceptual or internal relation between legitimate corporate behaviour and workplace democracy. In a larger sense, this will involve using Habermas's work as the basis for a theory of corporate legitimacy. We will try to show when corporate action can be said to be legitimate in Max Weber's sense of action or behaviour that is just and worthy of support (Thompson, 1994).

Corporate Legitimacy and Corporate Social Responsibility

The idea that business organizations owe certain responsibilities to the societies in which they operate is by no means a recent one. Yet, the contemporary notion of corporate social responsibility (CSR) is usually treated as a novel development. We will return to the question of why this might be a little later. In the meantime, since there seems to be no generally accepted definition of CSR, it makes sense to propose one. Leaving aside for a moment the specific case of the business organization, to say of any actor that they are 'socially responsible' means that they are able to give an acceptable account of their actions insofar as these actions have an impact on society. It means that, as a minimum, their actions are coherent with the moral norms and political-ethical values recognized as legitimate among those they affect. To be responsible is to respect legitimate norms and values.

The distinction between *moral* precepts and *political-ethical* rules, conventions and values is a very important one. We will follow Habermas (1996) in using the former to refer to universal standards and principles of justice, and the latter to refer to what is good for a particular community or reflects that community's authentic self-understanding. Hence, the imperative sense of moral norms is absolute or categorical, while that of political-ethical norms, although it certainly does not depend on purely subjective ends and preferences, is relative to the ordering of values and goals which defines a community.

Having clarified this distinction, we can say that when the actor in question is a corporation rather than an individual, it is appropriate to add to our definition of responsible behaviour the rider, 'to the extent that respecting political-ethical values is compatible with a viable business strategy'. While corporations cannot ever be absolved of the obligation to respect legitimate moral norms, it is arguable that under certain circumstances it is not illegitimate for them to challenge or even subvert the political-ethical values of the communities in which they operate. As Weber recognized, the undoubted benefits of the market economy and industrial production do not come without a price attached. In principle it makes perfect sense to argue that this is a price worth paying; in other words that effective business performance is itself a legitimate political-ethical value. The trick, as the American institutional economists realized, is to ensure that this price is not higher than is strictly necessary. Sumner Slichter, for example, argued that 'the kernel of the problem of industrial control' was 'how to prevent industry from unduly molding our opinions, how to prevent our ideals, our scales of values, from being too much affected by the standards of the market-place, how, in short, to protect life itself from being too completely dominated by the process of getting a living' (Slichter, 1931, cited in Kaufman, 2004, p.109).

So, while CSR is concerned in the first instance with determining the right thing for corporations to do, what this is thought to be depends at least as much on how 'the process of getting a living' is understood as it does on conceptions of what is morally and ethically tolerable. Responsible corporate behaviour therefore represents an appropriate or socially acceptable balance between the demands of material reproduction and community values. In this sense, as we suggested above, the essential problematic of CSR is not a new one.

Nonetheless, there are two particular elements in the contemporary notion of CSR that distinguish it from earlier conceptions of legitimate business behaviour. First of all, while CSR refers to the full range of business activities,[1] for most of the 20th century corporate behaviour was deemed legitimate or illegitimate primarily on the basis of its direct impact on labour. Second, while most approaches to CSR assume that corporations themselves should take the primary responsibility for assessing the social importance of particular approaches to business strategy and industrial organization in relation to the existing values of the community, this role – conceived in the limited sense of the regulation of the employment relationship – has historically been delegated to social institutions that operate beyond the corporation: the legal system and the machinery of industrial relations.

What all this suggests is that the basis on which corporate action is perceived as legitimate or illegitimate is not historically constant. Not just ideals and values but conceptions of the demands of the market, of the unavoidable aspects of 'the process of getting a living', are in constant flux. The experience of the 20th century suggests that corporate practice has periodically fallen out of step with this social evolution, giving rise to crises of legitimacy. We would argue that these crises have acted as

---

[1] There are six common areas of attention: first, the environmental and community impact of production and consumption; second, the social and cultural impact of advertising and marketing campaigns; third, the effect of corporate political lobbying; fourth, the effectiveness of consumer protection; fifth, labour standards in the supply chain; and sixth, fair trade and the conduct of relationships with suppliers.

catalysts for an intellectual engagement with the presenting problems, which in turn has informed political debate. The eventual result in each case was the reform of social and economic institutions with a view to bringing corporate action into step with contemporary conceptions of legitimate behaviour. In the next section, we will briefly discuss the principal crises of the last century, as well as that through which we are currently living.

From the 'Labour Question' to Anti-globalization: Crises of Corporate Legitimacy in the 20th Century

The emergence of the so-called anti-globalization movement towards the end of the 1990s was symptomatic of what was merely the latest in the series of legitimacy crises that have punctuated the long life of the capitalist economic system. In the ebb and flow of public confidence in the market economy, we can discern perhaps three earlier periods during which the perceived injustice or ineffectiveness of the system has been such as to prompt significant intellectual and political responses.[2]

The Labour Question

The first such period began in the late 19th century and ended sometime in the aftermath of the First World War. The wave of labour conflict and protest that swept the industrialized world in these years represented a direct challenge to capitalism. Euphemistically known as 'The Labour Question' by those who had the most direct interest in making it go away, the question in fact concerned the most basic concepts of production for profit, wage labour and the private ownership of capital. Bruce Kaufman suggests that despite the severity of the conflict, it was only in the face of the exigencies of organizing wartime production that any substantial political response was forthcoming (Kaufman, 2004, p.78). Nevertheless, the outcome was of considerable importance. What came to be accepted was the idea that efficiency – in effect, worker co-operation and industrial peace – could no longer be achieved simply by insisting on the property rights of the owners of capital. Rather, it was henceforth to depend on the representation of labour in the regulation of industry. This involved two things: first of all, the establishment of basic workers' rights and labour standards; and second, the negotiation of wages and terms and conditions via collective bargaining. Symbolic of this new order of industrial citizenship was the widespread

---

[2] The group of nations to which we are referring when we talk of the pattern of political, economic and intellectual development in the 20th century includes the United States, the United Kingdom and the other industrialized nations of the Anglophone world, and continental western Europe. Without wanting to minimize cross-national social and cultural differences, we will take it as having been established that, on the very largest scale, the recent history of each member of this group has been marked by the same events and by the same currents of thought. The broad outlines of social and economic policy across these countries have followed a remarkably similar pattern in response.

recognition by governments of the legitimacy of worker self-organization[3] and, perhaps even more importantly, the founding in 1919 of the International Labour Organization (ILO). Established as part of the Treaty of Versailles, the ILO was intended to be an institutional manifestation of the principle that 'universal and lasting peace can be established only if it is based upon social justice' (ILO Constitution, preamble). The ILO would be a 'parliament of labour' in which employers and workers had equal representation in the creation of regulations that would govern the employment relationship. An *international* system of regulation was needed because 'the failure of any nation to adopt humane conditions of labour is an obstacle in the way of other nations which desire to improve the conditions in their own countries' (ibid.).

The Great Depression

The second period of crisis was the Great Depression, sparked off by the stock market crash of 1929. In contrast to the 'red scare' of the pre-war years, the threat to capitalism this time came from within. The inability of industrial and financial leaders to prevent a disastrous deflationary spiral focussed attention on the need for government intervention in the economy. In particular, it came to be generally agreed that governments should engage in, or at least encourage, counter-cyclical economic measures such as the management of demand via public spending, the strengthening of institutional support for collective bargaining or the establishment of systems of social insurance. In the USA, the result was the New Deal and the Wagner Act; in Europe – although not until after the Second World War – the outcome was the social democratic welfare state in its various national incarnations.

The broad policy consensus that emerged from the two crises of the first part of the 20th century was a victory for the idea that there was a balance to be struck between economic and social goals. Both 19th century economic liberalism and the apparent alternative, the dominance of labour, were rejected in favour of an institutionalized balancing act that sought to establish a kind of socio-economic equilibrium based on the conciliation of class interests.

Productivity and Deregulation

The third major crisis of legitimacy, essentially a crisis of confidence in the solutions that had been designed to resolve the first two, warrants rather closer attention.[4] For a

---

[3] In Britain, for example, a Ministry of Labour was created in 1916 with a trade unionist at its head. The Ministry was to be a committed advocate of collective bargaining (Davies and Freedland, 1993, p.39). In the USA, union leaders, employers and the public were given equal representation on the National War Labor Board and several other economic agencies (Kaufman, 2004, p.82).

[4] The section that follows draws on Cradden, 2004. This work involved an analysis of the arguments used by trade unions, employers associations and political parties in the debate on industrial relations policy in the UK and Ireland between the late 1960s and 1997.

period of around twenty years, running from the mid-1960s until the mid-1980s, the characteristics and mode of social oversight of the employment relationship, and the broadly Keynesian orthodoxy in economic policy, were subject to intense academic and political questioning. The most obvious problem at the beginning of this period was that the seemingly effortless economic progress that had characterized the years after the Second World War was stalling. A sharp decline in the rate of expansion of the market for mass-produced consumer goods led to a shift in the emphasis of management from increasing production to increasing productivity. However, the combination of full employment, effective union organization and the expectation of tangible year-on-year improvements in living standards meant that attempts to cut costs and to increase managerial control over the production process were doomed to fail. In fact, they were met with a wave of industrial conflict that was unprecedented in its scale and international scope (Brecher, 1972; Shalev, 1992) The concession of real wage increases in the context of stagnant productivity growth – whether simply as a means of settling disputes or in return for agreement to changes of dubious value in working practices – had the inevitable inflationary effect.

The policy solutions that were canvassed fell broadly into two groups, depending on whether the problems of 'stagflation' and industrial conflict were understood to be caused principally by the behaviour of workers and trade unions or that of managers and the owners of capital. These competing diagnoses were underpinned by very different assumptions about the mechanics of economy and society that had, in turn, very different implications for the calculation of the appropriate balance between effective business strategy and established social values and ideals. Indeed, it would not be going too far to suggest that there were two mutually incompatible theories of society in play.

At first, the policy debate was dominated by those who did not question the fundamental assumptions of the post-war 'social compromise' (Crouch, 1977). They argued for the consolidation and modernization of the existing system rather than its replacement. For this group it was evident that the values and interests of workers and those of the owners of capital and their agents in management were and would always be conflicting, but also that these two sets of values and interests were equally legitimate in themselves. Neither could be permanently privileged as representative of the public interest. However, since capital and labour each relied on the other for the realization of their goals, there had to be some way of achieving the required degree of cooperation. The only rational way to proceed was for each of the parties to participate in the negotiation of a modus vivendi based on a realistic appreciation of the social, political and economic weight of the other. It was argued that managers were wilfully refusing to accept that the balance point of the socio-economic equilibrium had permanently shifted. They were at fault both morally – for failing to recognize the legitimacy of trade unionism as a social force – and technically – for failing to recognize that the de facto political and economic strength of the labour movement and the wide extent to which the aims and values it pursued were recognized as valid among workers, meant that neither the suppression nor the manipulation of workers was possible in practice.

From the theoretical perspective of the functionalist sociology that informed this 'pluralist' position (Kerr, 1964; Fox, 1966), the maximization of organizational effectiveness depended on the *joint* optimization of decision-making along both an economic/technical dimension and the socio-political dimension of workers' interests. From the normative perspective, on the basis of the most fundamental principles of natural justice and democracy, it was clear that workers were entitled to at least equal participation in the making of decisions that had an impact on their values and interests. Collective bargaining was therefore understood both as a technical process by which the optimal mode of the organization of production was determined, and as a political process in which the conflicting values of labour and capital were – at least intermittently – reconciled.

The range of policy solutions proposed in the pluralist vein ranged from modest reform of the institutions of industrial relations to the introduction of radical forms of industrial democracy and economic planning.[5] What unified these positions was a belief that social and political progress had disturbed the equilibrium between economy and society, and that it was the economy which would have to make the necessary adjustment. The variation was due not just to differing beliefs about how much ground the owners of capital could reasonably be expected to concede, but, more importantly, to differing assessments of which management decisions had an impact on the values and interests of workers. At one end of the spectrum there were those who held the traditional view that it was only those decisions with a very direct impact on the terms of the employment relationship that ought to be the subject of collective bargaining. At the other, there were those who argued that in practice it was impossible to draw a line between 'industrial relations' issues and the other areas of management. Ultimately, everything that management did had an impact on workers and hence there was no logical limit to the scope of collective bargaining. This implied that workers should be represented at every stage and in every area of management, whether strategic or operational. There were two areas in particular that were candidates for increased worker influence. First of all, it was frequently argued that it was appropriate for unions to bargain not just about pay and terms and conditions, but about what Allan Flanders called 'managerial relations', which is to say the authority relationship that exists between workers and managers. Flanders distinguished managerial relations from market relations on the grounds that, 'in the broadest sense of the word these relationships are political, not economic' (Flanders, 1975, p.88). In other words, they are premised on or assume certain values and interests. Since it was taken as a given that these were always contested as between workers and managers, it was thought to be wholly unacceptable to grant to one side the unilateral power to decide whether the relationship was legitimate. Second, it was proposed that tripartite economic planning be extended. Although the involvement of worker representatives in economic policy-making was already a common feature of government in the industrialized nations, what emerged in the 1970s were a series of much more radical conceptions of industrial democracy. In the UK in the early 1980s,

---

[5] We need to note that while the USA suffered from the same economic and industrial malaise as the rest of the industrialized world, and despite the fact that the pluralist model of industrial relations was essentially an American invention, the idea of extending the range and scope of collective bargaining was not seriously canvassed as a solution there.

for example, the joint policy of the Labour Party – at this stage the parliamentary opposition – and the Trades Union Congress was for the economy to be run on the basis of both collective bargaining and 'joint control' by working people in trade unions. The idea of joint control was related to a national economic planning framework which would 'give workers the opportunity to exercise a positive influence over all aspects of economic decision-making', the quality of which would be enhanced by their 'knowledge and skills' (TUC-Labour Party Liaison Committee, 1982, p.5). Unions were to be involved in all stages of a national and sectoral planning process, and were to be partners in the development plans which major enterprises would be obliged to negotiate with the (projected) government Department of Economic and Industrial Planning.

Despite the wave of attempts to improve and extend collective bargaining and other forms of industrial democracy throughout the 1970s, the persistence of the economic crisis handed the initiative to the neoliberal critics of the trade union movement. These critics argued that it was precisely the economic policies and structures of workplace governance that had characterized the post-war consensus that were to blame for the contemporary malaise. In resisting the reform of industrial relations – the aim of which was simultaneously to make management control more effective and to remove undue 'rigidities' in the labour market – and in continuing to insist on economically interventionist government, the unions and their supporters in politics were preventing the only effective resolution of the problem. This resolution was based on a revived economic liberalism characterized by the denial that it was possible to achieve a negotiated balance between economy and society and the rejection of the idea that there was any significant room for political or moral choice in economic and business policy decision-making. Rather, the single dimension that mattered was the economic. It was held to be simply an objective truth that the interests of both workers and shareholders were directly dependent on the success of the corporation. Since in this sense there was no political contest, what was imperative was to allow markets, whether for capital, products or labour, to operate as freely as possible. It was assumed that the benefits of economic liberalization in terms of wealth-creation, innovation and opportunity would always outweigh the inevitable social costs. Thus it was not just pointless but economically and politically dangerous to attempt the conscious management or negotiation of this trade-off in the way that the US institutional economists had suggested was possible. One right-wing think tank summarized the problem in this way:

> In the UK over the last few years more and more economic decisions have been taken outside the market. The result has been intense pressure group activity in the political arena, the growth of direct action by employees, and greater social unrest generally as even the meekest and most law-abiding of citizens have come to realise that economic rewards are increasingly disbursed through the political system and according to criteria which attach greater importance to the strength of a man's voice than to his ability and contribution (Centre for Policy Studies, 1975, p.14).

The crucial contrast in this approach is between the (supposed) impersonality and disinterestedness of market mechanisms and the 'strength of a man's voice'. The economy was not thought of as part of the political structure of society. Rather, it was a backdrop; part of the context for social action rather than being its object. The argument went as follows: since it could be scientifically demonstrated on the basis of theoretical economic models and empirical evidence that the best possible material outcomes for all arose from a policy of strict non-intervention in the naturally-occurring mechanics of the economy, it was surely folly to accept that those whose role it was to understand and respond to those mechanics should have to compromise the technical optimality of their responses in order to meet the demands of one powerful section of society. It was therefore simply mistaken to believe that setting the price of labour on the basis of what was politically acceptable would not inevitably lead to difficulties. It may have been sustainable for certain periods under certain conditions, but in the end the market would demand a correction.

Viewed in this light, collective bargaining appeared to be defensible only if conceived as a direct economic mechanism for setting the price of labour. If this was the case, then insofar as it was their role to agree a collective contract to secure a supply of labour, managers were simply the agents of the buyers of labour (capital) and unions the agents of the vendors (labour). The roles of both management and trade unions were principally economic, and 'political' aims and values were viewed as an unnatural intrusion. The most important implication of this conception of the relationship between workers/unions and management was that the extension of bargaining to managerial relations was unwarranted. It was assumed that the authority exercised by managers within the employment relationship did not require any positive act of legitimation beyond the initial agreement of the employment contract. Similarly out of place in this scheme was the idea that, beyond the individual enterprise, it is the role of the unions to articulate a socio-political interest as against the economic interests represented by management. Collective bargaining did not involve a compromise between economy and society. It was a purely economic phenomenon: the negotiation of the price of a particular type and quality of labour in the context of the supply of, and demand for it. In this light, unions were only one among a large number of economic interests whose voice deserved to be heard on the national policy stage. They had no privileged position as the sole carriers of the socio-political component of the public interest. What is more, bargaining over pay and conditions could not be conceived as a means to win the co-operation of a workforce that had already been engaged. Rather, co-operation was what wages paid for. By entering into a market relationship with an employer, workers were accepting that their actions would be governed by the demands of the market. In this sense, they were accepting the legitimacy of these demands, and hence they were accepting that they had a responsibility to conform that was more than simply contractual. The public interest demanded wealth creation, and the greatest amount of wealth was created when enterprises responded appropriately to their market environment.

By the middle of the 1980s, the conception of business management as requiring a joint optimization of economic and socio-political factors – in political terms, a conciliation of the values and interests of capital and labour – had been replaced in the policy debate by a one-dimensional emphasis on the overarching need to obey the imperatives of the market and competitiveness. The opinion that there was a permanent and inevitable conflict between the interests of capital and labour had largely been abandoned. Hence, the public interest was defined in almost exclusively economic terms. This analysis was gradually adopted by the majority of the political parties in the industrialized world, a process that only accelerated after the collapse of the Soviet Union and the other planned economies of Central and Eastern Europe. It was simply no longer credible to believe that the market economy could be avoided or significantly reformed.

Anti-globalization and the New World Order

That we are currently living through yet another crisis of corporate legitimacy is not quite so clear as in the earlier cases. There are, for example, no economic problems on anything like the scale experienced in the 1970s or during the Depression. Indeed, the global economy has arguably never been so stable. However, Martin Parker (2003) has pointed to four phenomena that amount to compelling evidence for the existence of a crisis. First of all, there is the anti-globalization movement itself, which Parker suggests exemplifies 'an explicit impatience with the supposed inevitability of market-led globalization and forms of managerial self-interest that justify inequality and environmental damage' (p.197). Second, there is the emergence of Critical Management Studies within business schools, an approach that challenges 'hegemonic' ways of thinking about organizing. Third, contemporary cultural representations of corporations and their managers are frequently highly negative, emphasising their supposed concern with increasing shareholder value at any cost. Finally, Parker cites the wave of corporate scandals that have emerged since the turn of the millennium. He concludes, 'To put it simply, many people in many places do not trust the market managerial version of the new world order' (ibid.).

David Courpasson and Françoise Dany (2003) concur that there is currently a crisis of managerial legitimacy, but trace it to the 'absence of a clearly established knowledge base' (p.1245), a problem they argue has been exacerbated by the tendency of managers to follow closely the 'fads and fashions' of the day. This mistrust of the technical capacities of management is one possible explanation for the lack of faith in the managerial new world order that Parker identifies.

We will suppose, then, that we are in the midst of a fourth, unresolved crisis of corporate legitimacy. Like the third, it has arisen in reaction to the resolution of the previous one – although in truth the neoliberal settlement, despite its success as an institutional orthodoxy, has never achieved the degree of popular consensus enjoyed by the social democratic welfare state. While neoliberalism is clearly the dominant espoused theory in contemporary approaches to political economy, it is such by default, because of the lack of any clear and theoretically coherent alternative. At the moment, the opponents of neoliberalism do not possess a theory of comparable status.

This having been said, many of the arguments against neoliberalism are very effective. At the core of contemporary objections to the legal and political structure that supports the existence of corporations is the role of management. These objections are directed both at the decision-making power of managers itself and at the specific use that has been made of it. The latter set of objections point to specific instances where corporate managers have violated valid social norms beyond the acceptable degree of challenge and subversion we discussed above. Most notably, campaigners have focused on damage to the environment, on unfair trade practices and on poor labour standards. The former set of objections are of rather more interest for our current purposes. They centre on the prerogatives that neoliberalism grants to management. In the neoliberal vision of the world, it is managers who have the more or less exclusive right to interpret what it is that the market demands from workers, corporations and society. Since in effect there is no longer any requirement to take account of an independently articulated socio-political interest before decisions are made, this right gives corporate managers enormous power. Jem Bendell (2004) has identified two grounds for the critique of corporate power. One group of critics focuses on the fact that corporate decision-making follows the logic of capital accumulation driven by stock markets. Social and environmental objectives are hence systematically excluded. The other group is concerned less with what drives decision-making than with who has the right to be involved in making decisions. From their perspective, corporate power is to be opposed simply because it is undemocratic.

The Corporate Theory of Society

Although these critiques of corporate power are rarely addressed directly by corporations themselves, we can nonetheless reconstruct a more or less coherent corporate response based on academic, political and 'public relations' argumentation in support of the existing prerogatives of managers. The corporate response aims to demonstrate or to make it understood that corporate power is *already* both procedurally and substantively legitimate: that the logic of decision-making is pragmatically and normatively sound; and that the exercise of the managerial right to decide is consistent with valid moral and political-ethical principles. At the core of the managerial argument is the claim that the contradiction between managerial power and the rights of workers and other members of society is unreal in practice. Because managerial action is in principle always rationally defensible, the benefits of employee consent and community support ought (in principle) to be available without employees having the right to withhold their consent, and without the community having any formal rights of oversight with respect to corporate behaviour. For managers, the important issue is that the rational defensibility of their actions is properly understood, both within the corporation and outside it. This will be the case only when a certain macro-level conception of society and of the role corporations play within it has been generally accepted. This 'corporate theory of society', has important implications for social and economic policy and for management practice.

The Autonomy and Objectivity of the Market

The core of the corporate theory of society is the assumption that markets are autonomous social structures that come into being as a consequence of the freedom of individuals to enter or not enter contracts. Since they are both inevitable and beyond conscious human control, the only rational attitude to adopt with respect to market forces is one of conformity. The claim that markets and economies are uniquely objective features of the social landscape is not unique to the neoliberal canon. Quite the contrary. As Andrew Sayer (2004) points out, the tendency for market forces to gain a degree of autonomy from actors' intentions and actions and hence to 'displace moral and traditional norms in structuring society' (p.2) has been identified by, among others, Karl Marx, Max Weber, Karl Polanyi and Habermas. Habermas has even argued that 'the strictly objectivating approach favoured by Marx, which examines mechanisms of integration from an external perspective, has successfully worked its way into various theoretical traditions' (1996, p.46). Where the corporate theory of society parts company from the critical progenitors of the concept is in adopting an unequivocally positive view of the autonomy of market forces. From this perspective, the market represents a kind of post-pluralist source of social goals; a positively conceived Rousseauian 'will of all', taking the place of the unattainable general will.

A direct implication of the autonomy of markets is that the structuring effect that they have on society does not reflect the contingent interests of capital but merely certain objective features of the economic landscape. This argument is perhaps clearest in neoliberal politics. The British Conservative Party under the leadership of Margaret Thatcher, for example, repeatedly accused the trade unions of wilfully ignoring the inability of corporations to concede just anything: 'Those who negotiate around the table must understand and be aware of the constraints within which they are operating, and must have a responsible attitude to those realities' (Howe et al., 1977, p.7). This obviously implies that the limits of the possible in bargaining are not set by the participants themselves. Rather, the range of settlements which maintain a corporation's conformity with market requirements are not set by what employers are prepared to accept, but exist independently of any agreement that may be reached.

Depoliticized Management

Closely related to the assumption that market forces are objective and autonomous is the claim that management is a technical profession. The argument that managers hold their posts by virtue of possessing some kind of expertise rather than because of a direct or indirect property relationship with the corporation is not a new one. In the 1930s, for example, the founding editor of the *Harvard Business Review* was already envisaging the creation of 'a body of [business] knowledge comparable to those that existed in older professions like medicine and law' (Stone, 1997). In fact, from the end of the 19th century, there had been a steady stream of research and argument that linked successful management with one predominant field of technical knowledge directly related to the production process.[6] Some of the principal candidates were rational bureaucratic administration (Max Weber, Henri Fayol), 'scientific' job design (Frederick Taylor), sociological interpretation of the dynamics of the work group (Elton Mayo), or the relationship between organization structure and different types of production technology (Joan Woodward). The novelty of the neoliberal conception of managerial expertise was both in its disciplinary focus and its scope. Starting in the

---

[6] The sources for the comments that follow are Pugh and Hickson, 1989, and Rose, 1975. Both of these works provide very useful overviews of the development of research on industry and organization in the twentieth century.

1960s, it was increasingly argued that organization structure was or ought to be a function of the business environment (Tom Burns, Paul Lawrence and Jay Lorsch). The emergence of this 'contingency theory' marked an important step towards the redefinition of the core managerial expertise in terms of exchange rather than production. Once the neoliberal revolution had put paid to the idea that there was a need to find a balance between economy and society, management could be conceived in a much broader and more flexible sense as the profession that interprets the objective but esoteric demands of the market and translates these into organizational structures and business strategies. This is a highly significant step because it extends the supposedly technical knowledge of management into an area which previously was thought to be a domain of political choice and compromise.

In the corporate theory of society it is not denied that management action involves norm-conformative behaviour. However, the authoritative actions taken, and recommendations made, by professional managers remain within socially established moral and political-ethical boundaries. The ends and values to which the managerial 'ought' refers do not go beyond that which is already recognized as legitimate. Hence the old pluralist argument that unilateral management authority involves 'the use of power to impose values on people, for their alleged benefit, which they would not freely accept' (Flanders, 1975, p.147) is rejected. The strategic choices that managers make on behalf of their corporations are therefore based exclusively on a technical assessment of the objective functional characteristics of the relevant market.

Flexibility

Once the market has been conceived as an objective and autonomous force, and once management has been conceived as a technical profession whose expertise lies in the construction of effective responses to that force, then 'flexibility' serves as a general motif for appropriate social and economic attitudes. The idea of flexibility encapsulates the assumption that 'rigidity' at any level will prevent the economy from functioning as envisaged in the theories of neoclassical economics. The policy aim is to dismantle not only the institutional but the behavioural obstacles to the functioning of the market.[7]

---

[7] While the academic literature on flexibility is vast, two pieces of work seem to have been particularly influential: John Atkinson's *Manning for Uncertainty – Some Emerging UK Work Patterns* (Atkinson, 1984) and Charles Sabel and Michael Piore's *The Second Industrial Divide: Possibilities for Prosperity* (Piore and Sabel, 1984). These two pieces of work brought together most of the ideas which have since been grouped under the heading of flexibility. Piore and Sabel's concept of flexible specialization unites labour market and labour process restructuring with niche or custom marketing, all of which is supported by the increased versatility in design made possible by new production technology. Atkinson's work, is more focused on concrete labour management considerations. he identified functional flexibility (changes in job design and skills utilization), numerical flexibility (the co-existence within a single organization of secure 'core' and insecure 'peripheral' workforces) and financial flexibility (the adjustability of employment costs in response to labour market supply and demand) as important developments in the management of the organization's human resources.

There are three propositions that underpin the concept of flexibility. The first, the inheritance of contingency theory, is that the possibility of competitive success will be maximized if the internal configuration of a corporation – its structures, processes, products and above all the size, characteristics (skills, attitudes, etc.) and mode of deployment of its workforce – match or are congruent with that corporation's market environment. The second is that we live in a time when, for most businesses, the market environment is unstable and characterized by intense competition. Putting this together with the first leads to the third proposition, which is that a business organization will be competitive to the extent that it is able quickly, smoothly and appropriately to configure and reconfigure itself internally in response to changes in its environment. While this reconfiguration can and should encompass business and marketing strategies, products and production systems, capital investment and so forth, the focus will tend to be on the human systems of the enterprise.

To facilitate this reconfiguration, flexibility is what is required not only of organizations, but of the society in which they exist, and of the people who work in them. Flexibility is a characteristic of the economy, encapsulating the idea of a national economic system which provides the best possible conditions for the global competitiveness of business and industry located within that economy. Perhaps the most important feature of such an economy is its ability to absorb the pressures both of internal growth and external shocks without the need for government resort to fiscal or monetary measures which are damaging to competitiveness, or to tariffs, exchange or import controls, or other protectionist measures.

A key aspect of the flexible economy is a flexible labour market, namely, one free of institutional or other rigidities, where price signals are clear, labour is mobile (both geographically and in and out of employment), wages move down as well as up in response to fluctuation in demand, and shortages or surpluses of particular types of labour are quickly remedied through the easy availability of effective training and retraining.

A key aspect of the flexible labour market is the flexible corporation, which is able to respond quickly and effectively to both product and labour market signals. The flexible corporation is characterized by two overlapping features. First, the relationship between its managers and workforce, that is the managerial ability unilaterally to design and implement working practices and 'remuneration systems' and to recruit, dismiss, deploy and redeploy staff to whatever extent and in whatever manner they wish without this being the cause of conflict, whether manifest or latent. Second, within the flexible corporation, the labour costs which employers are committed or semi-committed to meeting – whether in the short, medium or long-term – are minimized through the use of a variety of forms of non-permanent, non-full-time employment contract.

A key aspect of the flexible economy at all levels is the flexible worker. The flexible worker understands the nature, benefits and inevitability of the market economy. Consequently, she recognizes that the road to security is employability, expectation and attitude rather than a job for life. The flexible worker is mobile, multi-skilled, expects to have a 'portfolio of careers', understands and does not resent the business realities of short-term contracts, performance related pay and occasional wage cuts and is prepared to train and retrain as many times as necessary. The flexible worker is arguably the most important part of the picture. She is the theoretically perfect economic actor whose attitudes and action orientations are such that she will conform to the demands of the market without demur, whatever those demands might be. In a society of flexible workers, therefore, legitimate social action and the structural forces of the economy would be perfectly integrated.

Flexibility in this multi-faceted sense, despite its theoretical attractions, seems unlikely to arise spontaneously. Rather, it has to be achieved through policy interventions and management action. The institutional obstacles to flexibility are more easily dealt with than the behavioural ones. Political objections notwithstanding, the liberalization of international capital markets, the abolition of tariffs and subsidies, and the deregulation of product and labour markets are relatively easily achieved. What is very much more difficult is persuading workers and the community to accept that these measures are aimed at the promotion of the common good and that it is therefore incumbent on them to respond by behaving in the appropriate, flexible manner. The measures that have been taken with a view to prompting the required attitude of cheerful compliance with corporate plans and strategies fall into two categories, the first directed outward to the community, and the second directed inwards to the employees of the corporation.

CSR and Business Ethics

Although it may not be immediately apparent, CSR and business ethics can be understood as practices that contribute to the achievement of flexibility. A negative community reaction to corporate actions and practices – leading to consumer boycotts, legal challenges, reputational damage, etc. – can rarely be lightly dismissed and can in itself represent a substantial constraint on corporate freedom of action. Perhaps more importantly, it can contribute to pressure for regulation or other forms of political interference. For these reasons it is important that corporations are able to make a convincing public case that their behaviour involves the maximum possible respect for social norms and values.

We need to distinguish CSR as a managerial practice and area of business school teaching and research from the substantive concept of a corporation's state or quality of being authentically socially responsible with which we opened this chapter. From the perspective of the corporate theory of society, CSR practices are those monitoring and reporting mechanisms put in place by managers with a view to demonstrating that the corporation *already* applies widely accepted moral and political-ethical criteria in making decisions, that it is *already* responsive to social pressure in respect of the criteria that are applied, and that the decisions that are eventually made do in fact have positive outcomes for society. Similarly, policies and codes of practice that define the corporation's understanding of the ethical conduct of business are designed to show that the pursuit of profit is *already* limited by non-economic norms and values despite the absence of any formal social control over most of its areas of activity. In mainstream CSR research, for example, it is assumed that 'the societal expectations that define the role of a company in society will align the processes of strategy formulation and implementation with the social aspects of management. Thus the results will be socially tolerable consequences' (Scherer and Palazzo, 2005). In short,

CSR and business ethics practices are designed to show that corporations can be trusted to behave like any responsible citizen and that there is no need for external regulation.

HRM and Organization Culture

The measures intended to achieve flexibility within the corporation are often collectively referred to as human resource management (HRM). In the sense of a tactical approach to the achievement of flexibility, HRM emerged at around the same time as the concept of flexibility itself, although in fact the term had been in use for some time as a generic description of the practice of 'people management' or of manpower planning. Its emergence as a paradigm for the management of individual relationships in the workplace arguably dates from the increase in importance of personnel departments consequent upon the US civil rights legislation of the 1960s (O'Reilly and Anderson, 1982). In any case, HRM did not emerge fully formed and much of the initial analytic energy was expended on definitions and exercises in conceptual clarification (in the British literature see particularly MacKay and Torrington, 1986; Hendry and Pettigrew, 1987; Guest, 1987). Storey has argued (1992, pp.31-2) that confusion arose because it was, in the early part of the debate at least, often unclear whether research into HRM was concerned with prescription (setting up a normative model for the conduct of management), description (simply giving an account of developments in certain organizations) or conceptual modelling (providing a non-evaluative account of a theoretically coherent possible approach to management).

Aside from problems with the ontological status of HRM, two substantive issues were contentious in the debate. First, there was the question of whether HRM as an approach to management was genuinely novel. It was argued that it was little more than a thin veneer (mainly consisting of the title and its semantic implications) over a set of rather stale normative prescriptions based on the idea of seeking to 'humanize' business through encouraging co-operation and participative management styles. These had been preached for some years, and to little avail, in the shape of progressive personnel management (Legge, 1995). The second point of contention was whether HRM represented a single phenomenon, apparently very different 'hard' and 'soft' variants having been identified. The 'soft' variant of the practice seemed to emphasize the older normative prescriptions of participation and co-operation, stressing the possibility that management could be a positive sum game with benefits in terms both of competitiveness and of the working life of employees. The 'hard' variant was suspected of complicity in the neoliberal project, reflecting an approach to management in which the primacy of market forces was the key element and in which an instrumental use was made of behaviourist psychology to manipulate workers into compliance with managerial wishes (Guest, 1999).

With respect to the novelty or otherwise of HRM, two particular elements have, on balance, emerged as innovative. The first of these is the more important in practice, arguably representing the most clearly identifiable and widespread change in thinking about management, both within the ranks of managers themselves and in government. The second element, while not nearly so manifest in practice, is the more theoretically interesting.

The first element is the assertion that the 'human resource' is the key source of competitive advantage in business organizations and therefore that the active management of the (individual) employment relationship should be a – if not *the* – primary focus of managerial effort (Storey, 1995). Different market circumstances demand different organizational configurations. Thus the aim of actively managing the employment relationship must be to ensure that it matches or is congruent with the market strategy of the business (Purcell, 1995), and that it is internally consistent so that the various aspects of the organization's human resources policies are mutually reinforcing. Rather than a focus on the design, administration or operation of a bureaucratic structure, the manager's central task is the maximization of the utility of the human resource in whatever way is appropriate to the market circumstances. Thus the manager interprets and reinterprets the demands of competitiveness and puts these into operation through the management of the employment relationship. There are therefore no solutions to problems of work organization, remuneration, training and development, and so on that are universally applicable, transcending the concrete circumstances of the particular organization in its particular environmental context.

The refocusing of managerial effort on the capabilities and the performance of the individual employee is, in one light, little more than common sense. It amounts to a straightforward recognition that the full talents of each individual employee can and should be harnessed to the interests of the organization and that this can be a positive sum game. Perhaps more importantly, however, it represents a recognition that placing the emphasis on (inflexible) structures and processes within the organization is counterproductive. The design of the innerorganizational system is heavily downplayed in favour of an increased focus on the cues for organization behaviour provided by the system environment. This implies a diminution in the importance of the formal interconnection of action consequences within the organization (rules) in favour of an emphasis on action orientations (attitudes and values). However, if this is not to mean a loss of control by management, there is a need to control the reproduction of these action orientations. While in the literature this attempt is most obviously represented by the emphasis on the role of management in fostering *commitment* to the organization and attitudes conducive to high *quality* production or service, these are in fact particular or specific action orientations which are likely to be beneficial to the organization. The management of action orientations in general is represented both by the concept of the flexible worker, and by the second novel element in HRM, the management of organizational culture.

The *Harvard Business Review*, introducing some comments on the future of management provided by major management thinkers, noted that each thinker had 'identified challenges that are not so much technical or rational as cultural... The continuing challenge for executives, their collective observations suggest, is not technology but the art of human – and humane – management' (Harvard Business Review, 1997). These comments reflect a particular normative orthodoxy at the soft end of a spectrum which runs from what has been described as 'behavioural Taylorism' all the way to vague incantations to be nice to people. What they have in common – and what makes this second element of HRM sit so comfortably with the first – is a recognition that it is not the construction and administration of formal structures and hierarchies or elaborate communication and reporting systems which is the core of the management task. Rather, it is the attempt not just to try to promote co-operation, but to build it into the very fabric of the organization such that not co-operating appears irrational, even pathological. Management should manage in such a way as to have an impact both on the values of employees and on their cognitive repertoires; it should effectively evangelize a philosophy of the employing organization such that their point of reference is not the day-to-day tasks that they do or the rules according to which they do them but an almost pre-rational conception of 'the way we do things around here', which is related to 'our view of the world'.

Conclusion

In the theory of society that underpinned the post-war social compromise, the pragmatic and normative components of decision-making about the organization of production were not only conceptually separate, but were also thought to be coterminous with the conflicting values and interests of two different social groups: those who were obliged to work for a living and those who lived by virtue of their ownership of capital. Hence it was thought to be rational to institutionalize the search for an appropriate balance between the exigencies of material reproduction and the norms, conventions and values that defined the community – the process of defining legitimate corporate behaviour – as a bargaining process involving the representatives of labour and capital. This process itself was conceived both from a detached sociological perspective, and from the internal perspective of the actors and social groups involved. In the former sense, it was understood as a functional mechanism for the establishment and maintenance of an appropriate socio-economic equilibrium (Dunlop, 1958). In this light, the attitudes, values and behaviour of the actual participants in bargaining appeared less important than the political and economic realities that formed the backdrop of the process. In Habermas's terms, 'all *intentional* integrating achievements disappear from view' (1996, p.47; emphasis added). In the latter sense, however, bargaining took on the characteristics of political exchange and contestation. What was important was the capacity of the actors involved to agree compromises that could then be justified to those they represented.

This ambivalent social ontology opened the possibility of conceiving bargaining in two very different ways. Either it was the process in which the imperatives of the market and competition (along with the socio-political imperatives against which they must be balanced) were *identified*, or it is where these imperatives were *defined*. In the first case, the process of bargaining involved the mutual communication of information about the external pressures for action faced by each party, together with an exploration of where the equilibrium position between these two sets of pressures might lie. Ideally, the agreement eventually reached would be an accurate reflection of the real or objective or empirically possible equilibrium between socio-political and economic forces. If it was not, economic crisis or social unrest would be the outcome, regardless of the will of the bargainers. We can call this a 'systems' conception of bargaining. In the second case, the process of bargaining involved a mutual agreement that each party accept certain constraints on their freedom of action. It was assumed that market imperatives simply represented the contingent 'will' of capital, just as the socio-political imperatives articulated by the trade unions represented the will of labour. In participating in bargaining, the representatives of capital and labour, recognizing their inescapable interdependency, agreed to accept certain obligations that had the effect of limiting both the returns capital could expect on its investment and the extent to which the social and political goals of labour were realized. Since these limits were agreed, then however restrictive they may have been they would by definition be neither socially nor economically damaging. We can call this an 'action' conception of bargaining.

Over the course of the 1970s and 1980s, the exponents of neoliberalism – the progenitors of what we have called the corporate theory of society – were able to exploit pluralism's ambivalence with respect to the social ontology of the bargaining process. In effect, management was treated as if it were participating in systems-type bargaining, and unions as if they were participating in action-type bargaining. Managers were deemed to be communicating external imperatives, while the role of the unions was to recognize these imperatives and to choose to behave in such a way that they were satisfied. It was assumed that while economic forces were beyond the control of management, the social force of organized labour could be directed by the conscious choices of its leaders. Whereas the logic of sociological pluralism suggested that union behaviour should have been taken as a given, it was instead treated as the outcome of decisions that could and in many circumstances ought to have been otherwise. Unions were subject to moral censure for disrupting the smooth functioning of the unitary social system responsible for material reproduction by insisting on the realization of non-market goals and values. This negative argument gradually developed into a positive exhortation to embrace the ends and values of the market, of competitiveness and of efficiency. In the end, the discourse of flexibility dissolved the normative demarcation of economy and society, equating our 'scale of values' with 'the process of getting a living' and making a nonsense of the possibility of conflict between the two.

There can be little doubt that the greatest theoretical success of neoliberalism has been this collapsing of the distinction between two socially-embodied sets of values and interests. Mainstream socialist parties and even the trade unions themselves are now entirely willing to recognize that economic prosperity is a universal interest and that achieving it involves respecting certain more or less objective market parameters – parameters which no-one has consciously intended and which are not subject to human control. This willingness seems also to reflect the increasing difficulty of identifying a coherent 'working class' which is socio-culturally and/or economically clearly distinct from management.

Although contemporary critics have not yet arrived at a convincing theoretical response to the corporate theory of society, it is nonetheless clear that a return to the conception of socio-economic equilibrium that informed the pluralist model is very unlikely. The 'disembodiment' of the interests and values implicated in material reproduction – their detachment from any fixed association with particular organized groups in society – has in fact been of great significance in determining the direction that thinking about corporate legitimacy has taken over the last twenty years. As we noted above, the debate about the social acceptability of capitalism is no longer focused on the protection of the (historically contingent) work-related interests of the members of established trade unions in the industrialized world.

What remains in dispute is the assimilation of normative choices to supposedly pragmatic or technical economic ones. The corporate theory of society dismisses the issue of how to *achieve* a balance between economic and other social values. It insists that such a balance will arise naturally, on the basis of the technical choices of managers made within the general normative framework of society – as long, that is, as the need for flexibility is recognized within this framework. However, the claim that a purely technical apprehension of the parameters of corporate action is possible can be and has been challenged. Indeed, the corporate theory of society has been accused of representing a purely instrumental justification for actions that are of selfish or strategic origin. In this vein, the management techniques and practices associated with HRM and the practice of CSR and business ethics have frequently been denounced as fraudulent (Legge, 1995; Bendell, 2004). Whether or not the behaviour of corporations can be deemed illegitimate in this way depends on whether – or perhaps more accurately, to what extent – the corporate theory of society is a defensible view of the world. In the next chapter we will argue that it is not.

Chapter 2

Challenging the Corporate Theory of Society

In this chapter, we will consider some arguments that challenge the two basic components of the corporate theory of society: the non-political nature of management decision-making and the autonomy and objectivity of market forces.

Policy Decision-Making, Pragmatism and Politics

Habermas has proposed a general process model of social opinion- and will-formation – in effect, policy decision-making – in which 'pragmatic recommendations' are distinguished from interests and value preferences. Pragmatic discourses are those 'in which the rational choice between possible alternatives is justified' (1996, p.163). While the choice between alternatives is made with reference to interests and value preferences, these are merely hypothetically presupposed in the pragmatic discourse itself and remain external to it:

> The validity of pragmatic recommendations... does not depend on whether the directives are actually adopted and followed. In such discourse itself, there is no internal relationship between reason and will, between practical deliberation and acceptance of the results... Pragmatic discourses extend only to the construction of possible programs and estimation of their consequences. They do not include the formation of the reasonable will that adopts the program only in a further step, by *making its own* the goals and values hypothetically presupposed by the problem (pp.163-5; emphasis in original).

The distinction between pragmatic recommendations and positions taken on political-ethical goals and values is clearest where there is a significant technical component in decision-making. Take, for example, the field of public health. Some of the issues involved are wholly and unavoidably technical in the sense that there are facts involved that are unrelated to contingent goals and values and that no amount of discussion will change. What cannot be inferred from these facts alone, however, is the optimal mode of the *social organization* of prevention and treatment. There will always be certain pragmatically valid (technically effective) programs which are ruled out on the grounds of their political-ethical inadmissibility (for example, universal, compulsory HIV testing), just as certain measures which would otherwise be unacceptable from a political-ethical perspective (for example, limits on freedom of movement and association) may in certain circumstances have to be implemented because of the objective characteristics of the health issue in question (e.g. the need to place those suffering from serious contagious diseases in quarantine).

We can identify three more specific characteristics of this kind of policy decision-making process. The first is that the measures that are eventually taken will involve a *trade-off* between pragmatic/technical and political-ethical factors. They have to be technically effective, but also socially and politically acceptable. While there is obviously a degree to which technical effectiveness influences political possibility and vice versa, in the end it remains the case that certain established values may be set aside or downgraded because they are incompatible with a minimally effective policy, and certain technically effective measures may not be taken because they are incompatible with certain norms and values that are essential to a community's self-understanding.

The second characteristic is that the trade-off involved in determining the measures to be taken cannot be represented as a negotiation. Since the technical factors are objective and necessary, there is only one interest position in play, which is to say the general or public interest. While there may be those (usually the technical professionals) who champion the case for technical effectiveness over political possibility, they do so from the same public interest perspective as those whose primary concern is to minimize the disruption to established political-ethical values. In principle, although the policy measures that emerge represent a joint optimization which may not maximize conformity on either dimension, they are nonetheless optimal in an absolute sense with respect to the public interest.

The third characteristic is that the experts involved in the decision-making process can only have an advisory role. While their expertise qualifies them to give a view on the nature of the technical issues, beyond their ordinary capacity as citizens they have no special competence when it comes to weighing the pragmatic/technical aspects of policy against the political-ethical aspects. In short, they are not qualified to make a unilateral judgement on the validity of the trade-off between the two factors, and thus they cannot veto a decision made by those whose involvement in the decision-making body arises from the democratic process and who are accountable to the public.

'Politicized' Decision-Making

For all that it is very clear that political-ethical questions are central to decision-making even in the most technical policy spheres, the accusation of 'politicization' is nonetheless frequently directed at governments and administrations. In fact, the charge laid against decision-makers in such circumstances is that they have allowed private or partial preferences and interests to influence their choices and recommendations rather than focusing exclusively on the general interest. It is, of course, entirely possible that this occur. Staying in the field of healthcare, for example, those involved in decision-making may attempt to ensure that policy with regard to teenage pregnancy or the prevention of HIV infection conforms with conservative or religious opinions on sexual morality which they know are not widely shared. Alternatively, participants may seek to ensure that particular types of drug or treatment are preferred because of some private commercial or financial interest.

The contrast between the pragmatic discourse that is the means of establishing the technical parameters of decision-making and the strategic or instrumental use of reason and evidence that characterizes decision-making that is 'political' in this negative sense can be stark. On the one hand there is the (perceived) disinterested professionalism of the technical advisors and the idealized efficacy of the solutions they propose; on the other, the partiality or simply self-interest of the political appointees. A rejection of political modes of decision-making may follow, which leads easily on to calls for decision-making to be put entirely into the hands of technical advisors on the grounds that the validity of the solutions they propose, as Habermas points out, is independent of moral and political-ethical considerations. The distinction between the technical and normative aspects of policy is thereby entirely lost. Whereas the technical basis of policy is in principle open to challenge, the normative assumptions that also underpin regulation are latent or unspoken, and thus remain insulated from the policy debate. The validity of pragmatic/technical recommendations is conflated with the validity of the political-ethical goals and values presupposed by the problem that that recommendation is intended to address. In these circumstances, we can talk about an unwarranted de-politicization of decision-making.

'Falsely Technical' Decision-Making

Where such a de-politicization has occurred we can refer to the decision-making process as 'falsely technical'. In these cases, the validity of the policy aims and regulatory norms that arise from decision-making is grounded in the first instance by reference to the technical or professional competence of those involved in drawing up the regulations. Since professionalism is by definition disinterested, the implication of grounding validity in this way is that the norms promulgated are objective or technically necessary. There can be no question about their coherence with the general interest both because the substantive content of the norms is implied directly from certain true propositions about the nature of physical necessity, and because these propositions are identified through a value-free process of professional discourse.

To argue against compliance with the conclusions of such falsely technical decision-making processes can be very difficult. Challenging these conclusions involves questioning the validity of the trade-off between pragmatic/technical efficacy and existing political-ethical standards. This argument must in turn be justified on one or both of two possible grounds. First of all, the truth of the propositions about the nature of physical necessity which form the technical basis of regulation can be contested. It may be the case that existing norms and values whose validity is well-grounded are to be set aside in pursuit of a technical approach which is mistaken or less effective than claimed. Second, the validity of the latent political-ethical assumptions which underpin the proposed regulations can be contested. It may be the case that certain technically effective measures are not to be taken because of the wish to respect norms and values which are invalid or non-generalizable.

In the first case, it is inevitably difficult for those without a formal competence in whatever is the relevant technical area to challenge the opinion of the professionals. In the second, those wishing to challenge policy must first establish the nature of the latent political-ethical assumptions in question, identifying value-judgements and biases which are inherent in the established practices of professional groups, or which may have shaped the opinions of participants in decision-making. In other words, either the disinterestedness of a profession, or the professionalism of its members has to be put in question.

Policy Decision-Making in the Economic and Organizational Spheres

We suggested above that the technical effectiveness of public health policy is improved by its normative acceptability, and that if the technical effectiveness of certain measures is widely trusted, this will improve their normative acceptability. It remains the case, however, that the technical elements of the situation are logically separate from its normative aspects. The human immunodeficiency virus, for example, has certain necessary, objective characteristics which cannot be altered by human will or behaviour (although there may, of course, be some dispute about what these characteristics are). This is emphatically not the case with social systems, whether organizations or economies. The technical or functional characteristics of social institutions are as they are only insofar as (as Weber put it) there is a probability that certain persons will carry out the normative order governing those institutions (Weber 1977, p.49). As Anthony Giddens argues, the norms which are the basis of social action are inseparable from the functional characteristics of the social structures in the context of which that action takes place (Giddens, 1984). To change the normative regulation which governs social interaction in structural contexts is also to change the nature of the social structures themselves. Hence, in systemic contexts, a clear line cannot be drawn between pragmatic/technical and normative reasons for action. Whereas the latent normativity of the kind of technicized policy decision-making we discussed above is to do with values inherent in professional practice or individual action orientations, in cases where the technical component of decision-making relates to the characteristics of social and economic structures and institutions, the latent normativity is inherent in the claims about the nature of the structures in question. To argue that a social structure *is* a certain way is in an important sense to argue that it *ought* to be that way; or at least, to have passively accepted the legitimacy of the system of normative regulation which gives rise to it. It is hence to isolate a block of sociality from the possibility of criticism or challenge on the basis of its normative validity, assimilating it to objective reality and thereby restricting the possible critique to the 'technical' level of empirical social science.

Management as a Technical Profession

The problem here is that the members of the class of supposed technical professionals in economics and industrial organization have a private, partial interest in the system of relationships from which existing social and economic structures are constructed. Managers, for example, have an interest in being able to require that employees respond in a certain way to their plans, strategies and instructions. While they cannot pursue this interest directly – they cannot openly argue that the regulatory norms which govern social organization be designed to promote their interests alone – they are nonetheless able to pursue it indirectly by using their status as professionals to make claims about the effectiveness of certain organizational models on the basis of their technical knowledge of the functional characteristics of markets and economies. Pointing to a professional consensus on the (objective) technical superiority of a particular model of social organization of production – a model supported by statistical correlations of firm performance with the use of certain types of approach to the organization of relationships within the firm – they argue that the internal and external regulation of firms should conform to and support that model. Since managers are also the supposed technical professionals when it comes to the implementation of systems of production, distribution and exchange, in the managerial argument it is they themselves who are best placed to determine what counts as conformity and support in this respect.

The Trebly False Technicality of Management Decision-Making

In economic and industrial contexts, then, the de-politicization of decision-making is rather more complex than simply being a question of the illegitimate transfer or drift of normative authority to technical specialists. Beyond the possibility of 'normal' problems like professional conservatism or corruption and other forms of malpractice, there is a much deeper sense in which governance by 'experts' is potentially damaging to the general good.

First of all, the professional practice of management (and of the other members of the academic-industrial-advisory complex in whose hands both national and supra-national structures of economic and industrial governance are increasingly concentrated) is inherently normative: to argue that economies and organizations have a particular set of functional characteristics is also to argue that particular sets of social relationships between economic and organizational actors are legitimate. It is to exclude the possibility that these relationships might be otherwise. Simply to take the professional opinion of managers and their academic sympathisers at face value, then, even in a policy process which is otherwise properly democratic, already represents a significant de-politicization.

Second, the identification of what it is about successful organizations or economic policy interventions that makes them so is not a value-free process. Even the very definition of what constitutes success can be partial, the 'shareholder value' movement being a very good example. Perhaps the most significant potential for interested interpretation is to be found the very casual attitude to causality which characterises mainstream approaches to management research. Even though it is hardly controversial to argue that the formal organizational structure of an enterprise does not begin to give a full picture of the social relationships which exist within it, researchers cheerfully continue to focus on management interventions alone, correlating effects – in the sense of what enterprises actually do – with only a very small part of the spectrum of possible causes. In a recent review of the development of organization theory, for example, Michael Lounsbury and Marc Ventresca argue that 'as organizational theory emerged as a management subfield, conceptualizations of both social structure and organizations became increasingly instrumental, driven by functional imperatives, and animated by the prominence of narrow exchange approaches to behavior' (2003, p.462). Hence, we would argue that there is a tendency for management researchers both to oversimplify the nature of social organization, and to overestimate the ability of managers to control it. We can represent this tendency as a de-politicization because it exists at the cost of a proper appreciation of how much room there is for choice and variability in organizational configurations and practices.

Third, research into HRM and the other new management techniques associated with the pursuit of flexibility has demonstrated that they are applied selectively, with little regard for the overall coherence of the managerial approach and with a focus on the short-term resolution of local problems. The *integration* which is arguably the defining characteristic of a genuinely scientific or professional approach is notable by its absence. It seems, then, that these techniques are useful to managers only to the extent that they provide a potential for grounding and justification of increased managerial control. In this regard it has been argued that management is a 'constructed expertise' whose function is rhetorical rather than logical or scientific (Legge 1995; Townley 1993). The de-politicization of decision-making in the day-to-day practice of management would be obvious, then, even if it were not for the well-established antagonism between new management techniquess and worker self-organization. As we saw in Chapter 1, the market-referenced, unidimensional 'expertise' of managers is used to counter worker resistance which is justified by reference to moral and political-ethical factors. It provides a way for managers to avoid the need to respond to workers' arguments by deeming irrelevant the normative considerations on which trade unionism is based.

Challenging the Professionals of the Academic-Industrial-Advisory Complex

So, how might we go about puncturing the case which the technical professionals of organization and the economy have constructed for themselves? The first, more straightforward question we might pose is the same as that which arises in the context of non-economic de-politicization. Even if we accept that the exigencies of material reproduction give rise to certain types of social necessity or facticity which are in principle susceptible to being known in a technical sense – market pressures, international trade regulation, etc. – it is still not at all clear by what right a limited, self-appointed group can consider itself exclusively entitled to weigh the value of moral and political-ethical standards against the goal of pragmatic/technical efficacy on behalf of society. As we argued in Chapter 1, the traditional answer to this question has been collective bargaining in which the role of the unions is to act for society in the negotiation of the trade-off between social norms and economic efficiency. However, the idea of a *bargained* accommodation between capital and society is a defensible solution only if the social necessity against which normative standards have to be weighed is conceived from the perspective of workers alone; that is, if capital and its demands are placed outside society, beyond control and beyond the possibility of mutual understanding.

This conception of capital as something alien and apart was largely left behind in the 1980s and 1990s along with the planned economy and the cold war. But although it is now accepted as an integral part of society, capital is still treated as a sovereign institution, entitled to govern itself without considering the impact it might have on the rest of society. We deny ourselves access to the traditional social veto powers of regulation and, particularly, collective bargaining, but have not replaced them with any new way of ensuring that the actions of capital are coherent with a democratically-achieved conception of the good society.

The rejection of regulation and of bargaining has been a consequence of the success of the neoliberal argument that the public interest cannot be separated into economic and socio-political components with capital and labour each being assigned the task of defending one component against the encroachment of the other. However, despite the fact that in itself this argument has no implications for the organization of material reproduction, it has not been used as a springboard for the development of new modes of social oversight of the activities of capital. Instead, following exactly the pattern of the rejection of politicized modes of decision-making that we discussed above, the right to decide has simply been handed over to the technical professionals.

This brings us to a second question, which unlike the first is unique to economic and organizational contexts. Two things should be clear from the discussion above: (i) the technical professionals of the economy and the organization have a freedom to interpret the facts which is not available to those whose expertise relates to the physical world; (ii) in providing 'scientific' explanations of how organizations and the economy work, they are also giving an interpretive account of *how we are* – of the sets of political-ethical aims, values and interests that define societies and the smaller social groups that exist within them. Hence, the problem of corporate accountability is not simply a question of how to avoid potentially authoritarian responses to technical policy issues. Because the technical, supposedly necessary elements of the action situation can be interpreted to suit the aims of the professionals – and we do not suggest that they are necessarily aware of this – the line between the normative and the pragmatic/technical can be drawn in such a way that to all appearances, policy propositions are derived only from the most uncontroversially valid norms and the most objective economic and organizational facts. Hence, it can be argued the plans and policies of the professionals are so evidently in the general interest that democratic participation in decision-making would be pointless.

In order to make a significant impact on this argument, the challenges to corporate power that have arisen in the context of the anti-globalization movement are not sufficient in themselves. It is not enough simply to oppose the concrete policy propositions of the professionals, or to challenge their right to make unilateral judgements on issues of social organization – although the capacity to do this naturally remains important. Rather, what has to be contested is the very possibility of a value-free apprehension of the 'facts' of the economic or organizational situation. In the absence of such a contestation, the arguments of the technical professionals of capitalism in support of their own power are virtually impossible to oppose.

Contesting the Autonomy and Objectivity of Market Imperatives

As Lounsbury and Ventresca argue, the conception of the environment for corporate action as something that is 'abstract, unitary and exogenous to the actual workings of organizations and social life' (2003, p.463) is relatively recent. It was only with the development of organization theory in the 1960s and 1970s that the social context for organization behaviour began to be conceived in the very narrow sense of the market economy. The contemporaneous (re)emergence of neoclassical economics in academia and politics reinforced the message that what mattered most both in terms of explaining the actions of corporations and the individuals within them, and in terms of producing recipes for economic success, were relationships with the market.

Yet, the attempt to understand economic behaviour as a product of political and social processes as well as more strictly economic motivations has a long and distinguished history. Discussing the relationship between economics and sociology, for example, Milan Zafirovski (1999) recalls Durkheim's argument that the division of labour is a social phenomenon rather than a purely economic one, as well as Schumpeter's view that prices are obviously social phenomena, and Weber's observation that economic values should be understood as sociological categories 'in that, for example, 'they result from power constellations'' (p.498). Both Durkheim and Weber were important influences in the development of a school of economic analysis that has provided perhaps the most sustained and systematic critique of the classical and neoclassical approaches: German historical-social economics and its close American cousin, institutional economics. Currently undergoing something of a revival, arguably precisely because of its unrivalled purchase on the inadequacies of the neoclassical economic orthodoxy, this approach is based on the belief that 'all economic relations take place within specific cultural and institutional settings and that these background factors significantly shape the outcomes generated by supply and demand and other such economic forces' (Kaufman, 2004, p.57). To talk of cultural and institutional settings is to talk of moral norms and, more especially, political-ethical values, as well as their expression in laws and other forms of regulation. It is precisely the exclusion of norms and values from economic analysis that enables the justification of the claim that the market can be understood as an objective structural force.

Although the exclusion of the normative first arose as an empirical observation made from a critical standpoint, it has evolved into a positive theoretical commitment. Habermas has proposed a compelling reconstruction of this evolution, arguing that from the perspective of the strictly objectivating approach favoured above all by Marx, 'the image of social integration occurring through values, norms, communication, and even law disintegrates into mere illusion' (1996, p.46). Once faith in the unfolding of the grand historical telos of communism collapsed, what was left was a vision of society as a monolithic 'matrix of sheer compulsion' (p.47) held together by a single mechanism of integration, 'the exchange of economic equivalents' (ibid.). It is in the next stage of the evolutionary process that systems theory entirely loses its critical edge. The recognition of the growing complexity and increasing differentiation of society renders implausible the insistence on a single mechanism of integration. Instead, the systems functionalism of Parsons, and more recently Luhmann, conceives society as differentiated into multiple subsystems that 'meet at a horizontal level, so to speak, and stabilize one another by observing one another and, lacking the possibility of direct intervention, by reflexively adjusting to their mutual environments' (ibid.). The sense of compulsion, of an illegitimate obstruction of valid life-plans is here entirely lost, giving way to an affirmative systems theory that seeks to explain a varied and diverse society without starting with the self-understanding of actors.

It is not coincidental that perhaps the single most influential work in the pluralist industrial relations tradition, John Dunlop's *Industrial Relations Systems* (1958), was intended specifically as a piece of Parsonian systems theory. As we saw in Chapter 1, one facet of the pluralist approach was the conception of collective bargaining as the process of identifying the characteristics of an appropriate socio-economic equilibrium. One of the most important figures in British industrial relations research, Alan Fox, suggested that collective bargaining could be understood as an 'integrative subsystem which acts as one of the self-equilibrating mechanisms ensuring the survival and adaptation of the total system' (1974, p.282). Interestingly, Fox himself was sceptical of this approach precisely on the grounds that its functionalism left little room for critique. If there was little room for criticism, it was at least true that normatively-driven social forces like the labour movement could be incorporated into the grand theoretical picture. Habermas argues that by radicalizing Marxian systems analysis, both systems functionalism and structuralist social theories from Lévi-Strauss to Foucault 'avoid the narrowness and normative ballast associated with the holistic concepts of a philosophy of history. An unobstructed view is opened up for the wide range of variation, contingency, and diversity in highly complex societies' (1996, p.47).

The corporate theory of society actually takes the evolutionary process back a stage, reintroducing the holistic notion of society as a totality integrated by a single mechanism, the market. The difference is that the 'sheer compulsion' of the market is viewed as something positive, or at the very least as something neutral like a force of nature that we are obliged to live with. Non-economic norms and values simply do not appear on the theoretical radar. Rather, they are given the role of ensuring that actual empirical behaviour conforms with the corporate theory of society. Morality appears 'as a means to ends defined by economic rationality' (Fevre 2003, p.4). Politics is merely a support for economics. In this light, flexibility, HRM and other new management techniques are designed to produce a particular kind of economic behaviour that has no natural analogue.

The Problematic Status of Norm-Excluding Theory

There are three reasons why the exclusion of norms and values from what might be called the operational aspects of a theory of society – their relegation to an instrumental supporting role – is problematic. The first, as we have already argued, is that detaching the normative in this way obliges us to accept that the efficiency of material reproduction comes first, and that only once its demands have been satisfied can we sit down to consider what can be salvaged from the remains of our social and political priorities. There is no way to include norms and values *within* decisions about how to organize goal-achievement. At the same time as this kind of economic rationality can appear cruel and inhumane, it is also dangerously seductive since, as Polanyi argued, it allows us to 'delude ourselves that destitution and suffering [are] nobody's fault' (Fevre, 2003, p.13).

The second problem, quite simply, is that to assume that norms and values play no role in economic behaviour is wrong. It is straightforwardly untrue that normative factors are incidental or marginal to the functioning of the economy and the predictions of any theory that excludes them are likely to be inaccurate. Kaufman puts the argument with admirable clarity and is worth quoting at length:

> it is impossible to separate ethics and economics even on purely 'positive' grounds of prediction and understanding. With incomplete contracts, self-interest can quickly turn dysfunctional and anti-social. Because of bounded rationality, imperfect information and lock-in from fixed costs, economic agents have an incentive to cheat, lie, misrepresent, renege and extort both in the ex ante process of making a contract and the ex post process of contract implementation. This corruption of the economic exchange process can cause markets to self-destruct and bring great injury to the exposed party. In an imperfect world, legal sanctions can never fully eliminate such behaviour and, indeed, legal sanctions can be used by the powerful to exploit the weak. Thus, crucial to a well-functioning economy, and thus to economic theory, is a commonly accepted and observed moral code that protects the contracting process from breakdown and abuse. Also crucial to economic theory is one particular ethical value – justice (equity). Neoclassical economics neglects justice on the grounds that it is a metaphysical concept or non-scientific value judgement. Real people, however, judge economic transactions by not only price but also fairness, and transactions that are deemed unfair lead to predictable negative consequences, such as quitting, holding back work effort, striking and forming a union. Thus, institutional economics recognizes, not as a matter of special pleading but as a statement about how the world works, that free trade in property rights must also be fair trade and that exchanges that violate the canon of fairness will introduce their own form of inefficiency and welfare loss (2004, p.108).

Two recent pieces of work by economists associated with the institutional approach add further weight to the argument that there are not just moral but technical dangers in the neoclassical economic orthodoxy. In a paper discussing the possibilities for a theory of innovation, William Lazonick (2003) argues that markets – which he characterizes as offering 'profound economic and political freedom that, once acquired, is to be highly cherished and protected' (p.21) – are an outcome rather than a cause of economic development. It is organizations rather than markets that allocate resources to those innovative production processes that generate economic development. Whereas the conventional theory of the market economy would have it that 'participants in the economy have no possibility of strategically changing the technological and market conditions that they face…[,] the strategic transformation of technological and market conditions is what innovation is all about' (p.24). Lazonick characterizes the innovation process as collective, cumulative and uncertain: collective, because it depends on the integration within the organization of the knowledge, skills and effort of large numbers of people; cumulative, because the 'possibilities for the transformation of technological and market conditions in the future depend on the development of those conditions in the past' (ibid.); and uncertain, because the processes that can transform the corporate environment to 'generate higher quality, lower cost products are unknown at the time at which commitments of resources to these processes are made' (ibid.). On this basis, there are three 'social conditions' – which is to say, three characteristics of the business organization – which are necessary for successful innovation. The first is 'organizational integration', which means that it is the organization rather than the market that creates incentives that affect how people allocate their skills and efforts within a hierarchical and functional division of labour. The second is 'financial commitment', which is the allocation of financial resources 'to sustain the process that develops and utilizes productive resources until the resultant products can generate financial returns' (p.29). The third condition is 'strategic control', which is insider control of resource allocation as opposed to control by those with whom the corporation has only market relations, most notably shareholders.

Morris Altman's argument (2002) is that market criteria do not permit a socially rational choice to be made between high- and low-yield work cultures. Having assessed the available empirical research, he argues that there is 'rapidly amassing evidence that a certain set of work practices yield relatively large permanent increases in labour productivity, yet these work practices are simply not adopted and more often than not resisted by management' (p.274). These practices include employee participation, co-operative employment relationships associated with a minimally hierarchical management system, a relationship between wages and productivity, and employment security. Altman characterizes these high-yield work cultures as fulfilling Leibenstein's criteria for 'x-efficient' firms, that is, they operate at 'the outermost production possibility frontier' (p.278). However, achieving this level of productivity involves opportunity costs and, hence, 'the x-efficient firm might be characterized by the same average costs as the lower productivity x-inefficient firm if higher productivity and corresponding costs rise in an offsetting fashion. It is, therefore, quite possible that the x-inefficient firms can compete on the basis of low rates of labour compensation and a smaller investment in organizational capital' (p.280). If this is the case, then it is very unlikely that the high-yield work cultures will be adopted, despite the clear advantage to society in terms of greater per capita output and the private advantage to the workers of higher rates of pay. Altman argues that since it is not employees but managers who determine what the work culture will be, the costs of adopting and developing the new culture, mistrust between workers and managers, and an institutional investment environment that privileges short-run returns are likely to combine such that 'members of the firm hierarchy may find it utility maximizing to maintain their firm's competitive position within the framework of the traditional work culture, even if this involves reducing the level of their employees' pecuniary and non-pecuniary benefits or keeping them below what they otherwise might be' (p.283).

The arguments made by Lazonick and Altman both point to the same conclusion: the achievement of certain highly desirable economic outcomes is significantly less likely when non-market aims and values are excluded from the decision-making process. From the perspective of the corporate theory of society, Lazonick's social conditions of innovation and Altman's high-yield work cultures appear as market imperfections or rigidities. Belief in this theory 'tends to render ungovernable those corporate executives and political elites who wield power over the allocation of resources' (Lazonick, 2003, p.38), leaving decision-making exclusively in the hands of those who frequently 'do not incorporate into their objective function the utility generated to their employees by higher levels of income and improved working conditions' – Altman's marvellously academic way of describing those managers who simply do not care about the lives of their employees (2002, p.283).

The third reason why the corporate theory of society is problematic is the possibility that it will become self-fulfilling: that belief in this theory will gradually lead to the demoralization and de-legitimation of economic behaviour, with all the attendant risks that Kaufman, Lazonick and Altman identify. The claim that individuals *ought* to behave in a certain way because a particular theoretical model of their behaviour is *known* to be accurate is an important characteristic of neoliberal politics (Cradden, 2004, especially Chapter 2). To the extent that this sort of appeal is effective, it is not only because of a response to moral imperatives. There may also be a cognitive effect related to the propositions of the theory itself. That behaviour can be influenced by theoretical 'knowledge' about and conceptual models of that behaviour is well established. Steiner, for example, cites experimental evidence that 'suggests a large difference in the extent to which [trained] economists and non-economists behave self-interestedly... economists are more likely than others to free-ride' (Frank et al, cited in Steiner, 2001, p.450). The authors conclude that 'it would be remarkable indeed if none of the observed differences in behaviour were the result of repeated and intensive exposure to a model of unequivocal prediction that people will defect whenever self-interest dictates' (ibid.). Hence, insofar as neoliberalism can dominate political discourse, it is likely to have a cognitive as well as a normative impact. Even those actors whose economic knowledge is limited or nil can end up behaving as if they were knowledgeable. The 'embodiment' of particular models of economic rationality in government policy and regulation, as well as in the algorithms that inform computer modelling of the economy and financial markets means that there is a real sense in which society is moulded to fit the theory rather than vice versa. As Philippe Steiner puts it,

> formally rational economic knowledge is directly embodied in major institutions, to the point of turning rational economic knowledge into tools commonly implemented by people trying to achieve their economic goals. In such a situation, real actors are compelled (by law, by computers and by their own enlightened interest) to behave in the very rational way supposed by *virtuosi* (p.452).

Reintegrating Morality and Ethics into Economic Analysis: Institutional Economics, the Structure-Agency Problem, and Habermas's Social Theory

For all that the corporate theory of society is widely preached, and for all that it has no obvious competitor, the extent to which it has become embedded in society is questionable. The absence of any concerted contestation of the theory in mainstream politics may be due more to the lack of a clear and attractive alternative than to any positive acceptance of the concept of objective and morally neutral markets. The belief that economic behaviour involves an element of moral choice, and that just any behaviour cannot be justified simply on the grounds that it is 'demanded' by the market is pervasive (Steiner, 2001). This is perhaps one reason why the exclusion of norms and values from economics and the sociology of economic behaviour – and hence the conceptualization of the market as objective and autonomous – is increasingly being called into question, particularly in the context of the revived interest in institutional economics.

Stephen Ackroyd has argued that while 'the effects of organisation are beyond control, it is not yet clear that organisations themselves are beyond control' (2000, p.105). He goes on, 'However, a first step in taking control of them, or rendering it a possibility, is to understand better how far organisations are already in control of participants, but, also, how participants are persuaded that they are not' (ibid.). Ackroyd's argument suggests that the successful reintegration of moral norms and political-ethical values into economic analysis depends on our ability appropriately to conceptualize the relationships between the structural forces to which corporations respond and contribute, corporations themselves, the individuals who constitute them and the ideas these individuals have about the nature of the corporation and the market. In attempting to construct a theoretical picture of corporate legitimacy, then, we come hard up against one of the most intractable problems in sociological theory, that of the relationship between structure and agency. Everything we have seen so far strongly suggests that a reliance on purely structural, 'subject-less' explanations for macro-level social phenomena is likely to be misleading, but at the same time the relationship between micro-level processes of opinion- and will-formation and aggregate outcomes at the level of society is not at all clear.

This is where we are obliged to cross the frontiers of institutional economics, which is obviously limited in its ability to treat these wider questions of social theory. This is not to say that we have to abandon its insights. Indeed, Zafirovski argues that economics should be thought of as a branch of a more comprehensive general theory of social action that 'achieves the conceptual integration of analysing individual actions and analysing social structures, establishing the micro-macro link' (1999, p.509). Such a theory would 'generate explanations of the nature, factors and consequences of human social action, and of the structure, functioning and change of the social system, via a conception of the social structuration of individual agency and of agency's construction of social structure, including the 'definition of situation'' (ibid.). In order to pursue our aim of a theory of corporate legitimacy, then, it seems that what we require is a critical general social theory that permits the conceptualization of economic behaviour and economic structures as particular cases of social interaction and social structure rather than as something entirely apart.

To the extent that contemporary critical social theory has already found its way into those disciplines concerned with business and economics, not much light has been shed on this matter. It has been writers of a postmodernist tendency, particularly Michel Foucault, who have been most obviously influential (for example, Sewell and Wilkinson, 1992; McKinlay and Starkey (eds), 1998; Townley, 1993; Du Gay, Salaman and Rees, 1996). While many of the analyses in this tradition provide plausible accounts of the micro-pathology of processes of power and control *within* organizations, they nonetheless have little to say about the structural context against which power and control is exercised; about what goes on *outside* the organization in the sense of the market and regulatory environment within which enterprises have to operate. As Barbara Townley, one of the most influential management Foucauldians herself suggests, such approaches are less interested in the 'why?' or the 'who?' of power, than the 'how?' (1993). Hence they are of little use if one is trying to understand how structural forces are translated into motivation, and how the motives of actors affect the characteristics of social structures. Indeed, as Ackroyd points out, Foucault's work permits almost no grip on the idea of organizations as discrete social phenomena. His 'categories so cut across organization structures and boundaries, disassembling them into practices, that they do not exist in recognisable forms within his systems of thought' (Ackroyd, 2000, p.93).

Nonetheless, and in a more general sense, the insights of the 'linguistic turn' in the hermeneutic social scientific tradition are too valuable to dismiss. However, as Peter Hamilton points out, and as is hardly surprising given the debt owed by the discipline to systems functionalism, the tendency in industrial relations research has been to focus on the structural rather than the linguistic. Hamilton argues that we should unduly privilege neither: 'It is through the linguistic that we uncover the structural and vice versa as the structural influences our choice of rhetorical strategies and arguments' (Hamilton 1999, p.174).

Habermas

Fortunately there is a growing body of work which attempts to apply a 'critical modernist' or 'realist' social theory to problems in the sociology of work, industry, employment or organizations. Recently, the theoretical approaches of Anthony Giddens, Norbert Elias and Roy Bhaskar have all been canvassed as potential starting points for an industrial sociology that takes both structure and agency seriously (Barley and Tolbert 1997; Ackroyd 2000; Newton 1998, 1999; Reed 1997). Given the degree of interest in this area, it is perhaps surprising that beyond the very general discussion provided by Gibson Burrell (1994) there has been such limited attention paid to the work of Habermas, the most distinguished figure in the broad critical modernist camp, and, other than Giddens, the only one to have proposed a comprehensive general theory of society. We want to suggest that Habermas's work bears very close attention. His *Theory of Communicative Action* (1984, 1987) in particular seems to hold out the possibility of relating social structure and social action in a way that maintains what Mike Reed has called a 'stratified social ontology' (1997, p.21), which is to say assuming a realist stance with respect to social structures and social institutions while at the same time allowing that structures ultimately rest on shared meanings and are thus, at least in principle, susceptible to rationally-motivated change.

It is also arguable that Habermas's discourse ethics, outlined most comprehensively in *Between Facts and Norms* (1996), can provide institutional economics with a rational basis for determining the normative foundations of decision-making and policy choices. Kenneth Avio argues that institutional economics, while it takes as a basic premise the existence of normative, value-based action, skips rather too lightly over the distinction between 'a *belief* in legitimacy and legitimacy per se' (2004, p.720). Whereas moral and ethical claims might be legitimized by religion or culture, that is, given the appearance or aura of legitimacy, the *legitimation* of such claims is a different matter – if, indeed, legitimation in this sense of being *actually* just and worthy of support is even possible. Institutionalists,

Avio argues, typically adopt a 'quasi-relativist' attitude towards the concept of legitimacy, an attitude that reflects their scepticism with regard to the possibility of legitimation as a rational process. This scepticism is in turn a legacy of the 'hostility of Veblen, Dewey and John R. Commons to natural rights and to ultimate, a priori truths' (p.721). In processes of legitimation, institutionalists tend to seek a balancing of social power in which 'participants follow their strategic interests bounded by institutional rules designed to give each party an equal opportunity to sway the other to one's own point of view' (p.729). This formulation precisely avoids the need to distinguish between the validity of norms and their de facto acceptance. However, by assuming from the outset that bargaining based on the pursuit of strategic interests is the appropriate modus operandi for the coordination of economic action, it also pre-judges the issue of whether a true consensus based on the mutual recognition of generalizable interests might be possible. We would suggest that any serious attempt to respond to the corporate theory of society must start from acceptance of the idea that such a unitary economic interest is possible in principle. This in turn requires that participants adopt, using Avio's words once more, 'an entirely different performative attitude, one predicated on the desire to reach a mutual understanding on the validity of contested norms' (p.729). Habermas's discourse ethics is intended as a means of specifying the conditions under which a consensus on pragmatic, ethical and moral questions can be said to exist. It defines the characteristics of a process of legitimation whose outcomes can be said to have a rationally justified or cognitive status.

As we noted at the beginning of Chapter 1, Habermas's principal argument in *Between Facts and Norms* is that democracy is a necessary condition for the legitimation of law, that is, for political legitimation. The principal general condition for legitimate social interaction is an orientation to mutual understanding, which is to say an approach to action coordination in which participants aim to reach a consensus on a plan of action that is in the general interest of those involved. This condition rules out technocratic governance in which the right to decide is vested in a limited number of 'experts', but also the use of bargained or majoritarian forms of democracy, at least as a first resort. Rather, it implies the use of deliberative modes of decision-making in which only reasons valid from the perspective of all participants are acceptable. In short, Habermas argues that the validation of rules of social conduct is only possible on the basis that there are good reasons supporting them in themselves and not simply because they are the outcome of a compromise negotiated according to some agreed procedure. This is not to say that fair compromises do not have their place. However, it is only once it has been established that no adequate collective self-understanding is possible that a 'rational balancing of competing value orientations and interest positions' is appropriate (Habermas, 1996, p.108). Hence, for example, Habermas's work points clearly away from pluralist industrial relations towards non-bargained forms of involvement and participation. At first sight the types of employment relationship proposed in the literature on HRM and organization culture, and the types of relationship with the community implied by the literature on CSR and business ethics would seem to get close to the deliberative ideal. However, because of the insistence on the ultimate managerial right to direct corporate action, regardless of the democratic will of those inside or outside the corporation who are affected, they do not fulfil the validity conditions that Habermas proposes.

Objections to Habermas

Despite the prima facie interest of Habermas's approach, it has not been widely used in critical approaches to business and management. One possible reason for this is that he himself seems to support an objectivist conception of the market. In *The Theory of Communicative Action* he argues that meanings – normatively valid interpretations of social phenomena – can *only* be established in the social and cultural institutional spheres (the 'lifeworld') and, second, that in the political-administrative and economic spheres (the 'system') only a very restricted range of meanings retain any importance and that even these are fixed, their implications for action pre-specified rather than open to interpretation. In short, he argues that social action in economic contexts is not and cannot be conducted on the basis of valid norms. For our purposes this amounts to the admission that there is no way that the social and political aims of the labour and anti-globalization movements can be an integral element of action within a market economy. As Cannon argues, 'Habermas' reputation as a critical theorist rests on his defence of the lifeworld against the 'colonizing' tendencies of the system, but he is equally concerned to protect the system from the lifeworld' (2002, p.2). The remoralization of the economic system would, in his view, simply result in a loss of technical efficiency, and since technical efficiency is the very essence of what the economy is for, there is no point in trying to render it normatively accountable by attempting to democratize the interpretation of market forces. This self-imposed restriction is the more frustrating both because the connection between meaning and social action which Habermas proposes is highly convincing and because the mode of analysis that accompanies it – known as formal pragmatics – is innovative, sophisticated and powerful.

Fortunately, there is reason to believe that objections such as Cannon's can be surmounted, particularly if certain elements of Habermas's more recent work are taken into account. In *Between Facts and Norms* (1996), Habermas appears much more willing to concede that norms can have an impact on the functioning of the economic and political-administrative systems, although he is careful to insist that this impact is only possible when norms have been translated into the language of law. He argues that once 'normatively substantive messages' have been rendered in the complex legal code that is comprehensible in both the lifeworld and the system, they no longer 'fall on deaf ears'. 'Law thus functions as the 'transformer' that first guarantees that the socially integrating network of communication stretched across society as a whole holds together' (Habermas, 1996, p.56). This is a significant qualification of the stark separation of lifeworld and system that characterizes Habermas's earlier work. However, the precise implications of this qualification have yet to be drawn out.

Conclusion

The corporate theory of society legitimizes unilateral managerial decision-making. This is its purpose. It represents an ensemble of claims and assumptions about the social world and our relationship to it that provide grounding and justification for the absence of democracy in the corporate context. Whether this legitimization works as a *legitimation* is a different matter. This depends on whether the claims of the corporate theory of society can be sustained. In this chapter we have argued that many of the most basic elements of that theory are in fact false. We have suggested that the insights of institutional economics provide invaluable resources for the construction of a critique of the corporate theory of society, but we have also argued that in order properly to understand the relation between the micro- and macro-social processes of the economy, we need to combine these insights with the more general approach of critical social theory. We have proposed that the work of Habermas has great potential in this respect, although there are certain problems that must first be resolved.

The purpose of the discussion that proceeds over the following chapters is twofold. First, it aims to provide an outline of the theoretical scheme that Habermas develops in *The Theory of Communicative Action* and *Between Facts and Norms*. Second, it attempts to resolve the problems we have identified by showing that Habermas pays a price higher than necessary for the maintenance of the structural aspect of his scheme. After giving a brief outline of formal pragmatics and the methodological approach it implies, we go on to show that the concept of media-steering, proposed as a functional substitute for the substantive link between meaning and action which obtains in lifeworld contexts, is inadequate to the task of capturing the full range of possible meanings of the employment relationship. It will be argued that in order to comprehend social action in the context of the private business corporation, the concept of the lifeworld is not just advantageous but necessary, that the method of formal pragmatics is thereby admissible, and that the connection between structure and meaning is rather more direct than Habermas allows. This will enable us to construct an argument that a normatively-framed capitalism, and hence authentically legitimate corporate behaviour, is possible.

Chapter 3

Habermas's Social Theory

Habermas's two-volume *Theory of Communicative Action* was published in the original German in 1981. *Between Facts and Norms* appeared in 1992. Although these works are separated by more than ten years, they are best understood as a single project: a grand theory of economy, society and polity. The earlier work, which for convenience's sake we shall refer to as 'TCA', establishes the ontological and epistemological foundations of the theoretical approach. To borrow one of his own phrases, Habermas 'critically appropriates' and draws together the work of the principal social theorists of the 19th and 20th centuries, including Marx, Weber, Durkheim, Mead, Lukacs and Parsons, as well as his Frankfurt School predecessors Adorno and Horkheimer. The critical synthesis that he proposes involves leaving behind what he calls 'the philosophy of consciousness', that is, the attempt to found a theory of society on the perceptions of the isolated individual. Instead, he argues that *interactions* between individuals should be the fundamental unit of analysis. Running through all of his work is a desire to propose explanations that are adequate from the perspective of social evolution. The observation that natural language is the evolutionarily primary mode of social interaction leads to the theoretical emphasis on the logical structure of communication and to the normative emphasis on dialogue as a basis for social and political practice that are perhaps the best known characteristics of Habermas's approach.

The later work, which we shall refer to as 'BFN', is an extension and in some respects a clarification of the earlier. William Rehg has suggested that 'one might read [*Between Facts and Norms*] as drawing out the legal, political and institutional implications of [*The Theory of Communicative Action*]' (Rehg in Habermas, 1996, p.x). An important part of Habermas's aim is to show that democratic processes of opinion- and will-formation are the analogue of communicative interactions at the level of society. Just as communication undertaken with an orientation to mutual understanding is the foundation of normative legitimacy, deliberative democracy – as distinct from majoritarian or bargained forms of democracy – is a procedurally necessary foundation for legitimate law. The 'conceptual or internal relation between the rule of law and democracy' to which we referred at the beginning of Chapter 1 can be seen as merely a logical extension of the relation between communicative interaction and legitimacy that Habermas proposes in TCA.

In this chapter we will begin by outlining the basic elements of TCA, attempting in so doing to explain the choices that Habermas makes in the course of constructing his theoretical scheme. We will go on to argue that although in some senses BFN simply carries on further down the path established in the earlier work, it can also be read as representing a change of direction, albeit not a sharp one. One of the most important implications of TCA is that legitimate norms have no place in the economic and political-administrative spheres. What is more, the strategic motivation generated in these systemic contexts tends to drive out processes of consensus formation in language even in the social and cultural core of the lifeworld, something that Habermas calls the 'colonization of the lifeworld'. In BFN, by contrast, Habermas argues that 'the socially integrating force of solidarity... should be able to hold its own against the other two mechanisms of social integration, money and administrative power' (1996, p.299). The implication of this argument is that, given appropriate democratic procedures, it ought to be possible to exercise a degree of social control over social systems.

The Theory of Communicative Action[1]

Habermas suggests that there are two conceptual strategies that can be used to approach the analysis of the integration of social groups, that is, the ties that bind individuals in more or less coherent and ongoing association. Both of these strategies start from a definition of social association as the co-ordination of action, but where one approach stresses the achievement of co-ordination through the harmonization of action *orientations* – the reasons actors would give for acting as they do – the other maintains that that association is sustained through the functional interconnection of action *consequences*. Adopting the first strategy, society is conceived as the *lifeworld* of a social group. Adopting the second, society is understood as a self-regulating or boundary-maintaining *system*. Habermas argues that an adequate theory of society can only be constructed if both strategies are used simultaneously.

Rationality and Communicative Action

Before considering the idea of society as a lifeworld, we must introduce Habermas's concept of communicative action, which on his account is the fundamental mode of rational social action. For Habermas, modernization and rationalization are essentially synonymous processes. The modernization of society is a process of 'disenchantment', of the ever deeper penetration of rationality into the conceptual underpinning of our interpretations of the world. In the modern society there will be no 'sacred', no 'rationally impenetrable normative consensus' at the root of our interpretive commitments. Nothing will be immune from questioning or dissent, and everything will be rationally justifiable.

---

[1] The description of Habermas's theories which follows is based on a reading of Volumes 1 and 2 of Thomas McCarthy's translation of *The Theory of Communicative Action* (Habermas, 1984; 1987). It also draws on McCarthy's introduction to the whole work included in Volume 1 and on William Outhwaite's introduction to Habermas (1994). Some of the references below are to quotations from Volume 2 cited by McCarthy in his introduction. The translation of these passages is in some cases slightly different to the published translation of Volume 2.

Unlike Weber, Habermas argues that rationalization need not mean the exclusion of norms and values from social action in the public sphere. It is crucial to his argument that rationality can, indeed must, extend beyond the realm of the objective or material. According to the paradigmatically modernist 'cognitive-instrumental' conception of rationality, rational actions are those which contribute to the successful pursuit of some material aim – whether pursued by an individual or a social group – in the context of a known objective world and its properties. This strategy is based on the assumption that the material or objective world can be shown to exist in a way which clearly differentiates it from those categories of phenomena which are merely subjective, i.e. which are insusceptible to proof or disproof. Action that occurs within the realm of the subjective is neither rational nor irrational as it cannot be justified with reasons which are in principle refutable.

There are two problems with this approach. First of all, the distinction between objective and subjective leaves social phenomena in an ambiguous position. While it would be difficult for even the most hard-line philosophical realist to argue that they did not exist, at the same time they are insubstantial, consisting in the final analysis of nothing more than norms and conventions. Social institutions also provide the context for human action which must surely be describable as rational or irrational rather than neither.

Second, along with Hume, Nagel and many others, Habermas accepts that this kind of simple differentiation between categories of phenomena in terms of their supposed ontological status is in any case not sustainable. Indubitably true, foundational knowledge is unattainable. It is no more possible to prove beyond all doubt that the computer on which this chapter is being written exists than it is to prove that Microsoft does, or that Bill Gates is an identifiable and distinct entity.

However, this does not mean that we cannot act rationally, nor does it mean that we have to abandon the concepts of knowledge, truth and objectivity. In attempting to ground his theory of society in a way adequate to the resolution of these difficulties, Habermas begins by defining rational action as action for which there are good reasons or grounds which could in principle be defended in argument. This is a significantly broader conceptualization than that of cognitive-instrumental rationality. Specifically included within the category of good reasons or grounds are not only objective 'facts', but valid or legitimate social norms and authentic or sincere subjective desires, intentions and experiences. On this scheme – and other things being equal – it is as rational to take some action because it is conventional or right, or on the basis of some internal impulse, as it is because it is the action is likely to be effective in the prosecution of some material aim in the context of an objective world.[2]

This 'communicative' conception of rationality – so-called because the rationality of action is defined in terms of an actor's ability to make an argument that her action is rational – implies a change in the core problematic of philosophy and the social sciences. We must abandon both the attempt to establish indubitable chains of

---

[2] By way of example, Habermas suggests that it is irrational, indeed arguably impossible, simply to want a saucer of mud, but that it is rational to want a saucer of mud *in order to enjoy* its rich river smell.

reasoning connecting some reliable perception of a transcendent, ontologically self-sufficient world to our descriptions of it, as well as the assumption that it is only if we manage to do this that we are justified in using the concepts of truth and objectivity.[3] Having rid ourselves of this baggage, the interesting issue then becomes 'the intersubjectivity of possible understanding and agreement'. Rather than trying to answer the questions 'do I know?' and 'how do I know?', we should instead begin by trying to explain how we, the members of society, come to agree or otherwise to accept that we know what we know in common.

If the crucial feature of rationality is reason-giving, then knowledge must rely on agreement or understanding between two or more actors. It is important to understand, however, that the process of reaching understanding *cannot itself be reduced to some kind of comparison or alignment of meanings which have been previously apprehended by individuals*. To agree that something is the case is not simply to share a recognition of something in the objective world and its properties. 'Coming to an understanding is not an empirical event that causes de facto agreement' (Habermas, 1984, p.392). It is not a question of the objective, real or platonically essential world 'acting on' individual human subjects such as to stimulate some cognitive response which may or may not be correct and about which two or more individuals can subsequently agree (or disagree). Rather, coming to an understanding 'is a process of mutually convincing one another in which the actions of participants are co-ordinated on the basis of motivation by reasons' (ibid.).

Whereas the paradigmatic case of cognitive-instrumental rationality involves the relationship of an isolated individual to something in the objective world, communicative rationality involves a relationship between two or more individuals in which there is no restriction on the admissible categories of subject matter – objective, social or subjective. Because rationality is founded on reason-giving, and therefore on a relationship between two or more individuals whose ability to agree or disagree with each other is unrestricted by external forces, we can say that it is itself a normative or social phenomenon. Habermas argues that '[i]n contrast to *representation or cognition, coming to an understanding* requires the rider uncoerced, because the expression is meant to be used here as a normative concept (ibid.; emphasis in original).

We come to know and understand only through communication which aims to achieve an unforced and therefore valid agreement. While *de facto* agreement on an issue may arise for any number of reasons, this does not necessarily make for a valid

---

[3] Habermas is on this reading a philosophical realist. The implication of his argument is that since it is logically certain that we can never be certain, then our use of terms like truth and objectivity cannot be based on this unattainable certainty. However, he would, for example, reject Richard Rorty's claim that all we have are unending chains of semantic connection and that any interpretation is as valid as another (see Rorty, 1979). Rorty's criteria for the success of any one interpretation of the world over another – for example the convenience or attractiveness of an interpretation at a particular point in time – would be rejected by Habermas as insufficient. The 'force of the better argument' will exclude a range of possible conclusions because they are not *coherent with the evidence*.

consensus. Objectivity, in other words, depends on the attitude and intentions of participants in dialogue. It requires actors to engage in *communicative action* rather than, somehow, to ensure that the facts they want to communicate have been apprehended in a value-free way. Knowledge is subsequent, rather than prior to communication.

Habermas argues – perhaps more accurately implies – that it would be pointless to deny that reality is 'constructed' in the sense that the ultimate source of epistemic authority can only be agreement between 'speaking and acting subjects' who are free to argue and question without reservation. For this reason, what we call reality is in principle always susceptible to *re*construction or *re*definition. There can never be absolutely final and unquestionable truths, but for Habermas this does not mean that we are condemned to relativism. It simply means that we need to look for a yardstick of objectivity which does not depend on being able to demonstrate some kind of correspondence between the content of an utterance and a transcendent reality.

This yardstick is the extent to which the force of the better argument prevails as the basis for the definition of situations. While he briefly discusses the theory of argumentation, he leaves open the question of criteria for the assessment of what constitutes the better argument in any given situation. This is, of course, an entirely logical consequence of his epistemology. Given the appropriate conditions – the 'ideal speech situation', in which participants in discussion are free to argue unreservedly, are equally capable of so doing and participate in the negotiation of the situation definition with a communicative attitude – then the better argument is quite simply that which prevails.

Rather than chasing the red herring of criteria for truth, then, Habermas devotes his energy to clarifying what he calls the formal properties of communicative action. In line with his more general commitment to avoiding explanations based on some characteristic or state of the individual – the philosophy of consciousness – he argues that the analysis of the 'communicative attitude' cannot be understood as a psychological task: 'It is not my aim to characterize behavioral dispositions empirically, but to grasp structural properties of processes of reaching understanding' (Habermas, 1984, p.286).

There are two aspects or stages to this rather technical argument. First, and perhaps more important, the communicative use of language has to be distinguished from its strategic or instrumental use. We must be able to identify the actor who aims with her sentence to say what she says and to do nothing more than this. This is in contrast to the actor who, although prosecuting her aim through the use of language, intends to do *more* or to do *other* than say what she says; to act *strategically* with an egoistic orientation to the success of their individual plan rather than with a view to the harmonization of plans of action. Second, communication must be shown to be the original or evolutionarily primary mode of language use on which other, instrumental forms of language use are parasitic.

Drawing on Anglo-American philosophy of language, and in particular on J. L. Austin's theory of speech acts, Habermas argues that the structure of language is such that in saying anything at all, actors unavoidably 'raise claims to validity'; that is, they assert the validity of the premises of their statement. These premises are references to what he calls the three worlds of human experience: the one objective world of existing, factual states of affairs; the common social world of norms, conventions and institutions; and the speaker's own subjective world of emotion and inner experience. A validity claim, then, is a claim that an objective state of affairs is *true*; that a norm or convention is *legitimate*; or that a subjective experience is *authentic* or *sincere*. To understand the meaning of any sentence is to understand the objective, social and subjective conditions to which a speaker tacitly refers: those conditions the validity of which needs to be assumed if the sentence is to be taken at face value.

The communicative actor undogmatically believes in the validity of the claims she raises. Consequently, in accepting another individual's 'offer' of communication – in taking it at face value – a hearer is accepting as valid the implicit arguments underpinning the sentence. She is accepting that the speaker could, at least in principle, produce good reasons to support the validity of her statement. As we noted above, Habermas is keen to stress that coming to an understanding in this way is a normative event. Having accepted that the claims raised in a statement are valid, the hearer is subsequently *bound* to act in a way which is coherent with the offer of communication she has accepted. She is subject to the binding or bonding force of criticizable claims to validity.

Habermas's own example helps to illustrate the point. Suppose that a seminar participant has the following request addressed to him by a professor: 'Please bring me a glass of water.' The participant can either take the request at face value and go and fetch a glass of water or,

> he can in principle reject this request under three validity aspects. He can either contest the normative rightness of the utterance:
>
> > No. You can't treat me like one of your employees.
>
> or he can contest the subjective truthfulness of the utterance:
>
> > No. You really only want to put me in a bad light in front of the other participants.
>
> or he can deny that certain existential presuppositions obtain:
>
> > No. The next water tap is so far away that I couldn't get back before the end of the session (Habermas, 1984, pp.306-7).

Habermas shows that the seminar participant's understanding of the professor's utterance consists in his either accepting or rejecting the claims raised by the professor. In each of the four cases – acceptance, or rejection on any of the three grounds suggested – the participant's understanding of the content of the utterance cannot be separated from the positions he takes on the validity claims raised.

If the professor is acting communicatively, then all of her meaning, all she intends to say is contained in the propositional content of her utterance. There is nothing more. For the seminar participant to respond to her request by saying something like 'Yes, I'll just be a moment' indicates that he has accepted the validity claims which constitute the meaning of the professor's statement. If he had refused the request on any of the grounds suggested, his refusal would of necessity have been based on *the same* understanding of what validity claims the professor was raising. However, it would also have required that he impute some intent to the professor which bore no internal or logical connection to the propositional content of her utterance. There is nothing in the meaning of the sentence used by the professor that has any connection to the humiliation of the seminar participant, or to causing him to miss the seminar. However, had the professor wished to produce these effects for whatever reason, she could not have done so without the participant understanding the meaning of the sentence in terms of its underlying validity structure, accepting the claims raised, and subsequently being rationally bound to comply. The success of her strategic action requires that the participant comply with her request, and he will do so only if he understands by what she says the propositional content of her sentence and nothing more.

So, while speech can be used instrumentally, that this is possible relies on the communicative structure of language: 'speech acts have a certain independence in relation to communicative action, though the meaning of what is said always points to the interaction structures of communicative action (Habermas, 1984, p.295).

We will return to the subject of the structure of communicative action (and of the structural components of lifeworlds, which we introduce below) when we discuss the methodological implications of this part of Habermas's theory.

The Lifeworld

Habermas introduces the concept of the lifeworld as a complement to that of communicative action. He suggests that,

> If the investigations of the last decade or so in socio-, ethno-, and psycholinguistics converge in any one respect, it is on the often and variously demonstrated point that the collective background and context of speakers and hearers determines interpretations of their utterances to an extraordinarily high degree... [T]he literal meaning of an expression must be completed by the background of an implicit knowledge that participants normally regard as trivial and obvious (Habermas, 1984, pp.335-6).

It seems obvious that in the overwhelming majority of communication situations, participants do not *explicitly* assess the validity claims raised by their interlocutors, in the sense of consciously following a train of thought which identifies and tests the claims underpinning any statement.

The lifeworld – the term was originally coined by Husserl and was later taken up by Schutz in particular – is the 'world of everyday experience as opposed to the realm of transcendental consciousness' (Burrell and Morgan, 1979, p.243). Lifeworlds might be described as a social group's dictionary of accepted or established interpretations of particular experiences. They supply the 'always-already-there' set of interrelated and mutually-supporting background convictions drawn upon by actors in the course of interpreting the situations in which they find themselves. Put simply, we might say that a lifeworld is a socially accepted definition of reality: an 'indeterminate and inexhaustible background of... unquestioned presuppositions, a shared global preunderstanding that is prior to any problems or disagreements' (McCarthy in Habermas, 1984, p.xxvi).

Lifeworlds have three structural components corresponding to the three worlds of human experience we have already encountered: the objective physical world of existing states of affairs (culturally stored knowledge), the social world of legitimate norms of action (social institutions) and the subjective world of authentic expressions of self (personality structures).

Although it may seem fairly obvious, it is worthwhile setting out exactly why the idea of the lifeworld is of such central importance. The lifeworld of a society provides its participants with interpretive resources, 'embodying cultural reproduction (continuity of tradition, coherence and rationality of knowledge), social integration (stabilization of group identities, solidarity) and socialization (transmission of generalized competences for action, harmonization of individual biographies with collective forms of life)' (Outhwaite, 1994, p.87). It is a lexicon of the meanings, acceptable within the horizon of a society, of all the phenomena an actor can experience. As such it can both motivate actors to engage in, and place limits on action. A situation interpreted in one way defines a range of actions that it is rational or normatively acceptable for an actor to take in response to that situation. Interpreting the same situation in a different way will give rise to a different range of possible actions, rendering others non-rational or normatively unacceptable. Groups of actors who share a situation definition will possess the same or similar action orientations and thus their actions are co-ordinated.

The equation of society with lifeworld is therefore an attractive conceptual strategy. In modern societies, the sharing of situation definitions arrived at through mutual negotiation based on rational argument is the source of a rationally binding or bonding force. These ties are produced and reproduced through the medium of communicative action and stored in the lifeworld.

> In coming to an understanding with one another about their situation, participants in communication stand in a cultural tradition which they use and at the same time renew; in co-ordinating the actions via intersubjective recognition of criticizable validity claims, they rely on memberships in social groups and at the same time reinforce the integration of the latter; through participating in interaction with competent reference persons, growing children internalize the value orientations of their social groups and acquire generalized capacities for action (Habermas, cited by McCarthy in Habermas, 1984, p.xxvi).

Habermas identifies a problem with the argument that social groups can be equated with lifeworlds, however, in that it can only partially account for the dynamics of change in social structures. There is certainly a developmental or internal logic to the symbolic reproduction of the lifeworld that can account for some social change in the sense that there are certain aspects of social evolution that have to be seen as learning processes. This internal logic places limitations on the variation of concrete historical lifeworlds in the sense that societies can only support those ideas that are 'thinkable' – those social innovations that are normatively acceptable within existing limits. 'On the other hand, social reality is not exhausted by the ideas embodied in it; and these ideas *change in response to forces and factors that cannot be explained in terms of inner logic*' (McCarthy in Habermas, 1984, p.xvii; emphasis added).

Taken by itself, the lifeworld approach conceptualizes society from the purely internal perspective of participants and,

> remains blind to causes, connections and consequences that lie beyond the horizon of everyday practice... In this perspective, the reproduction of society appears to be only a question of maintaining the symbolic structures of the lifeworld; processes of material reproduction, through which the social system secures its physical existence in relation to nature and the other social systems, fade into the background (McCarthy in Habermas, 1984, pp.xxviii-xxix).

The System

This brings us to the idea of the integration of social groups conceived as system integration, an idea which Habermas argues can be attributed primarily to Durkheim. On Habermas's reading, Durkheim took the view that 'whereas primitive societies are integrated via a basic normative consensus, the integration of developed societies comes about via the systemic interconnection of functionally specified domains of action' (Habermas, 1987, p.115).

It seems obvious that at least some of the aggregate effects of interest-oriented actions are not intended by, indeed are not even visible from the perspective of, the individual actor. These effects are nonetheless real and have an impact on societies, as it were, from the outside. This comes clearly into view when we consider the material reproduction of society, which, although it requires that the activities of separate individuals be co-ordinated, cannot be represented as the *intended* result of collective labour. Rather,

> it takes place as the fulfilment of latent functions [of action] that go beyond the action orientations of participants... and cannot be grasped directly from [their] perspective. It calls instead for a counterintuitive analysis from the standpoint of an observer who objectivates the lifeworld. Whereas social integration presents itself as part of the symbolic reproduction of the lifeworld ... functional integration amounts to a material reproduction of the lifeworld that can be conceived of as system maintenance ... [it] only comes into view when the lifeworld is objectified as a boundary maintaining system (Habermas, cited by McCarthy in Habermas, 1984, p.xxix).

Systems theory conceptualizes society on an organismic or biological model. Its analysis of societies is structured by the focus on the conditions required for their survival, functioning, evolution and change. Burrell and Morgan suggest that the general principles of systems theory on the biological model include: that the system can be identified via a boundary differentiating it from its environment; that the system is essentially processual in nature, with the process involving input, throughput, output and feedback; that the overall operation of the system can be understood in terms of the satisfaction of system needs geared to survival or the achievement of homeostasis; that the system is composed of subsystems which contribute to the satisfaction of the system's overall needs; that these subsystems, which themselves have identifiable boundaries, are in a state of mutual interdependence, both internally and in relation to their environment; that the operation of the system can be observed in terms of the behaviour of its elements; that the critical activities within the context of system operation are those which involve boundary interactions, both internally between subsystems and externally in relation to the environment (Burrell and Morgan, 1979, p.63).

The system perspective cannot replace the lifeworld perspective, however, something which Durkheim also realized. He was unhappy with Herbert Spencer's strong version of the system thesis, which was that the market is a self-sufficient, entirely non-normative mechanism that spontaneously and unconsciously (in the sense of the absence of planning) brings about the integration of society by harmonizing the aggregate effects of egocentric, interest-oriented actions via functional interconnections. Durkheim did not want to allow that the integration of society could be entirely uncoupled from the value orientations of individual actors. In (contractual) relations of exchange considered in and for themselves, he could see nothing that resembled the kind of enduring regulatory influence required if societies are to hold together. Interest, he wrote, 'can create only an external link between [men]. In the fact of exchange, the various agents remain outside of each other, and when the business has been completed, each one retires and is left entirely on his own' (cited in Habermas, 1987, p.116). Developing this insight via the addition of a strong Weberian element, Habermas argues that although the conceptual strategy of presenting society as a self-regulating system on an organic or biological model is defensible, it must be understood that unlike in biological systems, there is no internal or necessary connection between a cause and an effect within a system connecting social actions: '[T]he structural patterns of action systems are not accessible to [purely external] observation; they have to be gotten at hermeneutically, that is, from the internal perspective of participants' (Habermas, 1987, p.150).

In social systems, the functional connections that exist are merely conventional and as such depend in the final analysis on the meanings that particular actions have for participants as judged against the context of an intersubjectively shared interpretation of the world and their place within it. Actions – causes – have particular effects because they *should* have, because this is what a particular action performed in a particular situation means. This symbolic mediation of systemic interconnections means that it is impossible to abandon the lifeworld strategy. Understanding social action necessarily involves the attempt to see the world from the internal perspective of members of social groups. On this basis, Habermas argues that societies must be conceived simultaneously as functional systems and as lifeworlds.

The prospect of an approach to empirical social science capable of dissolving structure and agency in the way that Habermas suggests is indeed tantalising. However, there is a need to make some significant modifications to Habermas's scheme before we can use the method of formal pragmatics to gain access to the 'structural patterns of action systems'.

Habermas's Two Methodological Approaches

The rather complex theoretical picture of society that Habermas paints does not lend itself very easily to translation into a methodological approach. Quite apart from any other considerations, it is a well-established criticism of his *Theory of Communicative Action* that its location of 'steering-media co-ordination within economic and political institutions, and communicative mechanisms of co-ordination within the remaining institutional spheres' (Mouzelis, 1997, p.116) is not coherent with the admission that social as well as system integrative processes play an important role in economic and political contexts of action. Habermas wants to deny that the concepts of communicative action and the lifeworld are applicable to the analysis of social interaction where relationships are formally organized. This is certainly unfortunate as this approach to social action, 'formal pragmatics', is very attractive in the context of recent debates about power and subjectivity in organizations.[4] While formal pragmatics opposes 'models of social order that take interactions between strategically acting subjects as fundamental, for example, models grounded in decision or game theory', at the same time it avoids the reduction of rationality to 'the standards of validity prevailing in any local context of communicative activity' (Cooke in Habermas, 1998, p.5).

In this section we will discuss Habermas's treatment of social and system integrative processes, giving particular consideration to the arguments that drive him to insist that two different methodological approaches are needed in the social sciences.

Applying the Concepts of Communicative Action and the Lifeworld: The Method of Formal Pragmatics

For Habermas, as we have seen, social action is crucially dependent on processes of consensus formation in language, and it is these processes which he aims to analyse with his first methodological approach, 'formal pragmatics'. Formal pragmatics 'aims at a systematic reconstruction of the intuitive linguistic knowledge of competent subjects, the intuitive 'rule consciousness' that a competent speaker has of her own language... It makes us aware that, as speakers and hearers, there are certain things we must – as a matter of necessity – always already have supposed if communication is to be successful' (Cooke in Habermas, 1998, p.2).

At the core of formal pragmatics is the argument that language has an inherent connection with validity. In methodological terms, it implies that the analysis of social action should focus on that connection, that is, on the logical structure of the contextualized utterances of participants. To give another brief example, a parent out

---

[4] Tim Newton, for example, poses the structure/agency problem for industrial and organizational sociology: how to avoid 'an orthodoxy wherein subjectivity remains largely a consequence of economic 'structures'' while at the same time addressing the issue of how modern selves 'resist, ignore, subvert (etc.) [discursive] practices within the context of particular socially constructed stabilities in power asymmetry' (Newton, 1998, p.441).

for a walk with his child might say to that child 'Look, there's a goat!' The child
might respond positively to this remark by saying 'Let's go and have a look'. In this
case she has accepted that her father's intention was to inform her of the presence of a
goat and nothing more, that he is right about the presence of a goat, and that his action
in telling her about it was the right thing to do. On the basis of their newly amended
situation definition, the child suggests that going and looking more closely at the goat
is an appropriate or rational thing to do, since being interested in goats is a perfectly
good reason for going to have a look at one if one is available.

She can respond negatively to her father's remark in one or more of the same three
ways which, as we saw above, are open to the student being asked for a glass of water.
She might say:

That's not a goat – that's just a rock.

In so doing, she is denying 'that certain existential presuppositions obtain', in other
words simply suggesting that her father was wrong about there being a goat. The child
might equally well say:

I don't care – why would I be interested in seeing a goat?

In so doing, she is contesting 'the normative rightness of the utterance', in other
words suggesting that as far as she is concerned it is not in her interest to look at goats
so her father can forget about pointing them out to her if he sees any more. Finally, it
is possible that the child might respond by saying:

Why did you tell me that? You know I'm scared of goats!

In so doing she is contesting 'the subjective truthfulness of the utterance', in other
words suggesting that her father's aim in pointing out the goat was not to tell her
about the goat but to frighten her.

In any of these three cases of rejection, and in the absence of other relevant factors,
going to take a closer look at the goat (or what the father claims or thought was a goat)
cannot count as rational action. The child will be at least confused if her father
subsequently insists on going to see the (alleged) goat anyway. Where the child has
accepted her father's statement, on the other hand, she is likely to be confused and
upset if her father subsequently *refuses* to go and look at the goat.

So, by analysing the structure of the father's statement – the argument about the
rationality of certain types of action which is implied by pointing out the goat in the
context of the micro-society of father and daughter – we are in a position to say what
social action is rational and what is not. On this basis we can point to reasons why co-
operation or conflict between the participants might follow depending on what course
social action actually takes.

It should be clear that in analysing the situation described above, we are
reconstructing the – in this case tacit – processes of argumentation which lead the
actors involved to act or not act. These processes of argumentation do not start from
first principles, however. It is obviously the case that participants in social action

approach situations with a host of already formed interpretations and assumptions about the world. In other words, action takes place against the context of a lifeworld. This, too, is open to a formal pragmatic analysis.

Even though it is a very simple social situation, the lifeworld shared by our father and daughter includes objective states of affairs (the presence or absence of the goat), legitimate norms (they will look together at things which interest the child) and subjective experiences and desires (the father's intentions in pointing out the goat; the child's interest in or fear of goats and other animals). However, their relationship also depends on a host of other more general interpretive commitments which they share not just with each other but with the other members of the wider society in which they live. In this case, among the most relevant of these would include the physical characteristics of their situation (how far away the goat is; the difficulty of the route between where they are and the goat; whether they have time to get to the goat and back before it starts to rain) and norms relating to the treatment of animals (that when they visit the goat they will not harm or frighten it).

For a hearer to refuse to accept a speaker's utterance is, then, for her to question the speaker's assertions about *their* lifeworld. If the father is acting communicatively, then a questioning of his utterance by the child ought to lead to a consideration of whether their situation should be redefined. For example the father might concede that his daughter was not after all interested in domestic animals and that he need not point them out in future; or he might recognize that what he thought was a goat is indeed a rock; or the daughter might agree that her father genuinely did not know she was frightened of goats and that he would not have mentioned the goat if he had known.

If, on the other hand, it is not possible for a speaker and hearer to establish or re-establish agreement about their specific situation, then the content of their lifeworld is called into question. An internal inconsistency or incoherence in their lifeworld will be made manifest. In the present case it ought to be relatively easy to establish the existential parameters of the situation (the presence or absence of the goat and whether going to see it is feasible), so if the relationship is to encounter difficulties then it is likely to be because of the parties' inability to agree norms of conduct towards each other, or their inability to accept the sincerity of each other's claims about subjective experiences. Father and daughter may not agree on whether the child is, or ought to be, interested in goats, or daughter may not accept that her father's intention was not to frighten her, or father may not accept that daughter is genuinely frightened of goats. If any of these situations arise, then father and daughter will certainly be unable to agree that they ought to go and see the goat. If action takes place in this particular social context it will give rise to conflict rather than co-operation.

In using Habermas's formal pragmatics to analyse the structure of meaningful social action, then, we are directed towards an analysis of the content of lifeworlds, both those specific to particular groups of actors and those having more general validity. On this basis we can point to reasons why co-operation or conflict between participants in social action might follow depending on what course social action actually takes. Conflict will arise when social action is internally or logically unrelated to an *agreed* situation definition, or when there is disagreement about some relevant aspect of a situation but action is taken without this disagreement being resolved.

The Logical Limits of Formal Pragmatics and the Need for a Systems Analysis

It is very clearly Habermas's view, however, that formal pragmatics cannot usefully be applied to the analysis of social action in the economic and political contexts. He intends this to be taken both as a methodological point and as an assertion about the nature of the social world. As he puts it, 'communicative action forfeits its validity basis in the interior of organizations' (1987, p.310) and so the analysis of social action in terms of the structure of validity claims will not reveal how action is co-ordinated and how conflict or co-operation arise. A different approach is required.

Juridical versus Communicative Rationality

The methodological approach implied by formal pragmatics assumes that actors act communicatively: their aim in participating in social interactions is to agree a definition of the action situation with their co-participants, from which appropriate co-ordinated social action can be inferred. If the possibility that this agreement be unreserved is to be kept open, then participants must have no unalterable prior commitment to the existence, non-existence, relevance or irrelevance of any element in that situation. However, economic and political contexts are defined precisely by the existence of rules that pre-determine the co-ordinated action that will be the outcome of certain kinds of social interaction. Decisions about action are in these contexts a result of a formal-legal or 'juridical' mode of rationality rather than communicative rationality. Juridical reasoning, suggests Andrini, consists 'of a sequence of acts which require – to reach a judgement or final sentence – that the elements considered significant or insignificant are included or excluded in relationship to the *quaestio facti* or *quaestio juris*' (1999, pp.6-7).

In other words, where rules exist, the elements of a situation are prejudged as to their relevance for action. Facts, norms and subjective states are deemed relevant or irrelevant to the validity of an argument before that argument is made. Evidence produced by an illegal police search, for example, is automatically irrelevant and is not permitted to form part of a chain of reasoning leading to a decision of guilt or innocence, regardless of the fact that it may establish the actual truth of the matter one way or another. What is important, then, is not the action situation as consensually defined by participants, but the relationship between that situation and a 'model'. If certain predefined elements are present in a situation, then it is deemed appropriate for participants to take certain predefined actions, regardless of any other elements of the situation which might otherwise have a bearing on decisions about action, but which the law or rule does not envisage.

On this reading, Habermas's view seems to be not that communicative action is impossible in political and economic contexts, but rather that it is unnecessary. In these contexts, participants

> act communicatively only *with reservation*. They know they *can* have recourse to formal regulations, not only in exceptional but in routine cases; there is no *necessity* for achieving consensus by communicative means... [there is] the legitimate possibility of redefining at will spheres of action oriented to mutual understanding into actions situations stripped of

lifeworld contexts and no longer directed to achieving consensus (Habermas, 1987, pp.310-11; emphasis in original).

Hence, since actors need not adopt a communicative attitude in dealing with their co-participants, the formal pragmatic analysis of communication will not necessarily provide a means of explaining the co-ordinated action that arises. Where participants do 'have recourse to formal regulation', the key to understanding action is to be found not in the participants' own interpretation of their situation, but rather in what Weber calls the 'order' that governs them; the formal rules and regulations that apply within the immediate group of actors, but which emerge from social processes taking place beyond the horizon of their lifeworld.

Why does System Integration Trump Social Integration?

In the passage quoted above, Habermas seems to leave open the possibility that communicative rationality be applied in economic and political contexts. As a consequence, he might be thought to accept that there are circumstances in which a formal pragmatic analysis of action is appropriate despite the systemic context. Nonetheless, he also takes the view that communicative mechanisms of co-ordination can always be discounted as major components in the explanation of economic and political action. These two positions sit rather uneasily together. Habermas's refusal to allow that the outcome of social interactions in systemic contexts can to any significant extent be the result of communicative action calls for some explanation.

Habermas argues that even if actors in economic or other formally organized contexts want or intend to act communicatively it is simply impossible for them to do so. Groups of actors in systemic contexts cannot reach a substantive agreement on the legitimacy of a particular goal because from an insider or social action perspective it is impossible to grasp the full consequences of any actions they might take in pursuit of that goal. System integration, it is argued, 'takes place as the fulfilment of latent functions [of action] that go beyond the action orientations of participants... and cannot be grasped directly from [their] perspective' (Habermas, cited by McCarthy in Habermas, 1984, p.xxix). Elsewhere, he argues that with modernization, 'the social system definitively bursts out of the horizon of the lifeworld, escapes from the intuitive knowledge of everyday communicative practice, and is henceforth accessible only to the counterintuitive knowledge of the social sciences developing since the eighteenth century' (Habermas 1987, p.173).

This argument can be approached from a number of different angles. First of all, as we have already seen, Habermas takes the view that society cannot simply be understood 'as the intentional complex of a free association of originally autonomous and equal members' (Habermas, 1996, p.44). Rather, he suggests that there has to be some way of integrating the 'realistic model of an anonymous, unintentional sociation taking place behind the actors backs' (p.46). For him, it is so evident that the economic and political-administrative systems are independent of conscious human control that the intentional coordinating achievements of individuals in these spheres are by definition epiphenomenal.

A second, more strictly logical approach starts from what formal pragmatics implies about the characteristics of communication in systemic contexts of action. As we have seen, Habermas argues that the defining characteristic of social integration in economic contexts is that it is premised on the coordination of action consequences rather than action orientations. In order to decide whether or not to undertake a particular action, market actors will look to the desirability of its outcomes rather than to the intrinsic nature of the action itself. Assessing the desirability of outcomes obviously involves calculating what these will be, which in turn involves making assumptions about the causal connections that exist between action and consequence. Assumptions about the functional characteristics of economies and political systems – economic and political 'laws' and principles – ultimately arise from inductive generalizations based on the external observation of large-scale consistencies in social behaviour. However, since economies and political systems are social phenomena, it must be granted that these consistencies are themselves conventional. They do not represent the manifestation of any necessary or 'hard-wired' characteristics of human behaviour. Hence, the generalization of the observed functional characteristics of economies and political systems into social scientific laws and principles can also be considered an interpretation of reasons for social behaviour in terms of the hypothesized validity of certain norms of action, conventions or rules. To put the same point another way, since there is clearly nothing necessary about the connections between cause (action) and effect (outcome) that inhere in social institutions like capitalism, sociological generalizations based on empirical observation amount to suggestions that participants in these institutions are behaving according to a certain norm or rule. Hence claims about the functional characteristics of social systems also amount to claims about the validity of certain norms.

For Habermas, the validity of norms in informal, non-economic social contexts is simply a matter of agreement among those involved. According to his discourse principle, 'Just those action norms are valid to which all possibly affected persons could agree as participants in rational discourses' (1996, p.107). However, action in the context of economic and political systems necessarily involves the assumption that certain norms are *generally* valid, that is, that their validity is recognized not just among the immediate group of actors but among all those participating in the economic system. The question that arises is whether this assumption of validity can ever be justified. For Habermas it is very clear that it can not, but this is not simply because the functional integration of modern societies is so great that it would be impossible to organize a meaningful process of rational discourse involving all the persons possibly affected by some instance of economic action. Rather, consensus formation is impossible even in principle because before any such action is taken, both its consequences and the identity of the affected persons are indeterminate. This is a consequence of the inductive epistemology of the law-like generalizations on which economic and political action is premised. By definition, statements about the functional characteristics of markets and political systems can only ever be *probably* true, something which remains the case no matter how many times such claims appear to be borne out by the outcomes of action. Hence, it always remains possible that unexpected outcomes will occur. Similarly, it is only possible to say that from the range of persons who might in principle be affected – for example, those who might be persuaded to buy a particular product or vote for a particular party – it is likely that a certain proportion will be. Exactly what that proportion will turn out to be, and exactly who the affected persons will be, cannot be known in advance. If it is impossible to say who the persons possibly affected by some norm of action might be, then obviously it is impossible to sustain a claim that these persons recognise the validity of that norm.

A third approach starts from the attempt to understand how social systems are seen from the perspective of individual actors. Habermas's point is neither that it is impossible that the social system and its effects are in the general interest, nor that a meaningful case in support of this possibility could not be made, nor that social structures are literally incomprehensible to ordinary social actors. For example, it is not even implausible, let alone incomprehensible, to justify free trade and its collateral social costs in terms of the general interest of the entire world. Rather, the point is that these types of justification involve the adoption of a third-party or externalist perspective on society that is no part of 'the intuitive knowledge of everyday communicative practice'. In this case, and even at the most simplistic level of argument, the justification would involve an analysis of the aggregate effects of free trade on such things as prices and employment. Adopting such a mode of analysis, however, involves assuming that certain things are necessary when in fact they are contingent, a step Habermas calls a 'methodological objectification'. In order for the analysis to be possible at all, it must be assumed, to use Weber's terms, that the capitalistic order of society *will* be carried out, even though it need not be; that hundreds or even millions of unknown individuals will behave in a predictable and calculable way. In other words, it has to be assumed that it is juridical rather than a communicative rationality that governs actions.

If we say 'we should institute a global system of free trade', then we are making a range of claims about the nature of economic systems which, as we have just argued, amount to claims about the contingent behaviour of participants in those systems. These claims are such that *if* they are true (i.e. if the norms involved are indeed valid), then a system of free trade can logically be shown to be the means of organizing trading relations which maximizes the benefit accruing to all participants in the global economic system. If the proposed norms of economic behaviour are not valid, then any claims made for free trade are also invalid.

Free trade is in the general interest only on the condition that the norms of economic behaviour that it assumes (the validity of which has been posited on the basis of induction or 'backwards inference' from empirical observation) are indeed valid and continue to be so. But since economic behaviour could clearly be otherwise, we can agree that free trade is in the general interest only if we all *accept and continuously reaffirm* the validity of these empirically-derived norms. Quite aside from the effective impossibility of organizing a public sphere involving all participants in which such a consensus might arise, there is also the logical objection we referred to above. Normative statements that assume the existence of a particular social-institutional structure, for example 'free trade is right', can be deemed valid or invalid only in the light of the outcomes of action within that structure. The connection between action and outcome, however, is merely probable and cannot be guaranteed. Before any action has taken place, then, such statements have an indeterminate validity status and thus participants in action simply cannot come to an agreement that they are valid – or rather, they can only agree with reservation, in the awareness that their actions may not be justified.

We are now in a position to see why Habermas takes the view that formal pragmatics is not applicable in systemic contexts. The formal pragmatic analysis of action in the economic and political systems is self-contradictory. It suggests that such action must be based on the assumption that certain norms and conventions are valid, while at the same time it shows that this validity cannot be established. Hence in systemic contexts, rational motivation cannot arise. Thus as a theory of integration, the idea that the co-ordination of action in the economic and political-administrative spheres proceeds primarily via processes of consensus formation in language must fail. It predicts that action in these contexts will not occur.

Habermas's Systems Approach

Habermas's systems approach, which owes much to the work of Talcott Parsons, is his attempt to construct an alternative theory of integration that can explain why the economic and political spheres of society hold together even though unreserved consensus on norms appears to be impossible. Such a theory must, on the one hand, be adequate at the level of meaning in the sense that the behaviour of individual actors in their relations with each other is comprehensible, and on the other, be able to account for large-scale patterns of social behaviour in terms of an aggregation of the outcomes of these individual interactions. The thrust of Habermas's argument is that the reservations of participants in action remain, but that these 'missing terms' in the equation that adds up to the motivation to act are substituted by the threat of punishment or the prospect of reward. Action is the result of rules that are consciously applied by participants in order to determine the outcome of interactions. Rules are followed not because of the reasons underpinning them, but because of the individual interest of participants in winning rewards or avoiding sanctions. The motivation to act is not rational, but empirical.

Starting from an action perspective, Habermas argues that participants in co-ordinated social action need not be linked (integrated) by the sharing of an entire lifeworld context. In certain circumstances, social integration is based on the sharing of a single *generalized* value. Generalized values have two peculiar characteristics. First, they bind all actors in the same way at all places and times. The actions of an individual pursuing a generalized value are therefore predictable. Second they are formal rather than substantive. Generalized values act as currencies of exchange between different non-generalizable (i.e. individual or partial) values and interests and are worthless in abstraction from their meaning as an expression of substantive aims and goals.

Generalized values are consistent and reliable because they are institutionalized in the form of 'steering media'. A steering medium could be described as the tangible manifestation of a rule or set of rules that determine(s) the outcome of social interactions. As we suggested above, the existence of such rules renders irrelevant most of the features of the participants' situation which would otherwise have a bearing on the outcome of an interaction and which increase the risk that participants will fail to agree about what they should do. As Habermas puts it, the 'demands and dangers' of coordinating action via reaching understanding in language,

> can be reduced through media that replace mutual understanding in language as a mechanism of co-ordination in certain well-defined contexts... Such media serve not only to reduce the expenditure of interpretive energy but also *to overcome the risk of action sequences falling apart*. Media such as money or power can largely spare us the costs of dissensus because they uncouple the co-ordination of action from consensus formation in language and neutralize it against the alternatives of agreed versus failed agreement (Habermas, 1987, pp.262-3; emphasis added).

The schematization of interaction involved in this stripping down of the criteria determining its outcomes is what justifies the methodological objectification involved in the adoption of a systemic perspective. Since action is determined by a restricted and determinate range of criteria, the sum of media-steered interactions represents a realization or playing out of the logic of these rules rather than some kind of expression of the collective or general will. Further, the reasons why individual participants follow the rules are unrelated to their content, the normative validity of the rules themselves. Instead, rule-following is motivated by a purely strategic desire to gain rewards or avoid sanctions. Social action and socially-valid reasons for action are no longer in an internal, necessary logical relation, and hence the economic and political-administrative systems that are the result of rule-following cannot be represented as the *intended* result of social action. Rather they become effectively autonomous and apparently objective forces in society, confronting participants in action with what seems to be the same immutability as the material world.

For the social scientist, the object of study is the set of rules by which the social system operates and where the logic of that operation leads. If the rules of a medium have been properly understood, and if participants in action are indeed bound only or principally by the generalized value the medium represents, then it ought to be possible accurately to deduce the aggregate outcome of social interactions. Where this kind of third party perspective can be adopted, then the otherwise impossible feat of prediction, i.e. the generation of testable hypotheses about social action in particular circumstances, becomes possible.

In the *Theory of Communicative Action*, Habermas does not discuss the research methodology of the systems approach. We cannot, therefore, sketch the outlines of a systems approach to research in the same way as we have sketched the methodological implications of Habermas's action approach. However, it is clear that when he talks about 'externalist' social science, what he has in mind are economics, empirical political theory, quantitatively oriented sociology, etc. There is, obviously, no need for us to discuss the methods of these disciplines here. In the remainder of this section, we will instead give a very brief account of the Parsons/Habermas concept of steering media.

Steering Media

In Parsons's original system theory there are four generalized values (utility, effectiveness, loyalty and integrity) corresponding to each of four social sub-systems.

However, Habermas argues – for reasons that need not detain us here – that steered interactions only take place in the economic and political-administrative subsystems, and that social integrative mechanisms retain their primacy in the remaining institutional spheres. The two steering media that he accepts have some currency, then, are money and power. At the level of meaning, media-steered interactions proceed as follows.

The money medium In relationships steered by the money medium, the 'standard situation' is exchange. One participant makes an offer, and the other either accepts or rejects it. The generalized value in this situation is utility, which is to say the ability to acquire use values. The initiator of the exchange makes a claim about the exchange-value of certain goods or services. The rationality criterion of the interaction – the rule that determines whether an offer is accepted or rejected – is *profitability*. If at the exchange-value proposed, the exchange would be profitable for the potential participant, then we assume that that person will accept the offer and act as required, regardless of any factors that might in other, non-economic, circumstances have an effect on the outcome of the interaction. A profitable exchange will be rejected only where there are opportunities for exchange at a more favourable exchange-value. To reject an offer of exchange, then, is to reject the claim that the exchange-value is as the initiator claims it to be.

The power medium The standard situation in contexts where social interactions are steered by the power medium is the issuing of a command by an office-holder in a bureaucratic or other formal hierarchy. The generalized value is effectiveness in the sense of the effective realization of collective goals. In giving an order, an office-holder claims that the order represents a binding decision, in the sense that it is within her formal-legal competence to require the compliance. The rationality criterion for the interaction is therefore the *sovereignty* of the office-holder: the successful establishment of a claim that the order is legal. It is assumed that if a decision specifies a course of action which is within the authority of an office-holder to require, then the person to whom that order is directed will accept it and act as required, again, regardless of any factors that might in other, 'non-administrative', circumstances have an effect on the outcome of the interaction. To reject an order is precisely to question the claim to legality, just as the rejection of an offer of exchange represents a questioning of the claimed exchange-value of the goods or services to be exchanged. The characteristics of the money and power media are summarized in Table 3.1 below.

Theoretical Developments in *Between Facts and Norms*

What we have seen so far in this chapter is that Habermas is compelled by his strict adherence to the logical basis of formal pragmatics to adopt a distinct theory of social action for those contexts in which action is premised on the assumption that an established set of rules will be followed. His systems theory ultimately remains dependent on the possibility of communicative action, however, because these rules

Table 3.1 Characteristics of steering media

Steering medium	Generalized value	Real value	Nominal claim	Rationality criteria
Money	Utility	Use values	That the commodities or services in play have a certain exchange-value	Interaction will succeed if it is profitable for both parties, i.e. if the claim about exchange-value is accepted.
Power	Effectiveness	Realization of collective goals	That the decision in question is legally binding	Interaction will succeed if sovereignty, i.e. the claim that the decision is legal, can be established.

Source: Adapted from Habermas, 1987, Figure 37, p.274.

are not without some foundation in valid norms. Systemic interconnections, insists Habermas, have to be gotten at hermeneutically. Nevertheless, on a strong reading of TCA it is difficult to resist the conclusion that the connection between system and lifeworld that this implies is primarily historical. The social evolutionary processes leading to the institutionalization of certain valid norms as money and as private and public law are more or less complete. Insofar as there remains a need for social institutions to have substantive validity it exists only in the requirement that new or amended legislation is properly enacted, that is, that it emerges from a formally valid parliamentary process which, at least in principle, translates into law a general interest identified through processes of consensus formation in language.

For Habermas, the logical rupture between social action and socially-valid reasons for action that characterizes political and economic contexts, which he calls the 'uncoupling' of system and lifeworld, has become so complete that he feels able to say that the economic and political-administrative systems represent areas of *norm-free* sociality. Although he does not argue that motivation on the basis of good reasons, normative and otherwise, does not occur in systemic contexts, and although he does not even suggest that this form of motivation is unimportant, he nonetheless implies that the external, empirical component of the motivation for action is sufficiently important to make an analysis of the lifeworld context of action in formally organized contexts pointless. As Mouzelis puts it, it is his view that 'the co-ordinating role of communicative understanding is peripheral or subordinate to that played by the steering media' (1997, p.115).

Yet, if law-making is conceived as it is in BFN, that is, as a process in which the normatively substantive message of social solidarity is translated into a language comprehensible in every sphere of society, and if, as Habermas suggests, social solidarity can thereby 'hold its own' against the competing integrative forces of money and administrative power, then it is difficult to maintain the reading of TCA that we have proposed in this chapter. It would seem to be rather more profitable to attempt to conceptualize the structural properties of communication in systemic contexts in the attempt to understand how moral norms and political-ethical values can frame and limit the functioning of the economic and political-administrative systems.

Law and Communication in Social Systems

As we saw above, social action in systemic spheres of action is based on the juridical logic of regulation rather than the communicative logic of mutual consensus. One might equally well describe this distinction in terms of language. Whereas the coordination of action in systemic contexts is achieved via the 'special codes' of profitability and sovereignty, in informal social contexts it is achieved via natural or ordinary language. Ordinary language

> possesses the merit of multifunctionality. With its practically unlimited capacity for interpretation and range of circulation, it is superior to special codes in that it provides a sounding board for the external costs of differentiated subsystems and thus remains sensitive to problems affecting the whole of society. The ways of defining and processing problems in ordinary language remain more diffuse, are less differentiated, and are less clearly operationalized than under the code-specific, unidimensional and one-sided aspects of cost/benefit, command/obedience and so on. In return, however, ordinary language is not tied down to just a single code but is inherently multilingual. It does not need to pay the price of specialization, namely deafness to problems formulated in another language (Habermas, 1996, p.55).

So, while communication in the special codes of the system is clearer and likely to be more immediately effective, it can only deliver and respond to certain types of message. One cannot say just anything using the binary codes of the economy and administration. However, as we noted at the end of Chapter 2, Habermas argues that normatively substantive messages can be rendered comprehensible in systemic contexts by translating them into the 'complex legal code that is equally open to lifeworld and system'. If this is the case, then the reverse should also be possible. Since ordinary language is universal, it ought in principle to be possible to produce a linguistic rendering of the content of systemic communication. If such a translation could be achieved, the problems to which systemic action gives rise could be formulated in ordinary language without thereby 'falling on deaf ears'. In other words, the legitimacy of social action in the context of the system could be considered in the light of its effects beyond the system itself. Eventually, any valid substantive norms that were violated by systemic action could be rendered in the legal code understood in the systemic context, thus redrawing the normative boundaries of the economic or political-administrative spheres of action.

Legitimacy and Action in the Systemic Context

It is not simply the case that substantive norms may limit the self-steering capacity of the system from the outside, however. Habermas concurs with Weber's view that social orders can only be maintained in the long run as legitimate orders, that is, as complexes of social action in which practices are based on a 'conscious orientation to a consensus presupposed as valid' (Habermas, 1996, p.67). Now, it is certainly true that the possibility of anticipating the behaviour of others that makes social orders useful need not be based on the mutual recognition of valid consensuses. Self-interest and custom can equally well give rise to enduring social orders. Nonetheless, 'an order which is adhered to from motives of pure expediency is generally much less stable than one upheld on a purely customary basis... The latter is much the most common type of subjective attitude. But even this latter type is in turn much less stable than an order which enjoys the prestige of being considered binding' (Weber, cited in Habermas, 1996, p.68). The synthesis of the long run requirement for legitimacy and the de facto, day-to-day variability of immediate motivations for compliance with social norms is the concept of legitimate law and convention:

> [A] legitimate order is not based solely on a normative consensus anchored intrapsychically through the internalization of the corresponding values. To the extent that its validity is not grounded through religious authority or in purely moral terms through value-rational belief, and thus is not protected by the corresponding sanctions (fear of losing religious benefits, feelings of shame and guilt) and the capacity to bind oneself, it has need of external guarantees. In these cases the expectation of the legitimacy of a social order is stabilized by convention or law (Habermas, 1996, p.68).

Convention and law therefore exist alongside and in support of normative consensuses. While this is coherent with Habermas's argument in TCA that societies have to be conceived simultaneously as systems and lifeworlds, it goes rather further than the claim made in that work that the legitimation of law requires nothing more than its enactment via a procedurally valid parliamentary process. In the later formulation, the legitimacy of formal regulation appears to be subject to the same discourse principle that governs the legitimacy of any social norm. It must always be open to participants in action in systemic contexts to comply with regulation because of an orientation to valid norms, even where their subjective attitude is in fact one of self-interest or habit. This is not intended merely in a normative sense. As Habermas puts it, 'Interests can be satisfied through generalized behavioral expectations in the long run only if interests are connected with ideas that justify normative validity claims' (1996, p.69).

Although the implications of this point for Habermas's overall theoretical project are potentially far-reaching, he makes no attempt to draw them out. However, an interpretation consistent with what we have argued above is that for any interaction conducted via one of the special codes of the system, there must be a rationally defensible structure of reasons that can be reconstructed and expressed in ordinary language. If this were the case, however, then the resort to special codes for the purposes of communication in systemic contexts would seem to be unnecessary, something that directly contradicts the argument of TCA and that Habermas clearly does not intend to suggest. At the same time, the idea that economic and political-administrative action and structures should be defensible from a normative perspective accessible to the individual actor is obviously essential for a theory of corporate legitimacy. We will return to this question at the end of Chapter 5, after we have given some consideration to the nature of communication in systemic contexts.

Conclusion

Central to Habermas's social theoretical project is the analysis of social action in terms of the logical structure of communication. Formal pragmatics proposes a procedural definition of both objective knowledge and normative legitimation, founding a universal epistemology on processes of consensus formation in language. This epistemology reaches its limits with modernization, however. The rise of juridical rationality and the increasing dependence on external support for normative regulation mean that social integration becomes dependent on the coordination of action consequences rather than on action orientations. Systems perspectives in the social sciences begin to provide a more realistic picture of society than those approaches, notably social contract theories, that privilege the conscious intentions of actors. Habermas's argument, however, is that societies have to be conceived as simultaneously subject to system and social integration. The question that he leaves unanswered is how any conflict between these integrative processes can be resolved. On a strong reading of TCA, the question simply does not arise because social and system integration are in effect confined to different parts of society. The logics of solidarity, cost/benefit and command/obedience are effective within their own spheres. While the latter two may in certain circumstances 'drive out' the former – the process that Habermas refers to as the colonization of the lifeworld – in any given social context there will be a principal integrative force that is sufficiently dominant to make any consideration of the effects of another irrelevant.

   Yet, a careful reading of BFN seems to suggest that the situation is more complex and that Habermas's position is rather more nuanced. The argument made in BFN suggests that the capacity of the law to carry substantive normative messages within the system is significant. Legal regulation has the potential both to limit the scope of system integration and to ensure that the economic and political-administrative systems themselves act as 'carriers' for legitimate moral and political-ethical norms. The crucial question that Habermas does not address is how and to what extent this may be possible. We want to suggest that the core of the issue is the interpretation of the politicocultural self-understanding of a community that permits the generalization of social scientific 'laws' that in turn explain the functional characteristics of systems. In Chapter 4, we will begin our attempt to address these questions by looking at the structure of communication in systemic contexts.

Chapter 4

The Structure of Communication in Systemic Contexts of Action

In this chapter, we want to argue that Habermas is wrong to suggest that communication in systemic contexts cannot be specified in terms of formal pragmatics. As we shall see, his discussion of the process of systemic social interaction from the participants' perspective – to be found in a chapter of TCA principally dedicated to Talcott Parsons – is lacking in detail and logically inadequate in certain important respects (Habermas, 1987, pp.261-82). He uncritically adopts Parsons' concept of media-steering, failing to provide a convincing account of how strategically-rational actors can make decisions about action coordination without engaging in processes of consensus-formation on substantive issues. In failing to give this issue the attention it deserves, he misses the possibility of providing a theoretical conceptualization of the relative influence of system and social integrative factors in any given situation, and is obliged instead to insist on the dominance of one or other set of processes depending on the action context.

Because of his mistaken assumptions about the 'action-level' characteristics of systemic action, Habermas does not try in TCA to extend the formal pragmatic analysis of action to cover economic and political-administrative contexts. However, in BFN he introduces an important clarification of his overall theoretical scheme by distinguishing between generalizable, universal moral norms and non-generalizable, political-ethical values and interests. Although he considers it possible to pursue non-generalizable values on the basis of an orientation to mutual understanding, he still does not pursue the issue of how the distinction between the two types of social norm might be reflected in the logical structure of communication. Given that the values and interests that animate corporate action are non-generalizable, and that our ultimate aim is to produce a theory of corporate legitimacy, it is important that we try to correct this omission.

In what follows we offer an alternative approach to the conceptualization of the action-level characteristics of systemic social interaction which supports the possibility of more or less norm-free interactions but also shows how normatively valid exchange and authority relationships can be compatible with the emergence and persistence of markets and political systems. First, we give a critical account of Habermas's approach to systemic social interactions from the participants' perspective. Second, we propose a structure of validity claims that seems to be adequate for the general case of the pursuit of non-generalizable norms and values. Finally, we suggest that it makes sense that this structure should also characterize the case of action in the systemic context.

Habermas on the Action-Level Characteristics of Media-steered Interactions

The plausibility of Habermas's approach to systems theory depends on whether we can satisfactorily reconstruct supposedly non-linguistic economic and political-administrative interactions from the perspective of the actors involved. Such an action-level reconstruction would need to be compatible with the system-level consistencies in social behaviour that we interpret as economic laws and principles and as the dynamics of political exchange. The existence of markets and of political systems needs to be coherent with the communication we understand to be taking place between participants in exchange and in administered relationships. More precisely, an adequate specification of the characteristics of a steering medium at the level of action must fulfil three general requirements. First, the specification should provide a plausible account of how strategically-rational actors can together determine the outcome of an interaction, in other words how co-ordinated action can take place without participants engaging in any processes of consensus-formation on substantive issues. Second, the aggregation of the outcome of interactions must logically lead to the existence of a system which is 'not the intended result of collective labour'; to something autonomous, beyond the conscious control of participants in the action that produces and reproduces it. Third, and a consequence of the first two requirements, the system that is produced must be reflexive: it must be the primary reference point for the decisions about action that produce it. There must be no need for any reference to sources of motivation or to reasons for action other than those arising within the system itself.

Before considering the money and power media in detail, we need to clarify one general point. In either case, it would be wholly implausible to suggest that social interaction could proceed without participants sharing a recognition of at least some of the characteristics of the objective, social and subjective worlds they inhabit. Certainly, it is possible that interactions be successfully resolved without there being any attempt to reach a consensus on what these characteristics are; but unless both participants *already* share approximately the same appreciation of the objective characteristics of the physical world, the de facto validity of certain social norms and the subjective intentions, needs and desires of human actors, then any kind of co-ordinated action would surely be impossible. As we will see, although it is clearly implicit in TCA that this is the case, Habermas fails to take this point into account in his specification of the two steering media.[1]

Money Steering

The Habermas/Parsons specification of the money medium fulfils none of our three requirements. Habermas appears to take the view that the only pre-existing connection between participants in an exchange, the only thing they know about each other, is

---

[1] At one point Habermas concedes that 'If all processes of genuinely reaching understanding were banished from the interior of organisations, formally regulated social relations could not be sustained, nor could organizational goals be realized' (1987, p.310).

their mutual adherence to the generalized value of utility. They are aware that all participants will seek to increase their utility, but are wholly unaware of the relationship between particular commodities and utility which holds for each individual, that is, of what commodities are worth to potential partners in exchange. The only form of communication in which they can engage is the process of offer and response: actors can only 'reciprocally condition their responses through their offers' (Habermas, 1987, p.264). The question that arises with respect to our first requirement – the possibility of strategic rationality – is whether participants in a bargaining process which begins from this situation will be in a position to determine the point at which it is rational to strike a deal. The answer depends on how we define strategic rationality. If we begin from the axiomatic assumptions of neoclassical microeconomics and assume that rationality involves profit-maximization and risk-aversion, then strictly speaking, bargaining ought never even to begin. Even if an initial offer is made that claims an exchange-value for a commodity in terms of 'units of utility' which is a very long way above its actual utility to the vendor (i.e. that is highly profitable), it can never be guaranteed that a buyer would not have paid more because there is no way of knowing anything at all about his utility preferences. Making an offer at all therefore involves the risk of a sub-optimal outcome.

Even if we loosen the assumption about risk-aversion a little, to take account of the fact that, for whatever reason, a vendor may have no option but to sell a commodity, we are still in difficulties. Consider a situation in which a commodity is worth 20 units of utility (utils) to a vendor and 30 to a potential buyer. Any exchange which prices the commodity above 20 utils and below 30 is mutually profitable, but on the information that Habermas suggests is available to the participants, and on the assumption that participants are profit-maximizing – the bare profitability of an offer will not necessarily lead to its acceptance – then there is no rational way for them to determine either the limits of that settlement range (beyond their own minimum requirements), or the point within it at which to strike a deal. This point needs some explanation. The only reason why a strategically rational actor might reject a profitable offer would be a grounded belief that a better, more profitable exchange is potentially available, whether from the same individual or some other. However, if we assume, as Habermas does, that bargaining takes place in isolation from any information other than the offers and responses of each participant, then there can be no such grounding. If our buyer initially offers to pay 15 utils, then we know the vendor will refuse, but the buyer will not know whether this is because the deal would not be profitable, or because the vendor is simply holding out for a better price in the hope of making a greater profit. Participants might simply guess that a better offer is possible, but if this were to be an established practice then the whole bargaining process would become irrational. Once bluffing is an accepted part of the game, then there is no way rationally to determine whether an offer is likely to improve, or whether a refusal is because the offer does not increase the participant's utility or because it does not increase it enough. Striking a deal would be left to chance since there is simply not enough information in the offers and responses to infer a likely settlement range. The possibility of strategic rationality is thus excluded, and with it the very existence of an economic system.

Certainly, it is not impossible that actors should not be interested in maximizing profit, instead being merely profit *seeking* in the sense that they will never either reject a profitable offer or make an offer which if accepted would earn them more than some minimum level of advantage (say, one util). However, participants would also have to be unaware of the ratio of profits earned by one participant to those earned by the other. Otherwise, unless they simply did not care about the *relative* gains made in the exchange, they would be paralysed by the risk attached to making the initial offer.

Quite aside from the fact that this seems highly implausible as an account of how interactions proceed at the action level, it is also the case that if strategic rationality were to involve profit seeking rather than profit maximization, there would still be no systemic context for action, and hence no possibility that this context be autonomous nor that it influence the outcome of interactions. The exchange-value settled upon in any given interaction would only ever reflect some minimal increment to the utility of the commodity to the participant who accepts the offer. In would not represent the average utility of a commodity. If we assume that the first profitable offer made to a vendor will be accepted, and that the buyer has no idea of the utility of the commodity to the vendor, then the only rational point at which to make an opening offer is zero. In the face of the rejection of this offer, the buyer will increase her offer until the vendor accepts or until her own utility threshold is reached (when she will walk away without a deal). If is deal is struck, then from an external perspective all we can say about the utility of the commodity to the buyer is that it is greater than the exchange-value. There could be no such thing as commodity prices in the sense in which we understand them since every agreed exchange-value would be valid only for one particular bargain. A stable system of exchange-values simply could not emerge and there would, therefore, be no such thing as markets. Exchange-values would remain firmly rooted in the use-value of commodities to particular individuals at particular moments and the aggregate result of interactions would be entirely unpredictable.

Power Steering

The power medium comes no closer to meeting our three requirements, although for very different reasons. In this case, the authority relationship is the key characteristic of an interaction. If participants in an interaction are to have the capacity to act strategically, then this relationship has to be separated from any dependence on substantively rational collective goals or substantively effective means of goal-achievement. The instructions that a superior within a bureaucratic or organizational hierarchy issues in the expectation of compliance, and a subordinate's actual compliance or non-compliance must arise *solely* from considerations of formal or legal validity. It is only in this way that the aggregate outcome of action can represent the playing out of the logic of the rules of the system, rather than the intention or will either of any individual participant or of all participants.

The problem here is that sovereignty requires supplementary legitimation. In the context of the money medium, the profitable transaction is an end in itself that requires no further justification. Since money can be transformed directly into the satisfaction of any type of material interest, it is a truly universal value. However, it cannot be assumed that the collective goals whose realization characterizes the successful power-mediated transaction are similarly generalizable. For this reason, Habermas admits that, when viewed from the action perspective, power-steered interactions are rather closer in character to communicative action than those steered by the money medium. The exercise of power, he suggests,

> requires an advance of trust that signifies not only 'compliance' – a de facto obedience to laws – but 'obligation' – a duty based on the recognition of normative validity claims... [Actors] have to be in a position to contest [the claim] that the goals set are collectively desired or are, as we say, in the general interest... Whereas no agreement among the parties to an exchange is required for them to make a judgment of interests, the question of what lies in the general interest calls for consensus among the members of a collectivity, no matter whether this normative consensus is secured in advance by tradition or has first to be brought about by democratic processes of bargaining and reaching understanding. In the latter case, the connection to consensus formation in language, backed only by potential reasons, is clear (1987, pp.271-2; brackets around 'the claim' in original).

Habermas argues that this requirement for legitimation arises from the need for the emergent system to be autonomous. Although counterintuitive, the point is well made. If in a power-steered relationship the collective goal is defined solely by the superior party, then the availability of sanctions will ensure that the outcome of an interaction is the contingent will of the superior. If this is the case in every interaction, then the resulting aggregate outcome at the system level cannot be said to be unintended. The outcome of co-ordinated social action will be exactly as those who coordinate want it to be. Thus, the requirement for system autonomy cannot be met. However, the attempt to correct this problem with the assumption of normative consensus about goals causes another problem that puts the possibility of media-steering in question. The presence of a legitimizable, substantive collective goal gives rise to the possibility that actors may feel bound to refuse a legal instruction on the grounds that it does not represent a contribution to the realization of that goal. It is difficult to see that if the motivating force behind compliance with commands is ultimately the realization of collective goals in which the individual actor shares an interest and in the definition of which he has the right to participate, an actor would comply with a command that appeared unlikely to result in a positive contribution to goal achievement. Thus on Habermas's model, it seems likely that the aggregate outcome of interactions steered by the power medium will be the realization of the collective goals in question rather than a playing out of the logic of administrative rules. Strategically-rational action would seem to be impossible since legitimate collective goals cannot be established via purely strategic interaction. Neither can the requirements for autonomy and reflexivity be fulfilled: the goals ultimately realized are those consciously chosen by the participants, and this choice is made with reference either to tradition or to consensual action orientations rather than to the political-administrative system itself.

Reasons for Action in Systemic Contexts

In BFN, Habermas proposes what is in effect a formal-pragmatic alternative to the characterization of systemic interaction set out in TCA. He argues that legitimate law embodies three types of reason: the pragmatic, political-ethical and moral reasons for action that we have already encountered. In terms of formal pragmatics, the first of these reasons involves a claim about the objective world, and the latter two claims about the social world. Since formal or legal regulation is what brings social systems into existence, we can say that systemic action is based on these same three types of reason.

Moral reasons are categorical or unconditional. Their subject matter is *justice*. They express the normative point of view 'from which we examine how we can regulate our common life in the equal interest of all… The imperative sense of [moral] precepts can be understood as an 'ought' that depends neither on subjective preferences nor on the (for us) absolute goal of a good, or not misspent, way of life (Habermas, 1996, pp.161-2).

Political-ethical reasons are, if not quite hypothetical, then at least not categorical. The values and interests of individuals or communities represent 'an 'ought' relative to the telos of our own good life' (Habermas, 1996, p.163). They supply motivation only for the persons or collectivities in which they are recognized. This motivation is relative to that arising from other values and interests, and may in any case only be temporary:

> Values always compete with other values. They state which goods specific persons or collectivities strive for or prefer under specific circumstances. Only from the perspective of the given individual or group can values temporarily be ranked in a transitive order. Thus values claim relative validity, whereas justice poses an absolute validity claim: moral precepts claim to be valid for each and every person (Habermas, 1996, p.153).

Political-ethical discourse is therefore located firmly in the concrete form of life of a community. The abstraction typical of moral discourse is absent. The kinds of questions that arise 'pose themselves from the perspective of members who, in the face of important life issues, want to gain clarity about their shared form of life… Serious value decisions result from, and change with, the politicocultural self-understanding of an historical community' (Habermas, 1996, p.160).

Pragmatic reasons, as we saw in Chapter 2, are entirely hypothetical in the sense that they are not motivating in themselves. Rather, they represent an operational complement to normative choices, whether moral or political-ethical: 'Pragmatic questions pose themselves from the perspective of an actor seeking suitable means for realizing goals and preferences that are already given' (Habermas, 1996, p.159). In themselves, they are valid to the extent that they represent an empirically accurate apprehension of 'the facts'.

Habermas includes in this category of pragmatic reasons both the relatively unproblematic physical characteristics of the objective world and the functional characteristics of social systems. Indeed, the 'facts' that are referred to in the title of BFN are precisely the social facts of legal regulation. However, at this point we come up against exactly the same problem that drove Habermas to propose his 'uncoupling' thesis in TCA. There is no recognition in BFN that, when considered on the aggregate level of social systems, these facts – facts about the functional characteristics of systems – are always contestable. As we have seen, the apprehension of the facts of the economic and political-administrative systems via the method of the social sciences can only ever be achieved in the sense of the construction of hypotheses that have a certain probability of being true. These hypotheses are based on empirical observation but also, more importantly, on an interpretation of the politicocultural self-understanding of the historical community in which they are thought to apply. Unless it is conceded that the essence of our shared form of life is something that can be observed 'objectively' from the outside and that it does not depend on democratic processes that clarify the way we are as a society, then the interpretations that underpin 'expert' analyses of social systems must remain subject to challenge from a political-ethical perspective. In order to see how such a critique might be conducted, we need to reconstruct the structure of validity claims that underpins legitimate law.

Politicocultural Reference Communities

We saw above that the binding/bonding force of criticizable claims to validity, the force of social or moral obligation, is necessarily related to a lifeworld context – the context against which the claims in question are redeemable – and thereby to a particular social group. Putting to one side for the moment the question of universal moral norms that in principle apply regardless of the social context, we can argue that the normative force that attaches to political-ethical values and interests emerges from what we can call a 'politicocultural reference community' (PRC): a concrete historical social group against the context of whose lifeworld the claims that give rise to that normative force are redeemable.

We need to draw a further distinction between two different types of PRC: those in which membership is voluntary and those in which it is compulsory or otherwise unavoidable. For the most part the latter type of PRC are political or administrative units, although they may also be non-governmental bodies with a state-sanctioned regulatory capacity, for example accrediting associations related to the practice of a trade or profession. This type of community is Habermas's principal focus in BFN. For our current purposes, however, we are interested primarily in voluntary PRCs, which represent a huge range of associational activity from informal groups of friends to trade unions to local history societies to sports clubs to professional partnerships. We will argue later that the two most important forms of voluntary PRC memberships are participation as a buyer or vendor in the market for a particular good, and participation in the business corporation, whether as an investor or an employee.

The distinction between these two categories of association is to be found in the nature of the 'legitimate order' by which they are defined. Compulsory PRCs operate on the basis that it is in the general or public interest that their order is respected, regardless of whether membership is universal or limited to a functional group within society. The nature of the 'ought' attached to the regulation arising from compulsory PRCs is closer to the categorical 'ought' of moral precepts than the purely hypothetical 'ought' characteristic of the pursuit of private interests. Compliance with the legitimate laws of nations and sub-national political units, as well as, for example, the deontological codes of professional groups is thus obligatory in the sense that non-compliance is considered a criminal act, which is to say an injury to society.

Compulsory PRCs are characterized by political-ethical aims and values that, if not generalizable in the same sense as moral norms, are expressive of a politicocultural self-understanding that has a very high degree of generality.

The rules and conventions of voluntary PRCs, whether formal or informal, cannot be characterized by this degree of generality. Rather, where the pressure of social convention or the law applies, it is simply to ensure that participants fulfil the obligations to their fellow members that, in choosing to participate, they have voluntarily assumed. In violating the rules of a voluntary PRC, a member is injuring only his fellow members and not the public in general.

At the same time, insofar as the members of voluntary PRCs have the opportunity to take legal action against those other members who are in breach of their contract of membership, the public interest makes its way into these private relationships of association. In regulating the definition of a valid contract of membership, the law divides voluntary PRCs into those that are *prohibited* and those that are *permissible* in the sense of representing political-ethical values and interests that are at once legitimizable from the perspective of the members of the PRC and, at least, not in conflict with the politicocultural self-understanding of the community as a whole.

The Structure of Communication in Voluntary Politicocultural Reference Communities

We can define permissibility as the acceptability on the level of society of forms of behaviour and social relationships that carry the binding/bonding force of criticizable claims to validity only against the particular lifeworld context of a voluntary PRC. Just as valid legal norms must be in accord with moral norms (Habermas, 1996, p.155), valid voluntary PRC regulation must be in accord with the legitimate norms of private and public law (as well as those of morality). We can break this general validity criterion down further. In order to be permissible, co-ordinated social action in pursuit of non-generalizable aims and values has to fulfil three criteria. First of all, membership of the PRC must be genuinely a matter of choice. All participants must freely have accepted the aims and values, and hence the collective goals, of the community. Second, the normative order that defines the PRC must be, at least, undamaging to the interests of society as a whole. It must be coherent both with moral norms and with the political-ethical aims and values of the compulsory PRC (in practice, the state) within which it is located. This is to say that there must be no conflict between different levels of social obligation. Third, any specific normative validity claims raised must be coherent with the overarching normative order of the PRC. Co-ordinated social action will be prohibited when any of these three criteria are not met.

In terms of the structure of communication, these three criteria take the place of the single, undifferentiated normative validity claim made in lifeworld contexts involving generalizable aims and values. If in the context of a voluntary PRC a speaker proposes some action involving the pursuit of political-ethical aims and values, then he has to win the hearer's assent to certain claims which are not raised in communication in the context either of moral discourse or discourse on the normative order of compulsory PRCs. First of all, the aims and values in question, while they *can* be chosen by anyone, are not such that they *should* be chosen by everyone. Communicative action within voluntary PRCs therefore involves most fundamentally the claim that certain goals and values are expressive of an authentic collective self-understanding in the sense that they have been freely chosen by both speaker and hearer. In this sense, despite being the 'location' of the content of the normative order of the PRC, this is not itself a normative validity claim. Rather, it is two separate claims with the same content. One of these is about the subjective world of the speaker, and one about the subjective world of the hearer. The communicatively acting speaker refers to his own sincere adherence to the normative order of the PRC, as well as his belief in the hearer's adherence to the same. The hearer can obviously reject either of these claims, in the former case questioning the sincerity of the speaker's claim to hold certain values, and in the latter rejecting those values himself.

The second validity claim is that the political-ethical order of the PRC is not in conflict with the established moral and political obligations that bind all members of a state or society. This claim establishes the wider social or normative context of the PRC. Such a claim cannot arise where co-ordinated action is undertaken in pursuit of generalizable moral norms or the political-ethical aims and values of the state since the relevant normative order is that of morality itself (human rights) or that of an entire society. This obviously cannot be in conflict with itself.

The third and final claim refers to the proposed co-ordinated action itself. The claim is that action is legitimate in the sense that it is coherent with the normative order of the voluntary PRC. Since the normative order of the PRC does not conflict with that of society as a whole, then neither will any action which is logically coherent with it.

In the context of voluntary PRC membership, then, the argument 'we should do this' can be rejected in three different ways. First, the 'we' in 'we should do this' may be rejected. Either the hearer has not chosen, or no longer wishes to be a member of the appropriate reference group; or the hearer rejects the speaker's claim to adhere to the values of that group. In the former case, the hearer is excluding himself from a particular lifeworld context. In the latter, he is rejecting the speaker's claim to share such a context and thereby questioning her motives. In either case, this kind of 'external' rejection will not lead speaker and hearer to attempt to achieve consensus. For the purposes of the communicative act in question, they are not members of the same PRC and therefore have no duty to reach agreement. To reject an offer of communication on this basis carries no necessary implication that the general aims and values of the PRC and the relationships and behaviour which arise from adherence to them are not perfectly permissible.

Second, and on the other hand, the claim 'we should do this' can be rejected either on the grounds that the aims and values of a PRC – its entire normative order – is in conflict with the established obligations that bind all members of a society, or because the means of pursuing a non-generalizable normative order proposed in the particular case are socially unacceptable. In this case it is the 'should' that is being rejected. It is important to note that a resolution of the second of the two possibilities (where a course of action is coherent with the otherwise permissible aims and values of the PRC but in conflict with more generally applying obligatory norms) will involve a modification of the general aims and values of the PRC in order to ensure that these are coherent with the normative order of society as a whole.

Finally, a hearer may recognize that the general aims and values underpinning the claim are norms he has chosen to adhere to, and that these norms are not in conflict with the established obligations applying in society, but may nonetheless reject an offer of communication for reasons which are *internally* connected to the proposed co-ordinated action itself. It is the 'this' in 'we should do this' that is the root of the objection. Unlike the first two types of rejection, this type of rejection will lead speaker and hearer to try to reach agreement on what *would* represent a valid means of pursuing the aims and values of the PRC given their particular situation.

An example may be helpful. We can imagine a situation in which two friends – the simplest and most informal possible type of voluntary PRC – are trying to decide what to do together one weekend. One suggests that they visit a particular exhibition of contemporary painting. The normative validity claim underpinning this suggestion may be rejected for five different reasons:

No, I find exhibitions of art very boring.

What are you after? You hate art exhibitions!

No, we should do something else because contemporary art is decadent and corrupting.

No, I know the exhibition is a good one, but we should not go because it is sponsored by
   a corporation that regularly engages in ethically questionable activities.

No, I've heard that that exhibition is very poor.

In the first two cases, the hearer is rejecting the speaker's definition of the way the two friends are together: the proposed understanding of their relationship. In the first case, our hearer is excluding an interest in art from the order defining the micro-PRC made up of herself and her friend. She would not enjoy any exhibition of art, regardless of its content or quality, and hence it cannot represent a valid element of the mutual self-understanding on which her friendships are based. The rejection of the speaker's plan therefore precludes any activity involving art of any kind and an entirely new suggestion will have to be made. In the second case, the hearer is accusing the speaker of having some ulterior motive in suggesting a visit to the exhibition since she believes that his implied claim to be interested in art cannot be sincere. Again, the self-understanding that defines the friendship does not include art because of the speaker's previously demonstrated preference against it. In suggesting a visit to an exhibition, he is acting outside the established terms of the PRC.

In the third and fourth cases, the hearer rejects the proposal from the perspective of the normative order of the wider society in which the friends live. In the third case, the hearer is rejecting the proposal on the grounds that an interest in contemporary art is illegitimate per se, and in the fourth because to support this particular exhibition would be socially damaging. In the final case, the hearer accepts that visiting an art exhibition is a legitimate norm, but rejects the suggestion on the grounds that the experience will not be enjoyable *for an art lover* because it is of poor quality. Unlike the first four cases, the content and quality of the exhibition is here of direct relevance to the decision about action. It is only in this last situation that it would be rational for the two friends to engage in a discussion about the quality of the exhibition as a prelude to deciding what to do.

In sum, then, we have the following proposition: Within voluntary PRCs, a successful interaction between communicatively acting participants requires that the following claims be established in place of the single normative claim raised where aims and values are generalizable:

1) **Internal validity of general aims and values**: Speaker and hearer are both members of the group. They have freely agreed to abide by the normative order that defines it.

2) **Legitimacy (permissibility) of general aims and values**: The normative order of the group conflicts neither with moral norms and principles nor with the obligatory political-ethical values that bind all members of the wider state/society in which it is located.

3) **Coherence of interaction with general aims and values**: The specific normative component of the communicative act (the 'this' in 'we should do this') is coherent with the normative order of the group.

Formally Organized Voluntary PRCs

At this stage we need to draw yet another distinction, this time between two different types of voluntary PRC: those in which the rights and duties of membership are formally specified and enforceable by law, and those that are externally supported only by social convention. Society will generally support the right of voluntary PRCs with permissible aims and values to take action against those of their members who do not fulfil the obligations of membership.[2] Obviously, society will not intervene to oblige friends to telephone each other when they say they will, or to force godparents to buy birthday presents for their godchildren. Nonetheless, it is clear that those who voluntarily enter relationships of friendship or of godparenthood subsequently have a moral obligation to behave in an appropriate manner, for all that this obligation may be externally supported only by what Weber called 'a general and practically significant reaction of disapproval' (cited in Habermas, 1996, p.69).

---

[2] One rather important exception to this rule in legal practice is to be found in British labour law as it applies to trade union membership. Trade unions are not permitted to take any disciplinary action against members who refuse to abide by a call for strike action, even where such a call is in accordance with the rules of the union as well as the law regulating industrial action. Not surprisingly, the continued existence of the principle of freedom of association in British law has been questioned as a result of this development, not least by the International Labour Organization (ILO, 1989).

The difference between informal social obligation of this kind and the rights and duties arising from legally enforceable contracts of exchange and of membership in private organizations is in one sense merely a matter of degree. In all cases, society provides an external guarantee for rights and duties arising from a normative order that is internally valid and legitimate (permissible) at the level of society. However, despite the conceptual linearity between the two cases, there is an obvious difference between those voluntary PRC memberships that carry legally enforceable rights and duties and those that do not. There is a difference in the nature of the rationality applied to resolving interactions: the difference between juridical and communicative rationality. In the former group of social contexts we find a formalized structure of claim and redemption based on the fulfilment of legal rather than substantive criteria. The outcome of social interactions is determined by the civil law and the law of contract and not on the basis of an informal shared understanding of the relationship between actors. In TCA, as we have already seen, Habermas argues that in these formally organized contexts of action, formal-legal or procedural claims to validity *entirely* displace informal, substantive claims. Communication takes place via special codes and not in ordinary language.

However, what we have just seen is that, regardless of whether the claims to validity underpinning communication are redeemable in a procedural or substantive sense, the *structure* of that communication remains the same. This is coherent with a reading of BFN that privileges the possibility of substantive legitimation for action in systemic contexts. Habermas's earlier argument that systemic interaction proceeds purely on the binary logic of cost/benefit or command/obedience misses the need to allow for a regular *reversion* to the perspective of substantive rationality in order to preserve the stability of the system. We need to be able to reconstruct the action-level characteristics of exchange and authority in such a way that interactions can be resolved *either* on the basis of procedural or substantive rationality within a single structure of communication. In this way, we can account for the emergence of social systems that evolved from, and whose stability ultimately depends on, legitimate norms.

The processes of offer and response leading to the agreement of an exchange or to compliance with a command should be specifiable according to the same basic structure of communication that we have outlined for the case of communicative action within voluntary PRCs. What this adds to Habermas's action-level specification of systemic relationships is an appreciation of the position of the other that goes beyond what can be communicated in the interaction itself. We saw above that strategic optimization requires more information than is available in the behaviour of the participants in the relationship. We want to suggest that this information is available in the systemic context itself.

Re-Specifying the Characteristics of Money-Steered Interactions

To give a plausible action-level account of the strategically-rational actor's agreement to an exchange, we need to bring the Habermas/Parsons specification of the money medium into line with the action model implied by neoclassical micro-economics. As we argued above, systemic interactions involve the comparison of an action situation with a model. In the case of the exchange of commodities, this model involves, first, elements of the objective world – it specifies the physical characteristics of the commodity in question – and second, the individual situations of other market actors as summarized or encoded in the price norms of the market. It is only the addition of this second element that enables participants to be profit-maximizing.

If we allow that participants share a lifeworld context at least to the extent of the contents of the objective world, then it is likely that they will have a separate but more or less congruent appreciation not just of the bare physical characteristics of a commodity, but also of the nature of human material need and the consequent substitutability of the commodity (the availability of alternatives that fulfil the same need). To put the point more conventionally, we must surely allow that participants have some idea of the *use-value* of a commodity and that in most cases – at least those involving basic commodities and unless participants are from very different cultures or societies – the individual assessments of use-value will roughly coincide without the need for any explicit consensus formation.[3]

To be able to assess the use-value of a commodity gets participants some of the way towards a strategically-rational deal, but it is not enough. The concept of utility is rather nearer the mark, combining use-value with the inherent desirability of a commodity and the purely subjective preferences or tastes of participants. Utility still cannot be the concept at the root of exchange, however, because the utility of a commodity to an individual usually declines as the quantity he already possesses rises. Thus the price at which he is willing to buy or sell also declines. The relevant factor in setting an exchange value, then, is not utility, but *marginal* utility: the utility of more of a commodity than an individual already has or has recently consumed.

The marginal utility of a commodity to an individual is a direct reflection of his individual (material and subjective) circumstances – his utility preferences – and as such cannot be known by other individuals unless that individual chooses to make it known. But it is only by using a well-grounded estimate of the marginal utility of a commodity to a potential exchange partner that participants can make a rational decision about the point at which to strike a deal, the point of maximum profitability. It is the market price that is the primary source of this estimate. A market price is in fact a perfect example of a sociological generalization in Weber's sense. Potential participants in an exchange are not and cannot be in a position to know with certainty the best price they can pay or be paid for a particular commodity. This would involve bargaining with every potential participant to discover the prices at which they are prepared to exchange. There is historical information available, however, in the form of those exchanges that have already taken place. Although in practice participants are unlikely to perform such an analysis in any precise sense, relying on some hazy concept of the 'going rate', we can nonetheless define the market price for a

---

[3] Not having sufficient information or expertise to judge the use-value of a commodity is obviously problematic if we consider the trade in specialized commodities like diamonds or racehorses. It would generally be considered foolish for an ordinary person to attempt to buy such commodities without expert advice.

commodity as *an estimate of the actually valid price for that commodity based on the statistical analysis of observed exchanges.* Where prices are unregulated, it is obviously highly pertinent to ask in what sense a price can be 'actually valid' since there is no process of consensus formation which can grant this status. A market price appears to be a norm deriving its validity solely from the fact that it is observed. As such, it is a perfect example of the empirically-derived, non-interpretively understood, probabilistic claims to validity we identified above as presenting such a problem for formal pragmatics. However, for the strategic actor, all that matters is that the market price indicates the statistical distribution of already agreed exchange-values for a commodity, and thus, given the reasonable constancy of perceived use-value, the distribution of marginal utilities. With this information in hand, he is in a position to estimate the probability that a particular exchange-value will be agreed.

If we now try to reconstruct the agreement of an exchange from the action perspective, we will find it rather more plausible (that is, if for the moment we put aside the range of questions that arise about access to information). Say that an actor wishes to acquire some commodity and that her individual situation is such that the commodity has a marginal utility to her of 30 utils. Having found another individual with that commodity available for sale, our actor examines the commodity and finds that it is of somewhat superior quality to the average. She assumes that the vendor is aware both of this and of the fact that the current market price is around 27 utils. What she does not know, and what the vendor will not divulge, is the commodity's marginal utility to the vendor – how much of the commodity the vendor has available, how desirable it is to him, and any other elements of his situation that may have an effect on price, for example the need to sell in order to acquire other, more urgently needed commodities. This, along with the commodity's marginal utility to the buyer (about which the vendor has no knowledge) is the information which is the subject of the process of offer and response. The most important contrast with the situation implied by Habermas is that the buyer knows that unless the vendor's situation is unusual in some respect, she is unlikely to be able to persuade the vendor to part with the commodity for less than 28 utils, since the market rate is 27 and the commodity is of better quality than average. The market rate tells her that judging from deals that have already taken place, the probability that there will be anyone willing to accept less than 28 utils is low. The vendor is equally aware of this, and therefore it would be rational for him to stick at this price. The buyer can certainly test the waters by trying to appear unwilling to pay more than a sum which is in fact less than she is prepared to pay, but since the standard of the market price exists, she has a reference point from which to depart in the hope that a better deal might be available, and somewhere to stick if it turns out that it is not. Knowledge of the use-value and availability of the commodity can also be brought to bear on bargaining. It may be known, for example, that a commodity has for some reason become difficult to obtain. In such a case, it would be rational for a vendor to hold out for a price above the current market price.

The Rational Structure of Communication in Exchange

Since the exchange interaction itself could potentially take place between any two individuals who are in the market for a particular commodity either as buyers or vendors, and since the price at which they settle will have an effect on the market price, which will in turn affect the prices of other commodities, we can argue that the relevant PRC consists of all potential participants in any kind of exchange, which is to say virtually all of a society.

The first step taken by our strategic actor is to decide whether he wants the commodity at all, i.e. to determine whether its marginal utility is greater than zero. Since we are dealing with strategic actors we can assume both that exchange is in principle an acceptable way of acquiring commodities (in fact, other than theft, it is the *only* way of acquiring them) and that the actor will do without the commodity, regardless of its marginal utility, if he cannot strike a profitable deal. It is the combination of the positive marginal utility of a commodity and the prospect of a profitable deal that turns the individual into a market actor, and thus a member of the PRC. As we have just argued, however, not just any level of profit is acceptable. Actors only want to agree the most profitable exchanges available. We can define the general aims and values of the PRC, then, as the exchange of a particular commodity at an exchange-value that *jointly* optimizes the profit to those involved.

The second step taken by the actor is to ensure that these general aims and values are permissible, i.e. that the commodity in question is legally exchangeable – that possessing it is not in itself illegal (e.g. proscribed drugs, stolen property), and that exchanging it for profit is permitted (e.g. no need for a licence to trade in the commodity). We assume here that the strategic orientation of market actors means that they will wish to avoid the sanctions attached to breaching the law.

The final step is to ascertain that the proposed exchange is coherent with the general aims and values of the PRC, which in this case is to say that the exchange-value implies the joint maximization of profitability. Since both participants are strategically-acting, each is entitled to believe that his potential partner will also attempt to maximize profit and that they will not agree to a sub-optimal exchange. Joint optimization therefore actually arises consequent on both parties separately attempting to maximize their gains. Starting from the basis of a market price which has been discounted or augmented to take account of any non-typical physical characteristics of the commodity, participants will negotiate in the attempt to discover the true marginal utility of the commodity to each other.[4] These negotiations will either result in an agreed exchange value – the participants independently accept that they are unlikely to be able to improve their profitability elsewhere – or one or other participant will not accept this and a deal will not be struck.

---

[4] In fact, taking into account any non-typical characteristics of a commodity is generally an integral part of the negotiation process. It is difficult to separate from negotiation on the more genuinely social elements of exchange-value. However, it is logically a separate operation, the physical characteristics of a commodity being wholly separate from their contribution to its value and not requiring the use of sociological generalization for their identification. Nonetheless, since our actors are strategic, we cannot say that there will be any genuine process of consensus formation involved in the identification of physical characteristics. Separate, but in most circumstances congruent knowledge about the characteristics of the commodity will instead be incorporated into the negotiating positions of each party.

Aggregate Autonomy and Reflexivity of Interaction Outcomes

On the basis of our specification of the action-level characteristics of exchange it should be fairly clear that all three criteria for media-steering are fulfilled. We have just seen that actors with a purely strategic orientation to action can nonetheless come to an agreement on an exchange value. Each completed exchange contributes to the statistical picture from which the price norms of the market are derived. We can assume that each particular exchange-value represents a compromise between the utility preferences of the participants. If either of these differ markedly from the market price, then it is likely that the value settled upon will also deviate from the market price, thus affecting subsequent bargains. Since these norms are all denominated in terms of a single medium, money, the totality of exchanges adds up to a dynamic system of interrelated exchange-values. This system is stabilized by the fairly constant relative use-value of commodities, but it also reflects the constantly changing average marginal utility of commodities to individual actors. In principle, no one exchange is any more important than any other in the determination of this average utility, and hence the emergent system is wholly beyond the control of any individual.

Re-Specifying the Characteristics of Power-Steered Interactions

Appreciating the position of the other in the context of authority relationships within private organizations involves making assumptions about the legitimacy of collective goals. As we suggested above, the communicatively acting member of a private organization – a voluntary PRC in which legally enforceable rights and duties are attached to membership – cannot claim that his interlocutor *ought* to adhere to the aims and values of the community in any absolute sense precisely because these aims and values are not generalizable. The only genuinely normative validity claim raised is that the aims and values are not in conflict with any valid political or ethical imperatives applying in wider society. Even where this claim is successful it is obviously not motivating in itself.

Where unrestrained processes of consensus formation in language do occur within a private organization, it makes no sense to think of the content of the eventual consensus as entirely open at the outset. If this was the case, what was it that brought the group together in the first place? Where is the sense in deliberately *joining* a group that initially has no aims and values at all, as opposed to simply finding oneself in association with a group of other individuals by virtue of genetic, geographical or other contingent factors? There must be, therefore, an irreducible core of subjective, individual choice at the root of the goals of a private organization. Members must have at least some minimal degree of individual commitment to or interest in the normative order of the organization *before* they join it, and hence this commitment cannot be truly normative. It does not arise via processes of consensus formation that take place *within* the organization.[5]

Just as in exchange relationships, then, members and potential members of private organizations do not need to come to any agreement with other members in order to judge whether membership (joining or remaining within the organization) is in their individual interest. In Hirschman's well-known terms (1970), the availability of the option of 'exit' means that the de facto validity of the normative order of the organization remains a matter of parallel individual agreement rather than joint agreement; of egoistic strategic calculation rather than the consensual recognition of redeemable normative validity claims. Thus, the context of the private organization per se ensures that authority need not be related to any substantively legitimate goals, and the emergence of a system remains a coherent possibility. We should note that 'legitimation' in this very limited sense of the existence of multiple individual agreement to the normative order of the private organization is the structural analogue in the power medium of the mutually positive marginal utility of an exchange.

The Characteristics of Power-Steered Interactions in Private Organizations

In becoming a member of a private organization, an individual agrees to carry out the normative order of that organization. Indeed, carrying out this normative order is what attracts individuals to membership in the first place. It is membership itself which is to be desired. However, the normative order also imposes costs – it involves obligation as well as entitlement – and it may be the case that an individual's net interest in membership is negative, in which case it will simply be abandoned. Only the individual can know the point at which membership becomes a net cost. This is structurally analogous to the potential participant in an exchange discovering that there are no deals available at a profitable exchange-value, and therefore simply doing without the commodity sought (or the profits from the sale of that commodity).

The primary obligation that arises from membership is compliance with valid instructions issued by office-holders. This obligation is owed to the organization itself, which is to say it is simultaneously owed to all of its members and office-holders. In a sense, the very concept of office within an organization is a means of saving organization members from their own strategic selfishness. Members' interest in membership will not be satisfied unless the organization actually functions, but the

---

[5] We will see in Chapter 7 that Habermas accepts that the existence of preferences which are the result of 'prior self-formative processes' are of relevance in exchange. The point we are making here is exactly the same: the choice of organizational memberships is influenced by pre-existing normative and subjective commitments. It could be argued that the root of the employment relationship is merely material need, and therefore that the employee cannot freely agree to the normative order of the corporation. But we might equally well argue, first, that for many workers, the choice of employer *is* a positive one; and, second, that the employee arrives at the workplace already equipped with cultural knowledge about work and the employment relationship which is a vital factor in his calculations about the balance between the obligations and rewards of organizational membership – about what it is and is not reasonable for an employer to expect from an employee and vice versa.

strategic rationality of members acts precisely in opposition to the possibility of this functioning. Office-holders articulate the interests of the members qua components of the organization, against the articulation of the interests of the member qua individual which is the role of the member on the receiving end of an instruction.

Given that members of the organization are strategic actors, it is rational for them to seek to avoid complying with instructions (something which we assume represents a cost to the member) if such avoidance is compatible with retaining membership. They will only comply, then, if in so doing their net interest in membership remains positive, and if by refusing they risk losing membership. In the vast majority of private organizations it will be within the competence of office-holders to expel individuals from membership if they do not comply with legal instructions. Members must therefore be able to distinguish legally valid and legally invalid instructions, or in Habermas/Parsons' terms, must recognize when an office-holder has sovereignty over them. For office-holders in the organization, the logic of interaction is parallel. Their role in the organization is to issue valid instructions, and they will seek to maximize the range of instructions with which members are prepared to comply while voluntarily remaining in membership. Office-holders obviously must also be able to distinguish legally valid and legally invalid instructions.

At this point it might appear that knowledge of the individual situations of members of the organization is of no relevance to anyone except the individuals themselves. Neither members nor office-holders appear to have any control over the scope of sovereignty of office-holders. If an instruction is valid, then an office-holder has no choice but to issue it and the member to whom it is directed must either comply or, if the instruction is such as to make membership a net cost, leave the organization. It is only the individual situation of the organization member that is of any consequence here. The legal specification of the membership relationship, however, can never be so detailed as to leave no room for interpretation. Certainly there are some issues which are straightforward, such as whether the participants are within the spatio-temporal confines of the organization, whether the person issuing the instruction is in fact an office-holder etc. However, there inevitably will come a point at which the scope of sovereignty of an office-holder cannot be unambiguously defined. Now, in a formal sense the office-holder is empowered to decide unilaterally what is a correct interpretation of the legal order. There is no explicit requirement for agreement as there is in the case of exchange where neither participant has a greater right to interpret the market.[6] Nonetheless, the office-holder has to be aware of the

---

[6] Habermas makes the point that power-steered relationships do not share the inherent structural balance of those steered by money, arguing that office-holders have the power to determine which collective goals shall count as valid, and thus have control over the definition of the generalized value of effectiveness in a way which is not possible with utility (1987, pp.271-2). Allowing for the distinction we have drawn between private and public organizations, this is in fact the same point. The solution in the public context, where goals are generalizable, is to introduce some process involving consensus formation in language – the aim of which is the agreement of collective goals – whereas in the private context, where goals are not generalizable, structural balance is achieved via the negotiation of rule-systems.

possibility that exercising his legal authority to the fullest possible extent risks losing members, as individuals decide – depending on their situation – that the obligations of membership outweigh its rewards. The office-holder obviously cannot know where this watershed will be for the members under his command. Similarly, for members to accept as valid *any* instruction that remains within the letter of the legal order of the organization would violate the strategic principle of maximizing returns by minimizing costs. We can argue, then, that the scope of sovereignty of an office-holder must in the final analysis be the subject of negotiation. Just as with exchange, a process of joint optimization occurs. Office-holder and member must *agree* an interpretation of the formal order of the organization that maximizes the office-holder's successful instructions (against the possibility of losing members) while minimizing the member's obligations (against the possibility of being expelled from membership).

So, actors in money-steered interactions will seek to maximize profit by comparing their situation with a model which includes known elements of the objective world – the use-value of the commodities in question – and a statistical summary of the unknown individual situations of members of the market. Actors in power-steered interactions will instead seek to minimize compliance/maximize obedience by comparing their situation with a model which includes both known elements of the *social* world – the formal legal context, to the extent that this is unambiguous – together with a summary of the (unknown) individual situations of the other members of the organization. Information on the latter subject comes not from the members themselves, but from sociological generalization. Participants refer to the historical evidence about those situations in which instructions were deemed valid, which is to say the statistically established patterns of compliance. The point is not to determine whether or not an instruction is valid in any substantive sense, but to assess on the basis of the empirical evidence the probability that a refusal to comply will lead to expulsion from membership, or the probability that insisting on compliance will lead to resignation. If situations arise that do not fit into these empirically established patterns, then the scope of sovereignty has to be redefined either through formal or informal bargaining processes, just as the scope of profitability is redefined through bargaining on price where the characteristics of commodities or the marginal utility of the commodity to participants are not those assumed or implied in the market model.

The Rational Structure of Communication in Private Authority Relationships

Once again, we can specify the process of command and response that leads to the agreement of the scope of an office holder's sovereignty according to the structure of communication that we outlined for the case of communicative action within voluntary PRCs. The relevant PRC is straightforwardly the organization itself. The interpretive precedent set by the agreement that an instruction is valid affects only those who have agreed to be bound by the legal order of the organization.

The first step taken by our strategic organization member is to decide whether the individually-accruing benefits arising from the objects, structures and practices of the private organization are desirable. We can assume both that accepting authority is in principle an acceptable way of achieving collectively desired goals and that the actor will do without the entitlements of membership, however desirable, if they do not outweigh its obligations in the sense of those instructions with which he is obliged to comply. The rational member will not simply accept any level of net benefit, however, but, assuming that the entitlements of membership are invariable, will seek to minimize his obligations. Actors will only comply with instructions if to refuse would lead to expulsion.

The second step taken by the actor is to ensure that the formal objects, structures and practices of the organization (including the particular instance of this normative order in the form of the instruction itself) are legally permissible. There are any number of potential examples of private organizations violating legal norms, which might include the exclusion of women, ethnic minorities or any other 'non-relevant' category of person from membership; the discriminatory allocation of membership entitlements, for example the reservation of office to particular individuals on some unjustifiable basis; or the socially or environmentally damaging consequences of the pursuit of certain objects.

The final step is to ascertain that the particular instruction is coherent with the formal objects, structures and practices of the PRC, which in this case is to say that the instruction falls within an agreed, jointly-optimal scope of sovereignty. Since both member and office-holder are strategically-acting, each is entitled to believe that the other will attempt to minimize or maximize the range of valid instructions and that they will not agree a scope of sovereignty where they believe there is a reasonable probability that it can be improved upon (from their particular perspective). Joint optimization therefore actually arises consequent on both parties separately attempting to optimise their gains. Starting from the basis of a scope of sovereignty redrawn to take account of any elements of the situation which are without a precise existing precedent but which lend themselves easily to interpretation, participants will negotiate in the attempt to discover the point where the value of membership to the individual balances the duty of the office holder (for the failure of which he will be held responsible) to enforce the legal order of the organization. These negotiations will either result in an agreed scope of sovereignty, which is to say that both participants independently accept that they are unlikely to be able to get more from their interlocutor, or one or other participant will not accept this and expulsion or resignation will follow.[7]

Aggregate Autonomy and Reflexivity of Interaction Outcomes

Just as with exchange, the strategic capability of individuals presupposes the existence of the legal order of the private organization. This legal order could not have come into being except through processes of consensus formation in language. However, once it is in existence, it is the strategically-motivated compliance of individuals that reproduces and validates that order. Participants refer to the de facto valid established

---

[7] In real world situations, i.e. within employment relationships, while high labour turnover can certainly be a problem, it is more usually the possibility of strike action or forms of employee recalcitrance other than resignation which office-holders seek to avoid.

interpretations of the system of rules in order to determine the outcome of interactions, but the unavoidable ambiguities in any legal order can lead to the renegotiation of the scope of sovereignty, changing the meaning of the rules for subsequent interactions. Not only do rules 'apply themselves' under these conditions, then, linking up in unforeseen ways, but the legal order of an organization is subject to unplanned and unintended change by virtue of the fact that members act strategically on the basis of sociological generalizations.

Respecifying the Characteristics of the Money and Power Media

Through a criticism of Habermas's account of the money medium, and a consideration of how the power medium might operate within private organizations (those with non-generalizable aims and values), we have shown that the two media can be specified in more detail and in much more precisely parallel terms than those proposed in the Habermas/Parsons account. We have construed both the market for commodities and the private organization as PRCs defined by non-generalizable interests, aims and values. Membership of these voluntary PRCs carries both obligation and entitlement. There are two major differences between the media. First, in the case of the power medium, agreement to membership, the fulfilment of obligations and the drawing of entitlements are temporally separated such that the membership relationship extends over a long period and involves many interactions. In the case of exchange, on the other hand, membership, obligation and entitlement, although conceptually separate, are exhausted in a single interaction that may last only seconds. Second, while neither of the parties to exchange has a privileged entitlement to interpret the market, the office-holder in a power relationship is formally entitled to insist upon a particular interpretation of the legal order of the organization – even though in practice he may be forced to accept a compromise position in order to retain members.

Table 4.1 summarizes the characteristics of the two steering media, setting out the logical structure behind a hearer's reaction to an offer of communication in our two media-steered contexts. Recalling our discussion of the legitimacy of non-generalizable norms, we can see that this rather complex structure is what takes the place of a normative validity claim as the rationally motivating force behind communication in systemic contexts.

We do not want to suggest that this is communicative action. It would not be accurate to say that the meaning of a speaker's offer or instruction includes the claim that the various conditions do obtain, since the speaker is in no position to know anything about the most crucial element, the situation of the hearer – at least not in the strict sense of knowledge dictated by the principles of formal pragmatics. Instead, the speaker's statement is made with the backing of pertinent statistical evidence, that is, probabilistic claims about the functional characteristics of the system. Whereas in informal contexts of action, communicative actors can be *certain* that if the claims underpinning an offer of communication are accepted then that offer will be successful, actors in formally-organized contexts can never be certain of anything. Even if a hearer accepts that the claims which underpin a statement made in a systemic context are, in their own terms, wholly redeemable (i.e. justified on the basis

Table 4.1   Action-level characteristics of social interaction in media-steered contexts

	Exchange – logical structure of the decision to accept an offer	**Private authority relationship – logical structure of the decision to comply with an instruction**
Internal validity of general aims and values	Actor's assessment of the marginal utility of commodity (based on its physical characteristics and actor's individual situation) is positive.	Actor's assessment of his interest in membership (based on the organization's objects, structures and practices and his individual situation) is positive.
	Actor accepts the principle of distributing commodities via exchange with a view to profit.	Actor accepts the principle of organizing goal-achievement via hierarchical bureaucratic authority relationships.
Legitimacy (permissibility) of general aims and values	Actor knows that exchange of commodity in question with a view to profit is legal.	Actor knows that organization's objects, structures and practices are legal.
Coherence of particular interaction with general aims and values	Actor compares proposed price with market price, taking objectively determinable differences in use-value into account in order to assess scope for negotiation; following negotiation to exhaustion (if needed), assessment made of the probability of a more profitable deal being available elsewhere in the light of the remaining divergence between proposed price and market price. If this probability is low, and providing the exchange is profitable at the negotiated price, then deal will be struck.	Actor compares instruction with de facto established interpretations of legal order, taking objectively determinable differences in the situation into account in order to assess scope for negotiation on scope of sovereignty; following negotiation to exhaustion (if needed), assessment made of the probability of retaining membership if instruction is refused in the light of the remaining divergence between instruction and established practice. If this probability is low, and provided the net interest in membership remains positive, then instruction will be accepted.

of the empirical evidence), this is still no guarantee that they will accept the 'offer of communication' and act appropriately. Speakers can only ever be sure that it is *likely* that from a range of hearers, a certain proportion will comply. This is precisely what Weber means when he says that an organization exists only insofar as we can say that 'there is a probability that certain persons will carry out the order governing the organization' (Weber, 1978, p.49).

Conclusion

Another of Weber's important insights is that 'Statistical uniformities constitute understandable types of action, and thus constitute sociological generalizations, only when they can be regarded as manifestations of the understandable subjective meaning of a course of social action' (Weber 1978, p.12). What we hope to have shown in this chapter is that one 'understandable subjective meaning' of the statistical uniformities which inform action in systemic contexts is that these uniformities are meaning*less*. It is perfectly possible to interpret them simply as the aggregate result of multiple social interactions conducted by strategically-rational actors. Although we have had to modify Habermas's account of social interaction in systemic contexts in order to argue that this is the case, it seems that actors can indeed treat the functional characteristics of social systems as if they embodied no legitimate norms, recognizing in the actions of the other actors who together form those systems only the same strategic, individualistic motivation by which they themselves are driven.

In modifying Habermas's approach in this way, we have shown that the structure of communication in formally-organized contexts parallels the structure of communication in the informal context of PRCs with non-enforceable rights and duties. In both economic and organizational circumstances, however, there is a need for a 'surrogate' for the lifeworld context that informs the resolution of social interactions in informal action situations. Habermas's account of systemic action is inadequate because it fails appropriately to conceptualize the social context of exchange and authority relationships. What is missing is the recognition that without the context of the system itself, in the sense of the historical or statistical record of completed interactions, strategic action is not possible. It is only the existence of a systemic context that enables actors to decide via strategic negotiation rather than consensus formation in language whether an interaction is coherent with the general aims and values of a PRC.

Chapter 5

Legitimate Action in Systemic Contexts

In this chapter, we want to argue that there is a clear alternative to interpreting as meaningless the statistical uniformities observed in the economic and political-administrative spheres. We will suggest that for every formal-legal element or claim to validity in the structure of communication in systemic contexts, there is an underlying substantive claim. Where these claims are redeemable, the association of action and outcome arises because a market price or an instruction is in some sense substantively valid, and hence actors will for all intents and purposes be rationally rather than merely strategically motivated to act. The observed statistical regularities of price and compliance with authority that characterize social systems can be interpreted as the result of non-strategic behaviour on the part of participants in exchange and authority relationships. They strike deals and do what they are asked because they recognize the legitimacy of the prices and instructions involved. In other words, the systemic context itself can be given a positive value status.

The sense in which this validity is substantive, as we have tried to demonstrate, cannot be exactly the same sense in which the normative claims raised by communicative actors are potentially valid. That which is merely probable does not have the same logical force as that which is certain. Nonetheless, we want to argue that there are plausible substantive explanations for observed patterns of conformity to the price norms of the market and the legal order of organizations which are perfectly meaningful, commonplace and logically coherent. In fact, since it is only the existence of the market or legal context that enables participants to act strategically, we are obliged to propose some explanation of this sort even if we ultimately wish to argue that media-steered interactions are valid only in an empirical sense. As Parsons put it, 'A social order resting on interlocking of interests alone, and thus ultimately on sanctions, is hardly empirically possible though perhaps theoretically conceivable *given the order as an initial assumption*' (cited in Habermas, 1987, p.208; emphasis added). Thus, the emergence of systemic contexts has to be explicable as the result of normatively valid social interaction.

Fairness: The Substantive Validity of Exchange and the Evolution of Markets

While we could easily expend an entire chapter discussing the nuances of the word 'fair', we will restrict ourselves simply to proposing a definition that applies in contexts where co-ordinated social action does not involve the pursuit of a general interest. Fairness, we suggest, involves taking the individual interests of all participants in co-ordinated social action equally into account. It involves the balancing of non-generalizable interests, taking the place of a general interest as the normatively valid goal of co-ordinated social action. Our proposal, then, is that the de facto validity of the price norms of the market could in principle be a consequence of participants recognizing that these norms express fair exchange-values. If this is the case, any exchange relationship that involves an exchange-value coherent with a market price will be a fair exchange relationship. However, this is still a circular argument. We need to consider what it is that can give the market this inherent normative validity in the first place. In other words, we need to define a fair exchange relationship in isolation from a market context, and to show how the market can emerge on the basis of such substantively valid exchanges.

We can say immediately that a legitimate exchange relationship, given that it involves aims and values which are clearly non-generalizable, will follow the structure of communication we outlined above with respect to voluntary PRCs. Exchange will be legitimate (that is, permissible and thereby morally or legally enforceable) where the parties freely agree to pursue their individual interests via exchange, where exchange involving the commodity or commodities in question is a permissible form of relationship and where the equivalence between commodities expressed in the exchange value is itself in some sense substantively rational.

In all of what follows it should be borne in mind that it is never going to be possible to give a precise formulation of what makes for a fair exchange. In any case that is not our aim. The point we are trying to make here is merely that the concept has some substance; that it is plausible to argue that exchanges can be socially sanctioned in a substantive sense such as to give rise to the binding/bonding force of criticizable claims to validity.

The Internal Validity of Exchange

We argued above that it is possible for an actor to decide to participate in an exchange and to keep her end of a bargain, *only* because the exchange in question appears to be the best available means of increasing her net utility. Where actors approach exchange with this attitude we cannot say that they recognize the rights of their exchange partner in any categorical sense. They owe their partner the fulfilment of their side of the deal only in a hypothetical sense, because if they do not fulfil it, then their own interests will not be served.

It is certainly the case that the actions of participants in exchange cannot be rationally motivated in Habermas's strong sense. At the core of formal pragmatics is the internal, logical or necessary connection between legitimate norms and co-ordinated social action. The only actions which are obligatory in a categorical sense are those which are logically coherent with the legitimate aims and values of a social group. As we have seen, in contexts where co-ordinated action is the logical consequence of a non-generalizable, non-legitimizable norm, the obligation to act that arises cannot logically be related to the action itself since categorical obligation can only arise from legitimizable norms. Nonetheless, it *can* derive from the agreement between participants; the mutual promise to undertake certain actions. There is every reason to suppose that the keeping of promises is a generalizable norm and therefore there is no necessary reason why participants in exchange should not look upon their contractual duties as binding in a moral as well as an empirical sense. The normative order to which they agree in entering a contract involves the aim of profit for both parties, and thus each party *owes* the other the increase in net utility that she expects to receive.

However, the agreement of the participants, no matter how sincerely intended, is not enough in itself to qualify an exchange as permissible. It is certainly a necessary condition, but it is not a sufficient one. The normative order of the exchange relationship must be permissible independently of the agreement of the parties to it.

The Permissibility of Exchange Itself

Exchange represents an agreement between the participants in interaction that they either currently have no social obligation to assist each other in their aims without the expectation of recompense, or that for the duration of the exchange they will suspend any such obligation. Rather than agreeing that they should identify common goals and find some means of pursuing them, speaker and hearer agree instead that they should conduct exchanges in order mutually to increase their individual net utility. They agree that they will not coordinate their actions in order to promote their common interest, but to promote their separate, individual interests. Now it is by no means obvious that exchange is an acceptable form of social interaction. Weber's *Protestant Ethic* (1992), for example, demonstrates brilliantly the non-naturalness of the principle of distributing commodities via exchange. It would not be appropriate to engage in a detailed discussion of whether exchange is defensible in principle. There are many arguments that could be made against it and in favour of some other mode of the distribution of commodities. Empirically, however, we can say that the principle of trade, of distributing commodities via exchange with a view to profit, is generally acceptable now and has been for many centuries and across many cultures. For our current purposes, we are concerned only with whether exchange has historically represented a legitimizable form of social relationship. There can be little question that it has.

That having been said, it is also true that exchange cannot be permissible in the unqualified sense applying to many other types of relationship with non-generalizable aims and values, like friendship. For example, as we noted above, the possession of certain commodities is simply impermissible and therefore so is their exchange. There are also commodities the possession of which is perfectly legal but whose distribution via exchange (for profit) is either impermissible or highly controlled. We should note that impermissibility and legality in this sense do not always coincide. To give a contemporary example, there are many who would argue that certain countries in Africa should be supplied with drugs for the treatment of HIV/AIDS either free or at non-commercial rates. However, the drug companies insist that they have the legal right to charge the same prices as are charged to, for example, private sector healthcare providers in Europe.

Clearly the most important qualification on the general permissibility of exchange, however, is that it applies only to *fair* exchanges. To be acceptable, the normative order of the exchange relationship must include the aim of taking equal account of the interests of all those who are involved in the co-ordinated action which is involved in carrying it out. For the moment we will assume that the market does not exist, and that the participants in co-ordinated action are only those individuals who are directly involved in the exchange.

The Fairness of a Particular Exchange-Value

The final part of the legitimacy equation is whether the exchange value settled upon in any given case is fair. As we suggested above, fairness is rather an elusive concept, but this certainly does not mean it makes no sense. In the absence of the market and of any consideration of the particular material situation of the participants, the only non-arbitrary basis for the determination of fair exchange is the physical properties of the commodities involved in the wide sense of their usefulness, scarcity, and substitutability. On this basis it could plausibly be argued, for example, that one chicken is equivalent to one rabbit, or to a leg of lamb, or to a kilo of cheese, or to a dozen oranges. In principle, there seems no reason why a fixed system of valuing commodities purely on the basis of their physical characteristics should not be developed.

However, we cannot maintain that the particular material situation of participants in exchange is of no relevance to the definition of fairness. It would seem very odd to argue that a person who has more of some commodity than she could possibly use should receive exactly the same in exchange for that commodity as someone who has a very small quantity of it.[1] Similarly, it would be unreasonable to say that someone who possesses a limited quantity of some commodity which is of great use to her should be expected to exchange it at the same value as someone who has no use for it at all. At the root of both of these intuitions is the recognition that the interests of participants in an exchange are relative to their individual situations, and therefore that in order to take the interests of both equally into account, not only commodities but the participants must be considered. Thus rather than use-value, it seems much more intuitively plausible to argue that it is not only the physical characteristics but also the *marginal utility* of a commodity – as we saw above, its usefulness to a particular individual given the amount of it she already possesses or has recently consumed – that form the conceptual basis of fair exchange. The fundamental normative principle here is that it simply is not right that someone should acquire or retain a commodity which is useless to her if it is useful to someone else; or to possess more of that commodity than she can use. By inference, the greater the 'usefulness-gap', the less right it is for the participant for whom a commodity has the lower marginal utility to seek to acquire or retain it by respectively offering or insisting on a more advantageous exchange-value. In simpler terms, what this means is that levels of profit should not be excessive.

---

[1] As with many of the arguments we are making here, the evidence in support of this point is primarily cultural and to make the case properly would require a discussion similar to Weber's in the *Protestant Ethic*. This is obviously not the place to enter into a full-scale discussion of that kind, but on the point that the substantive value of commodities or money is relative to the situation of the individual we might at least cite the Christian biblical lesson of the widow's mite (Mark 12:43), where the author's intention is clearly to demonstrate that the absolute, moral value of money depends on the resources of the person who gives or spends it.

If we assume that in principle the component of exchange value accounted for by the physical characteristics of commodities is both more or less fixed and universally known, then we can see that a socially-sanctioned exchange-value is genuinely normative. The variable component in an exchange-value expresses a contingent relation between two individuals in the sense of representing a judgement about the relative importance of participants' needs and desires in the light of their existing material circumstances. To say that an exchange-value is fair is to do more than comment on the relative usefulness and availability of the commodities involved. It is also to say that *the relationship between the participants* in the course of which those commodities are exchanged is permissible and hence worthy of the support of society.

Fairness and Legitimate Markets

Once even one exchange-value has been agreed and socially sanctioned, then others can be agreed simply by analogy, even if in subsequent exchanges participants act strategically. Exchange-values reflect or encode both the objective 'is' of the physical characteristics of the commodities involved and the social or normative 'ought' of the relationship between the participants. By definition, an exchange-value is fair if it has been agreed by reference to the relevant differences between the commodities involved and the participants' circumstances in the case in hand, and the same components of an already-completed exchange which is known to have been fair. We can assume that any relevant differences in the physical characteristics are clear to both participants and are taken into account in their offers and responses. Although participants will not know the particular circumstances of the individuals involved in the original fair exchange, it is nonetheless justified to assume that any differences in circumstances will be reflected in the exchange value. Even after the participants have taken account of any relevant differences between the commodities in the original exchange and those currently involved, it may still be the case that for one or other participant the adjusted exchange-value is either not profitable at all, or is insufficiently profitable. If this participant is able to persuade her potential partner to accept a deal at more advantageous exchange-value, then we can still argue that this will be a fair deal on the grounds that otherwise the other participant would not have accepted it. We are entitled to argue that this agreement is genuine only if both participants are free to walk away but are also both aware that the terms of the original deal are public knowledge and will be a universal reference point for offers and responses. Participants are in this sense free to investigate how different their circumstances are from those of the participants in the original fair deal, and whether there are potential partners in exchange with 'matching' differences in marginal utility in the other direction.

There is a problem with this idea of an original fair exchange, however, which is that once it is used as a basis for the derivation of other exchange-values, it arguably ceases to be a valid reference point itself. If an exchange is used as a reference point, then the actions of the participants in the second exchange are co-ordinated with those of the participants in the first. The relevant PRC is enlarged to include all four participants. While the first and second exchanges do not thereby become unfair in themselves, any subsequent exchanges will need to take account of *both* of the established exchange-values in reaching a deal in order that this third exchange-value take account of the situations of all six participants in co-ordinated action. And so the process continues, quickly reaching the point at which it is only the statistical distribution of agreed exchange-values that provides a comprehensible guide to fairness. Thus, the (variable) distribution of exchange-values takes the place of a single fair exchange as the objective reference point for fairness and we have a market.

What the institutionalization of utility as money adds to all this is ease of comparison between exchanges involving different commodities. Certainly this is possible without a medium of exchange – if a sheep is worth four hens, and two hens are worth a piglet, then a sheep is worth two piglets – but the expression of exchange-value in terms of a universal medium permits an instant assessment of the profitability of proposed exchanges and allows the consequences of variations in value to be assimilated into the market system quickly and smoothly. Above all, money makes it clearer that to participate in an exchange is to accept membership of the vast voluntary PRC represented by the economic system. Through the medium of money, the movements of commodity prices are inextricably interconnected. In agreeing a price, the participants in an exchange affirm, renew and contribute to the level and validity of the market price. This in turn affects the market price of other commodities.

As a consequence, and perhaps counterintuitively, the component of fairness that derives from the original exchange is only maintained if participants act strategically, i.e. if they have a view solely to profitability and do not attempt to strike a deal through the use of threats or normative appeals. Any exchanges within a market that do not proceed strictly according to the rationality criterion of profitability will disrupt the fairness of market prices. If the circumstances of some participant or group of participants are, for whatever reason, given more weight than those of everyone else by asking or offering a lower or higher price, then a market price affected by these privileged exchanges will be distorted. It will not be fair because it does not take equal account of the circumstances of all potential participants as encoded in their offers and responses. Every practice which violates the canons of free trade – for example monopoly, monopsony, tariff barriers or price-fixing cartels – amounts to a situation where the circumstances of one or more participants in a market count for more than those of the others. Monopolies and monopsonies are simply not markets since the only circumstances that count in price determination are those of a single supplier or buyer. Tariffs privilege producers in one country over those of another, and cartels one group of producers, however defined. These larger-scale examples of anti-competitive behaviour are generally unlawful whereas something like offering a special deal to a relation or neighbour is not, but they are nonetheless logically a single type. What should be clear is that the economic-technical criterion or assumption of perfect competition can also be understood as a criterion for the moral and political acceptability of the capitalist economic system.

We suggested above that the relevant PRC for the assessment of the fairness of exchange consists of everyone who is in the market as a buyer or vendor of any commodity, which is to say virtually all of society. A fair price should therefore take account of the interests of every member of society in their capacity as market actors. To put the point another way, if every exchange results in a distribution of commodities between the immediate participants which is fair, then the whole system of exchange will have outcomes which are fair. Therefore, returning for a moment to the characteristics of steering media, we can say that the 'real value' underpinning money-steered exchanges, structurally analogous to the realization of legitimizable collective goals, is not just 'use-values' but *the fair distribution of use-values*. The market economic system will be legitimate when this aim is achieved in practice.

Effectiveness: The Substantive Validity of Authority and the Structure of Organizations

Just as with exchange, we want to argue that it is possible for members of organizations to judge when a relationship is substantively rather than merely formally valid. Once again, we are guided by the structure of communication in voluntary PRCs. If members of a private organization are to recognize that they *owe* compliance with an instruction to all the other members in more than a hypothetical sense, they must agree three things. First, they must recognize the validity *for them* of the political-ethical order of the organization, in the sense that they accept that participating in the successful collective pursuit of its general aims and values will also give rise to the satisfaction of their own private values and interests. Second, they must agree that there is no conflict between the political-ethical order of the organization and that of society as a whole. Both its collective goals and the organizational structuring by which they are realized must be permissible. Third, in any particular case, they must agree that the office-holder who issues an instruction is acting within her legitimate area of competence in a substantive sense: compliance with the instruction must indeed be an effective means of realizing legitimate (permissible) collective goals.

The Internal Validity of Authority

The 'ought' attached to commands can be entirely hypothetical. Where a compulsory bureaucratic-administrative system is thought to be meaningless, compliance with authority is simply a matter of avoiding the sanctions that will be imposed in the case of non-compliance. In the case of meaningless voluntary association, compliance with authority is a matter of retaining membership and the individual benefits it brings. On the other hand, where authority is underpinned by moral norms or political-ethical values with a high degree of generality, compliance is clearly a *duty*; the 'ought' in question is categorical or near-categorical.

In the case of legitimate private or voluntary association, the motivation to comply with authority is rather more complex. Participants in private organizations recognize that their own personal values and interests will best be realized by participating in the pursuit of collective goals which, while not necessarily legitimizable from their own perspective, are at least not illegitimate. As we argued in Chapter 4, the political-ethical order of the organization cannot be legitimate in itself in the same sense that the political-ethical order of a natural community can be legitimate. Rather, the order of the organization is a composite order that owes its validity to the fact that, if fulfilled, it will indirectly *cause the fulfilment* of the values and interests of the organization's members. Thus every organization member depends on the collective effort of every other member for the satisfaction of her values and interests. To join the organization is to enter into multiple relationships of mutual dependence. As in the case of exchange, the promises thereby made are the root of the potentially substantive validity of the organizational order. In principle, since the satisfaction of the interests of each organization member depends on the efforts of every other, it would be perfectly reasonable for an individual member to feel that she owed the organization – all of the members, including herself – her full-hearted participation in the collective effort.

At this point, the precise analogy with the exchange relationship breaks down. Whereas in the case of exchange, there is no additional step between promise and performance, in the conventional organizational context the membership contract and bureaucratic authority structures intervene between the individual's commitment to participation and the outcome in terms of her contribution to the realization of the collective goal. Hence beyond the legitimacy (permissibility) of concrete collective goals, the individual's agreement to the organization's general aims and values must include an element of consent to the means of action coordination, which in the vast majority of cases will involve hierarchical relationships of authority.

Once again, however, the mutual agreement of the organization's members to the fulfilment of its order, although a necessary condition, is not enough in itself to legitimize the authority relationship. The goals and means of the organization must be legitimizable (in the sense of permissibility) independently of the agreement of its members.

Legitimate Authority Relationships

In this section we will briefly discuss the conditions under which authority can be legitimate in Weber's sense of normative authorization – giving rise to absolute or categorical obligation to comply – in order to inform by analogy our discussion of what might make authority within private organizations legitimate (permissible) from the perspective of society as a whole.

Following the rules of formal pragmatics, we can say that the normative validity claims recognized by those who accept authority must be such as to provide an internal or necessary connection between the relationship of command and response and legitimizable collective goals. In modern societies, where authority relationships based on some traditional principle of social stratification like caste, class or age are no longer acceptable, this logical link is provided by effectiveness. The 'advance of trust' of which Habermas speaks is the subordinate's trust that it is appropriate to obey the superior's instruction, even though prior to acting she is not in possession of a full understanding of why obedience would represent an effective means of realizing collective goals. If obedience *does* represent an effective means of realizing collective goals, then the subordinate should obey, but the subordinate will not be in a position to assess whether this is the case until *after* the action is completed. Hence the need for trust. This is in contrast to our art exhibition example (Chapter 4), where both actors are equally competent to decide on the validity of the proposed action before any action is taken. Similarly, in pre-modern authority relationships, participants will all have been aware that the rightness of obedience is not dependent on the empirical outcome of the interaction. Rather it is simply categorically right to obey the orders of one's feudal, class or caste superiors.

The idea of an advance of trust is important because it is only the inclusion of trust that enables a distinction to be drawn between commands (Weber's term for normatively authorized instructions) and mere suggestions or proposals. If a speaker and hearer's shared lifeworld context includes absolutely all the knowledge required to pursue their collective ends, and in the absence of any 'conditions of sanction', i.e. any formal-legal structure to their relationship, it is difficult to see in what sense even an imperative communicative act by a speaker involves the exercise of authority. *A priori,* it is at least as likely that hearer issue instructions to speaker as vice versa, and the speaker's act is surely better characterized as a suggestion or proposal.

The existence of authority based on trust, then, signifies an incomplete sharing of lifeworld contexts. More precisely, it signifies that the superior has access to pragmatic knowledge that the subordinate does not share. There seem to be two types of situation in which authority relationships can arise in informal social contexts. First, there are situations in which active co-ordination of action is required but where this involves no specialist knowledge or expertise, being simply a question of access to a perspective on action wider than that of the other participants.[2] This wider perspective is information the other participants in action do not possess and which the coordinator does not attempt to explain before issuing directions. Any person might intervene to direct traffic around the scene of an accident, for example, and expect to be obeyed on the grounds that it is evidently in the interest of all concerned that traffic flows as smoothly as possible and without further incident. The continuing authority of the traffic director is dependent on outcomes – precisely on whether following her instructions is effective in the goal of keeping the traffic flowing smoothly.

The second type of situation is perhaps more important. This is where one participant is in possession of some specialized knowledge or expertise relevant to the effective realization of the collective goal. Provided that the other participants accept that 'the expert' could in principle give good reasons for her instructions which are in an internal relationship to the collective goal, and where they accept that the action situation is such that providing such an explanation there and then would be inappropriate – for example, the delay involved might actually be damaging to the collective interest – then co-ordinated social action involving authority relationships

---

[2] This can occur even in quite complex organizational contexts, perhaps the best example being professional partnerships – in which category we can for these purposes include university departments or other academic organizational units – where managerial responsibilities are in many cases assumed simply on the basis of taking turns. Although rather different, Habermas's own example of a normatively authorized imperative, a member of an aircraft's cabin crew asking passengers not to smoke, also falls into this category. The crew member has been made aware of the no-smoking rule and the good reasons deriving from the safety of all on board the aircraft which underpin it. S/he is not an expert in aircraft safety, but by virtue of his training and position has a perspective on action which is wider than that of the passenger.

can be wholly consensual and thereby legitimate. For example, a passer-by helping a doctor at the scene of an accident complies with the doctor's instructions because they *both* agree that they must try to save lives (their goal is morally right), they *both* believe that in complying with the doctor's instructions the passer-by will be acting in pursuit of that aim (the doctor's instructions are objectively effective), and they *both* believe that the doctor's claims to medical knowledge are sincerely made (the doctor has no subjective intent to deceive). To win the compliance of the passer-by, the doctor need do no more than plausibly identify herself as such and issue instructions that are not obviously wrong, i.e. ineffective. In this particular situation, because the norms involved are legitimizable at the level of society, it would clearly be morally wrong (in some circumstances perhaps even criminal) for someone with no good reason to doubt the doctor's competence or sincerity of intent to question her instructions. In parallel, it would certainly be criminal for someone to claim the authority of medical knowledge without in fact having access to that knowledge. Such a person claims the right to obedience without there being good reasons, based in effectiveness, for that right to exist.

What this brief discussion shows is that in informal social contexts in modern societies, we can equate authority with claims about effectiveness that are redeemable *a priori*, before any action takes place. Where participants are acting communicatively, and where action is oriented to the fulfilment of moral norms or political-ethical values with a high degree of generality, it is clear that (objective) effectiveness and (normative) authority are inextricably bound up with one another. As we saw in Chapter 2, pragmatic recommendations only have normative force insofar as they represent a means of realizing consensual goals. At the same time, the obligation to comply can only arise where such recommendations can in principle be shown to be effective.

Permissible Authority Relationships and the Effectiveness of Particular Instructions

In a general sense, then, authority relationships are rationally justifiable, and therefore legitimate, in cases where the subordinate party's advance of trust is warranted by the specialized knowledge of the superior. The subordinate has good, if indirect, reasons to believe that compliance with an instruction represents an effective means to a shared end. She believes that a logical or internal connection between action and outcome could be demonstrated *if required*. In formally organized contexts, however, where the relevant pragmatic knowledge pertains to the functional characteristics of the administrative system, it seems that the required trust cannot rationally be extended because of the circularity in the argument linking an instruction with its outcome.

As Edmund Leach put it, 'structural systems in which all avenues of social action are narrowly institutionalized are impossible. In all viable systems, there must be an area in which the individual is free to make choices, so as to manipulate the system to his advantage' (cited in Bourdieu, 1994, p.96). In the case of administrative or organizational systems, this suggests that there can be no formal regulation so precise as to exclude the possibility of conflicting interpretations. Even where the members of an organization regard its formal or legal order as an accurate specification of effectiveness, there is still a need for some way of closing the gap between rule and action. Otherwise, the reliable prediction of consequences is impossible. Office-holders will not be able to guarantee that compliance with certain instructions will have a particular (desirable) outcome, because the model of the functional characteristics of the system that predicts this causal relation cannot itself be guaranteed to be accurate. The accuracy of the system model cannot be guaranteed because it depends on participants adhering to the general aims and values of the organization, which include not just its goals but also its structures of authority. Participants can be expected to adhere to these aims and values if they are valid, but their validity depends on their effectiveness; on whether the projected outcomes of coordinated action are *actually* achieved. In effect, the compliance of subordinates depends on the accuracy of a system model that already assumes their compliance. Hence, the effectiveness of an office-holder's instruction will be literally indeterminate before that instruction is carried out.[3]

We suggested above that actors can negotiate the closure of the gap between rule and action by engaging in a kind of strategic bargaining about the scope of sovereignty of office-holders in the context of observed patterns of conformity with authority. However, we are concerned here with the possibility of specifying a substantively rational means of legitimizing authority. We need to find an a priori, logically self-sufficient reason to believe that complying with an instruction is the right thing to do.

From the perspective of social evolution, it would not be correct to argue that formally-structured systems of social organization originally emerged on the basis of consensual conceptions of effective authority, in the way that markets can plausibly be argued to have emerged on the basis of substantive definitions of fair exchange. For most of human history, authority has been based either on empirical force or on rationally impenetrable inherited cultural traditions. However, as a heuristic device, it is useful to consider how power-steered systems might emerge from substantive modes of action coordination.

If a group of actors is fairly small, the gap between formal rule and action may be bridged by processes of consensus formation in language, processes which for most purposes amount to communicative action. The effectiveness of action can be guaranteed (or, equally, can be questioned) because each participant *knows* how the other members of the organization will react to particular instructions. Certain norms, certain ways of doing things are known to be valid within the PRC formed by the organization, because there are ongoing processes of consensus formation in which the validity of these ways of doing things is confirmed and if necessary revised. As the experience of participants grows, however, and it begins to be possible to associate

---

[3] It is important to note that, depending on the particular case, some or all of the specialized knowledge of office-holders may pertain to technical matters unrelated to system functioning, for example scientific or technological issues. In these circumstances, the subordinate party in the authority relationship can put his trust in the genuinely technical competence of the superior without reservation.

particular patterns of organization and modes of the division of labour with more or less successful outcomes, a degree of trust in the insight of certain individuals or in the efficacy of certain ways of doing things may emerge. Particular office-holders or groups of office-holders (those associated with successful interactions) may be deemed to have a certain expertise with respect to what 'works' and what does not. Organization members may come to believe that such office-holders could in principle explain the rationale behind their instructions in understandable terms, perhaps because the office-holders have always shown themselves willing to do so. Alternatively, the interpretation may be less personalized, instead taking the form of an understanding of what constitutes effective action within the organizational system, or a 'recognition' that the system has certain functional characteristics.

Effectiveness and Systems of Organization

As organizations grow and new participants arrive, formal regulation is likely to become increasingly important. Nonetheless, actors may continue to believe that the 'way things are done here' is the effective, and therefore the *right*, way to behave. They can thus invest the consistent patterns of behaviour that they observe with a positive value status, recognizing that the organizational system acts as a 'transmission belt' for legitimate political-ethical aims and values, just as the market can transmit socially-sanctioned definitions of fairness. As long as an interpretation of the formal order of the system that is consistent with observed patterns of conformity with authority can be correlated with successful outcomes – the realization of legitimate collective goals and the maintenance of an appropriate degree of dignity and mutual respect within administrative systems – then participants are likely to accept it. They are also likely to accept that that interpretation, along with the model of the functional characteristics of the system that it simultaneously explains and implies, is an accurate specification of effective coordinated action. As in the case of exchange, the strategic negotiation of compliance can result in changes to the interpretation of the formal order of the organization. These changes, however, will in principle reflect the changing value preferences and priorities of the organization's members. Given that this is the case, then the strategic negotiation of the scope of sovereignty ought actually to maintain the substantive validity of the organizational system rather than disrupting it.

The Procedural Specification of Legitimate System Outcomes

The market economy is founded on a procedural definition of the fair distribution of commodities. Since the value of one commodity in relation to another depends not just on its relative usefulness, substitutability and scarcity but on the constantly changing needs and preferences of individuals, the task of producing a permanently valid, absolute or universal ordering of material values (prices) is impossible. A fair distribution of commodities cannot, therefore, be specified in advance of the process of exchange. What is possible, however, is the specification of a means of conducting exchanges that will give rise to a variable distribution of commodities that at any given point in time can be said to be fair. As we suggested above, this procedural specification, based on economic laws and principles, is embodied in the abstract technical criteria for perfect competition.

In the same way, an organizational system should be founded on a procedural definition of the effective realization of valid collective goals. The value of one set of goals and means relative to another depends not just on the political-ethical value of the realized goal itself, but on the degree to which participation in the coordinated action by which the goal is realized contributes to the satisfaction of the individual values and interests of each member of the organization. Thus, the task of producing an absolute or universal ordering of political-administrative values (acceptable instructions) is impossible. Effective modes of organization cannot, therefore, be specified in advance of the process of administrative action coordination. What ought to be possible, however, is the specification of a means of conducting the interaction between office-holders and ordinary members that will give rise to an organizational order that at any given point in time can be said to involve the effective realization of valid goals. If we pursue the analogy with exchange, then at this point we should suggest that this procedural specification must be based on the laws and principles of organizational dynamics. However, despite many attempts, it has not proved possible to generalize observations of political and industrial organization into laws and principles whose coherence and explanatory power are comparable to those of economics. The variables that might in principle explain the dynamics of administrative systems are too numerous, and their interaction too complex and too dependent on local organizational histories to be generalizable. There are, then, no concrete technical criteria for 'perfect management' that can be deemed to be applicable to any organizational interaction in the way that the criteria of perfect competition are applicable to any exchange. However, this is not to say that a means of determining what these criteria might be in any particular organizational context cannot be conceived. We want to suggest that the procedural means of guaranteeing the validity of the organizational system, the analogue with respect to the power medium of the free market, is democratic management. We will return to this issue in Chapter 7.

Actors' Attitudes and System Outcomes

The most important implication of what we have seen so far in this chapter is that individuals need not approach action in systemic contexts with a strategic attitude. The adoption of such an attitude is not inevitable because of the possibility of interpreting observed patterns of conformity with market prices and organizational authority as the outcome of legitimate social action. Market and private organizational orders can in principle represent legitimate social orders in the sense that we discussed in Chapter 3: coordinated action in these systemic contexts can if necessary be justified on the basis of a rationally defensible structure of reasons that can be expressed in ordinary language. Perhaps more importantly, it also seems to be the case that approaching systemic action with an orientation to mutual understanding does not prevent the system from functioning. In principle, the strategic resolution of interactions is in the general interest. It is the system itself that 'carries' the legitimizable normative content of exchange and authority relationships: the fair distribution of use-values and the effective realization of valid collective goals. In pursuing their private strategic interest, individuals are acting in the general interest without thereby being obliged to undertake the impossible task of assuring themselves that the discourse principle is being respected in the strong sense demanded by formal pragmatics. Hence, the question we posed towards the end of Chapter 3 – why are the special codes of the system necessary if economic and political-administrative forms of action coordination are defensible in themselves – is answered.

However, because economic and political-administrative systems are constructed so as to operate on the basis of a variety of subjective attitudes including expediency, custom and habit, these systems are likely to carry on functioning regardless of whether the 'promissory note' of legitimizable outcomes is ultimately redeemable. So long as the aggregate outcomes of systemic action remain legitimizable – so long, that is, as the value status of the system itself is positive from the perspective of actors – strategic and communicative action are indistinguishable. There will be no difference in outcome and so there is no choice to be made. The point at which the idea of choosing an action orientation begins to make sense from the normative perspective is the point at which system outcomes cease to be legitimizable. At this point, the attitude of actors begins to have an effect on the resolution of interactions. Whereas the purely strategic actor who considers the system to be meaningless is unconcerned with whether the substantive validity claims implied in exchange and authority relationships are redeemable, the actor who *expects* the system to produce legitimizable outcomes will change her behaviour depending on whether the system is seen to function as it ought to. As we saw in Chapters 1 and 2, the question marks over the redeemability of contemporary capitalism's promissory notes are legion. We can expect, therefore, that if participants were to adopt an orientation to mutual understanding this would have a significant effect on system outcomes.

Exchange

Actors who approach exchange with a communicative attitude will be aware that a market price represents a social standard of fairness. They will also be aware, however, that buying or selling at the current market price does not in itself guarantee that an exchange is fair. Rather, fairness is defined by reference both to the market price and to the relative material situations of the parties to an exchange. A fair exchange is one in which the relationship between the parties implied by the conduct of the exchange in the context of their relative material situations is just and worthy of support. It is one in which the fairness of the overall social distribution of commodities is sustained or improved. In practice, this may mean that there is a difference between the price which it is empirically possible for one party to extract from the other, and the price that should (in the ethical sense) be charged. We argued above that the substantive fairness of an 'original' exchange can in principle be transmitted via or carried by the economic system as a whole on the basis of strategic action by subsequent market actors, but this will be the case only where certain conditions obtain. What we have to assume is that the parties to the exchange are aware that these economic-technical conditions frequently do not obtain in practice. This can be shown either directly, for example via the research programme of institutional economics, or indirectly on the basis of a failure of the system to produce the required outcomes. Since the fair distribution of commodities ought to be the aggregate result of properly conducted exchanges, the existence of disparities in wealth that are sufficiently large as to be socially damaging indicates that the procedural conditions for fair exchange are not being respected.

Regardless of how the conclusion that the system itself is not fair is reached, adopting a purely strategic attitude to exchange will tend not to result in a fair outcome. In these circumstances, the actor with a communicative attitude will not simply exploit any empirical bargaining advantage that she possesses, but will resort instead to a politicocultural definition of fairness as a reference point for the settlement of an exchange-value. Hence, unless the bargaining conditions are perfect, the adoption of a communicative as opposed to a strategic attitude towards the settlement of exchange-values will indeed result in a different outcome. What is more, the conscious reversion to a substantive cultural standard of fairness in price determination will tend to correct any deviation from that standard consequent on imperfect bargaining conditions.

Authority

The variability of outcomes depending on the initial attitude of actors is perhaps rather easier to appreciate in the case of private authority relationships. The strategic actor is not concerned in the first instance with the effective achievement of collective goals, but is instead seeking the most effective means of pursuing her individual interest. As with the case of exchange, however, these two situations ought in principle to be parallel – the subordinate's pursuit of her private interest should coincide with the effective pursuit of the order governing the organization; and where compliance with instructions is agreeable to subordinates, this compliance should be effective with respect to the realization of collective goals. But, once again as with exchange, this is often and perhaps even usually not the case. The existence of perfect management is even more unrealistic an assumption than the existence of perfect competition. In practice, managerial plans and strategies rarely if ever represent a perfectly effective means of carrying out the order of an organization, which is to say one that aligns the individual and collective interests of the membership. Where this is the case, a purely strategic approach to compliance with authority will not result in effective outcomes.

The organization member with a communicative attitude will approach interactions with a view to the realization of a valid political-ethical order; an order that represents her interest as an individual, as a member of the organization and, in certain cases, as a member of society as a whole. Where an instruction is understood not to be coherent with any such order, the actor oriented to mutual understanding will respond in such a way as to resolve any empirical conflict between her individual interest and compliance with the instruction in favour of the collective interest of the organization. Even where it is not in her individual interest to do so, the actor may simply refuse to comply, or may interpret the instruction in such a way as to correct the office-holder's misrepresentation of the collective interest of the organization's members. As in the case of exchange, the application of a substantive standard of effectiveness to bureaucratic interactions will tend to push modes of social organization back towards optimality where this is not already the case.

Conclusion

Legitimate relationships of exchange and authority are perfectly conceivable in informal social contexts. There are circumstances in which exchanges can be genuinely fair and authority genuinely effective. In fact, if we want our theory of systemic social action to be adequate from the perspective of social evolution, and if we accept Habermas's argument that communicative action is the evolutionarily primary mode of social action, then we are in any case bound to concede this possibility.

It is not so obvious that the legitimacy of informal exchange and authority is preserved once the action context is formally organized. We saw in Chapter 4 that a purely strategic approach to action is possible given the existence of a systemic context. What we have argued in this chapter is that legitimate social action against the backdrop of the same systemic context is an equally coherent possibility, as long as we accept that statistical evidence about prices or patterns of conformity with authority can be treated as information about the validity of norms. If the systemic context itself is seen as potentially legitimate – as meaningful rather than meaningless – then judgements about the value status of overall system outcomes will have an effect on behaviour.

Nonetheless, the circularity in this argument remains. The legitimacy of systemic social action depends on whether the systemic context is legitimate. But the systemic context is legitimate only if it can be assumed that the individual relationships from which it is constructed are themselves legitimate. Likewise, the functional characteristics of systems are as they are only because of the behaviour of individual actors. But actors behave in the way that they do only because they have taken a view about the functional characteristics of systems. We would encounter precisely the same problem if we were to attempt to argue that exchange and authority are not legitimate. Either way, there seems to be no way to determine either the value status or the functional characteristics of social systems. This is, of course, precisely the problem with the formal pragmatic analysis of exchange and authority that prompts Habermas to adopt a systems theoretic approach in the first place. In Chapter 6 we will attempt finally to resolve this difficulty.

Chapter 6

The Concept of Worldviews

Our problem at the moment is that we have not been able to reject the logic that drives Habermas to rule out the applicability of formal pragmatics as a theory of action in formally organized contexts. Quite the contrary: we have accepted that it is precisely the inherent and inescapable indeterminacy of the co-ordination of action on the basis of action consequences, rather than on the basis of action orientations, that gives rise to the risk of 'action sequences falling apart' and the consequent need for empirical motivation (legal sanctions) to ensure that they do not. However, in TCA Habermas does not treat the possibility of the failure of action co-ordination merely as a possibility. Rather he wholly rejects the alternative possibility: that sociological generalizations – claims about the nature of markets or about the dynamics of goal-achievement in administrative structures that are based on the examination of empirical evidence about the actual outcomes of action – can be established as de facto valid, to the extent that they can amount to elements of the reasoning behind rational, co-ordinated social action. These generalizations, he suggests, are not 'available as themes within the lifeworld'.

Despite this insistence that system-theoretic propositions cannot give rise to rational motivation – perhaps most clearly stated in the first section of Chapter VIII of TCA, where he discusses the relative positions of steering and communicative mechanisms of co-ordination within organizations – Habermas is nonetheless ambivalent about the actual existence of those conditions of developed modernity under which the validity basis of communicative action in systemic contexts is wholly undermined. He is, quite simply, not prepared to argue that the three spheres of validity are now finally and completely differentiated (1987, pp.185-97). It is interesting to note, then, that in considering the earlier stages of social development where there is no doubt that the differentiation of value spheres is incomplete, Habermas takes a line that appears to open the possibility of resolving the logical problems we have identified with the thematization of external perspectives on society in contexts of social action.

Mythical Worldviews

The resolution we have in mind centres on the concept of a 'worldview' that figures in Habermas's theoretical outline of pre-modern societies. In a general sense, a worldview is a 'cultural interpretive system' through which lifeworld contexts are understood and which reflects 'the background knowledge of social groups and guarantee[s] an interconnection among the multiplicity of their action orientations' (Habermas, 1984, p.43). The existence of such worldviews is most obvious in societies in which the cultural value spheres (objective, normative and expressive) are not fully differentiated. In the mythical interpretation of the world typical of tribal societies, for example, we find a

> mixing of two object domains, physical nature and the sociocultural environment. Myths do not permit a clear, basic conceptual differentiation between things and persons, between objects that can be manipulated and agents... magical practices do not recognize the distinction between teleological and communicative action, between goal-directed, instrumental intervention in objectively given situations, on the one hand, and the establishment of interpersonal relations, on the other. The *ineptitude* to which the technical or therapeutic failures of goal-directed action are due falls into the same category as the *guilt* for moral-normative failings of interaction in violation of existing social orders. Moral failure is conceptually interwoven with physical failure, as is *evil* with the *harmful*, and *good* with the *healthy* and the *advantageous* (Habermas, 1984, pp.47-8; emphasis in original).

For our purposes, the most important thing to note about pre-modern worldviews is that they cannot conceive morality and materiality as distinct from each other. This conceptual inseparability of the normative and the objective has implications for participants in action:

> The magical relation between names and designated objects, the concretistic relation between the meaning of expressions and the states-of-affairs represented give evidence of systematic confusion between *internal connections of meaning* and *external connections of objects*... Validity is confounded with empirical efficacy... Thus a linguistically constituted worldview can be identified with the world-order itself to such an extent that it cannot be perceived *as* an interpretation of the world that is subject to error and open to criticism. In this respect the confusion of nature and culture takes on the significance of a reification of worldview (ibid., pp.49-50; emphasis in original).

Where the objective, the normative and the subjective are still undifferentiated, then, an actor's worldview *is* the world. Actors do not recognize that taking action involves an interpretation of the world which is potentially erroneous: 'the concept of the world is dogmatically invested with a specific content that is withdrawn from rational discussion and thus from criticism' (ibid., p51). To give a brief example, the earth-centred cosmology favoured by the 16th century Roman Catholic Church was not simply an inference from the observation of the heavens. Rather it represented an amalgam of astronomy, theology and morality in which the proposition that the sun moved around a fixed Earth was supported not only by empirical evidence – it was, after all, simply common sense that the Earth was not moving at great speed through the cosmos since the things that were on it did not fly off – but by a whole range of intertwined normative, metaphysical and aesthetic commitments. To suggest as Copernicus did that the Earth may in fact move around the sun was therefore to do much more than suggest a more mathematically defensible explanation of the movement of the stars and planets:

> The essential dichotomy between the celestial and terrestrial realms, the great cosmological structure of Heaven, Hell and Purgatory, the circling planetary spheres with angelic hosts,

God's empyrean throne above all, the moral drama of human life pivotally centered between spiritual heavens and corporeal Earth – all would be cast into question or destroyed altogether by the new theory (Tarnas, 1996, p.253).

If the only issue had been how best to explain the observed movement of the stars and planets, the Copernican system (or better, Kepler's modification of that system with the addition of the assumption that the planets had elliptical rather than circular orbits) would clearly have won the argument immediately. Not only was it simpler and more elegant, it produced more accurate predictions of the positions of the stars at certain times.[1] However, the debate was not and could not be confined to the sphere of the objective in this way. In the contemporary Christian worldview, the three value spheres were insufficiently differentiated to permit such a discussion.

This immunization of world-concepts from criticism is even more apparent in the social and institutional arenas. While in traditional societies social organization may well be functional for material reproduction, this functionality does not form a separate part of the reasons for the mode of social organization. The relationships through which material reproduction occurs are God-given and thus normatively self-sufficient: 'In societies organized through kinship, the institutional system is anchored ritually, that is, in a practice that is interpreted by mythical narratives *and that stabilizes its normative validity all by itself*' (Habermas, 1987, p.188; emphasis added). Thus an objectively-grounded challenge to the functionality of the institutional system, even were such a thing to be conceivable, would represent a challenge to the norms of action on which that system was based and hence to the entire worldview; it would be a challenge to the gods themselves.

Pre-modern worldviews, then, are interpretations of the world that conflate different aspects of validity in such a way as to deflect criticism arising from within a single validity sphere. To accept a mythical worldview is to accept it in its entirety and, indeed, to discount any evidence that it is inadequate. This is not to say that worldviews are unassailable in the sense that they cannot change or decay or be replaced by differing beliefs about the world. Obviously they can. However, this kind of change cannot be the outcome of direct criticism of a worldview itself. Habermas draws a comparison between worldviews and portraits:

A portrait is neither a mapping that can be exact or inexact, nor a rendering of facts in the sense of a proposition that can be true or false. A portrait offers rather an angle of vision from which the person represented appears in a certain way. Thus there can be numerous portraits of the same person; they can make the character appear in quite different aspects, and yet they can all be experienced as accurate, authentic or adequate. Similarly, worldviews lay down the framework in which we interpret everything that appears in the

---

[1] It is interesting to note, as Tarnas points out, that both Copernicus and Kepler were drawn to the heliocentric view on aesthetic-theological as well as empirical grounds. They both considered that God's plan was surely more 'ordered and harmonious' than that reflected in the cumbersome, complex and inaccurate system of mathematics required to explain the apparently eccentric movement of the planets under the geocentric system.

world in a specific way as something. Worldviews can no more be true or false than portraits (Habermas, 1984, p.58).

Where worldviews differ from portraits, however, is in the fact that they '*make possible* utterances that admit of truth' (ibid.). If we accept that the concept of truth only makes sense as a universal validity claim, i.e. that a true statement merits assent regardless of the language in which it is formulated, then we can compare and hence (indirectly) criticize worldviews from the standpoint of what Habermas calls their *cognitive adequacy*: 'The adequacy of a linguistically articulated worldview is a function of the true statements that are possible in this language system' (pp.58-9). Hence, to return to our example, although theologically-supported geocentrism is unassailable from within or on its own terms, what is undeniable is that the assumption of a heliocentric universe means not only that astronomical charts and tables can be produced more easily, but also that they are more accurate. Given the economic importance of nautical navigation during the 16th century, there was a strong material incentive for the contents of the Christian worldview to change.

Religious-Metaphysical Worldviews, Ideology and Mediatization

For Habermas, worldviews are not necessarily global or totalizing in the sense that they can exist only where there is no differentiation between the three value spheres. Modernization – the process by which nature and culture gradually become disentangled; by which the objective, social and subjective worlds separate out from each other – is a gradual process, and the move from the archaic totalizing worldview to wholly transparent modernity does not occur in a single step. We can therefore identify stages of development intermediate between tradition and developed modernity characterized by different degrees of partial differentiation of the spheres of validity and hence different types of worldview which are less and less extensive in their reach. Habermas calls the major intermediate type of society 'civilization' and suggests that it is characterized by a religious-metaphysical worldview (Habermas, 1987, p.191). He argues that one of the major features that distinguish civilizations from archaic or traditional societies is that social organization is no longer normatively self-sufficient:

> In societies organized around a state, a need for legitimation arises that, for structural reasons, could not yet exist in tribal societies... the authority of the laws in which a general political order is articulated has to be guaranteed, in the first instance, by the ruler's power of sanction. But political domination has socially integrating power only insofar as disposition over means of sanction does not rest on naked repression, but on the authority of an office anchored in turn in a legal order. For this reason, laws need to be intersubjectively recognized by citizens; they have to be legitimated as right and proper. This leaves culture with the task of supplying reasons why an existing political order deserves to be recognized. Whereas mythical narratives interpret and make comprehensible a ritual practice of which they themselves are part, religious and metaphysical worldviews of prophetic origin have the form of doctrines that can be worked up intellectually and that explain and justify an existing political order in terms of the world-order they explicate (ibid., p.188).

While the political-institutional order can be clearly distinguished from (say) structures of theological authority, the legitimization of secular authority is nonetheless ultimately premised on the existence of a sacred world-order lying behind appearances. This world-order is codified and described in a religious-metaphysical worldview which is beyond rational criticism. What we have here could almost be described as the separation of policy and execution. The legitimacy of institutional structures is split into two aspects: on the one hand, there are the basic aims and values specified in the religious-metaphysical worldview which the institutional structures exist to pursue; and on the other, the efficacy of those structures with respect to this *raison d'être* given the particular physical and socio-cultural context.

Once an institutional logic of organization can be conceived separately from 'the structures of the prevailing worldview', however, it becomes possible that traditionally-sanctioned modes of social organization be seen as a barrier to the maximization of the efficacy of goal-oriented action. If institutional effectiveness is conceivable in isolation from issues of normative validity, the possibility of conflict between processes of functional and social integration arises. 'Rational' models of social organization may disrupt traditional structures and hierarchies, and may contradict traditional moral norms and principles. Since the religious-metaphysical worldview which is the ultimate basis of social integration is beyond rational criticism, this conflict cannot be resolved in favour of functional integration without, sooner or later, there being some 'structural violence' inflicted on the lifeworld. To put it simply, if functional and social integration are in conflict but neither are to be disrupted, actors must not be aware that *what they are actually doing* – their actions themselves and the outcome of those actions – is not consistent with *why they are doing it* – the normative basis of their actions:

> The conditions for the social integration of the lifeworld are defined by the validity basis of action-coordinating processes of reaching understanding in connection with the structures of the prevailing worldview; the conditions for the functional integration of society are set by the relations of a lifeworld objectified as a system to an environment only partially under control. [It may be the case that] a compromise between internal validity claims and external survival imperatives can be achieved only at the cost of institutionalizing and internalizing value orientations *not in keeping with the actual functions of the corresponding action orientations...* (Habermas, 1987, p.233; emphasis added).

The compromise between the moral and political-ethical validity claims that provide the direct justification for action and the functional imperatives of material reproduction holds only so long as the actual function of participants' action orientations remain hidden:

> Under circumstances such as these, the illusory character of the fulfilment of validity claims that carry a value consensus and make social integration possible must not be seen through. What is needed is a systematic restriction on communication, so that the illusion of satisfied validity claims can assume objective force (ibid.).

Taking the developed West as an example, we can say that 'external survival imperatives' demanded the rapid expansion of material reproduction; a system in which 'resources [could] be more easily mobilized and more effectively combined'. This resulted in the uncoupling of social labour from kinship relations and its reorganization on the basis of a stratified class society. But,

> [w]hat presents itself from a system perspective as an integration of society at the level of an expanded material reproduction, means, from the perspective of social integration, an increase in social inequality, wholesale economic exploitation, and the juridically cloaked repression of dependent classes... [to minimize the possibility of social integration breaking down,] the functions of exploitation and repression fulfilled by rulers and ruling classes in the systemic nexus of material reproduction have to be kept latent as far as possible. Worldviews have to become ideologically efficacious (ibid.).

Mediatization and Ideology

In using the phrase 'ideologically efficacious', Habermas intends to refer to those situations in which the worldviews of participants in action are such that they suffer from an 'objectively false' consciousness of their situation. This in turn will arise when lifeworlds are 'mediatized'. The separation of institutional structuring from direct dependence on the moral and political-ethical validity structures of the lifeworld, and the consequent possibility that system and lifeworld can influence each other, potentially leads to the mediatization of lifeworlds. This occurs when a traditional normative consensus is instrumentalized in support of system integration. It is a by-product of material reproduction; of the exigencies of the functional integration of society. Mediatization is what occurs when 'systemic constraints of material reproduction inconspicuously intervene in the forms of social integration' (ibid., p.187).

On Habermas's definition, ideology will exist where the mediatization of a lifeworld has given rise to the systematic restriction of communication. Communication is restricted when it is not possible to thematize certain issues against a particular lifeworld context; when certain reasons for action are in certain contexts automatically deemed invalid, just as certain elements of an action situation can be deemed invalid for the purposes of legal reasoning. As we have already seen, in the period between tradition and modernity, economic and political order depended on basic religious and metaphysical concepts that 'lay at a level of undifferentiated validity claims...[in which there was a] fusion of ontic, normative, and expressive elements' (ibid., p.189). Any argument in opposition to the existing order that contradicted these basic religious and metaphysical concepts was likely at best to be dismissed and at worst condemned as representing the seditious undermining of public morality. Hence, for example, in England up until 1867 it was a *criminal* offence for an employee to breach a contract of employment (for an employer it was merely a civil offence). Employment relationships were governed by the legal doctrine of 'master and servant' in which the right of an employer to command a worker was conceived as a moral absolute, an aspect of a system of social stratification justifiable by reference to a divine order. It was simply not relevant to question the authority of a 'master' on the grounds, for example, that by accepting it, his 'servants' were damaging their physical and psychological well-being in order further to enrich an individual who already had more wealth than he could possibly use. The physical conditions of workers were seen as inseparable from the moral condition of their class and the harshness of employment regimes was usually justified with reference to the duty of a master to have a view to the moral tutelage of his servants. An argument often made, for example, was that reducing working hours was wrong because increased leisure time was likely to be spent in sinful pursuits. Similarly, as Eric Hobsbawm shows, the possession of property was commonly thought to be a deterrent to the hard work that was the only possible moral salvation of the working classes (1962, p.183). Habermas refers to Weber's sociology of religion on this point, arguing that Weber 'showed how the world religions were dominated by a basic question, namely, the legitimacy of the unequal distribution of earthly goods among humankind' (1987, p.188).

The Modern Worldview, Fragmentation and Colonization

For Habermas, modernity is characterized precisely by the absence of any worldviews and, hence, the absence of mediatized lifeworlds and ideology. Along the path towards modernity, cultural interpretive systems gradually become less and less extensive until the 'vanishing point' is reached where there is no longer any kind of worldview that steers practice. In modern societies, nothing is rationally impenetrable. The sacred domain has disintegrated and culture has become disenchanted, losing 'the properties that made it capable of taking on ideological functions' (ibid., p.353). Worldviews, that is to say, 'global interpretation[s] of the whole, drawn up from the perspective of the lifeworld and capable of integration',

> had to break down in the communication structures of a developed modernity. When the auratic traces of the sacred have been lost and the products of a synthetic, world-picturing power of imagination have vanished, the form of understanding, now fully differentiated in its validity basis, becomes so transparent that the communicative practice of everyday life no longer affords any niches for the structural violence of ideologies. The imperatives of autonomous subsystems then have to exert their influence on socially integrated domains of action from the outside and *in a discernible fashion.* They can no longer hide behind the rationality differential between sacred and profane realms of action and reach inconspicuously through action orientations so as to draw the lifeworld into intuitively inaccessible, functional interconnections (ibid., p.354; emphasis in original).

As Habermas himself points out, what this suggests is that part of the condition of modernity ought to be open competition between system and social integration. To the extent that economic and state-bureaucratic imperatives impose themselves in socio-cultural value spheres, it should be clearly perceptible both that this is happening, and that the imperatives in question do not arise from any legitimate political-ethical consensus. However, at least in the case of the European welfare state capitalism of the post-war era, this is evidently not the case. As a means of explaining this contradiction, Habermas argues that late capitalism must have produced some functional equivalent for ideology that prevents active opposition to the assimilation of system imperatives in the lifeworld without relying on an intersubjectively shared, holistic interpretation of society that locates the ultimate justification for forms of social life in the realm of the sacred, and hence beyond the reach of rational criticism. He suggests that under the conditions of fully developed modernity, the task of grasping the 'play of the metropolis and the world market' (ibid., p.355) sufficiently well to permit the formation of a consciousness of the scope and effect of systemic forces is too complex to be achieved from the ground up, without the global overview of inherited cultural traditions: 'the everyday knowledge appearing in totalized form remains diffuse, or at least never attains that level of articulation at which alone knowledge can be accepted as valid according to standards of cultural modernity' (ibid.). This is not to say that the assimilation of system imperatives goes unnoticed. The problem is not false consciousness but *fragmented* consciousness. It is not possible to conceive society at a level of generality sufficiently high to allow the construction of a coherent, rational plan of opposition. This is the point at which Habermas introduces the metaphor of colonialism: 'When stripped of their ideological veils, the imperatives of autonomous subsystems make their way into the lifeworld from the outside – like colonial masters coming into a tribal society – and force a process of assimilation upon it' (ibid.).

Colonization, Action Orientations and Interpretive Commitment

Habermas says nothing specific about what the colonization of lifeworlds implies at the level of meaning. It seems reasonable to suggest, however, that colonization will be experienced as a kind of social dislocation in which the de facto valid ordering of cultural and political-ethical values is *visibly* an outcome of system imperatives; where social convention remains a powerful action-orienting force at the same time as it is apparent on reflection that the values of the day are not rooted in legitimate normative consensus. We might speculate that the 'vanishing point' of colonization would be the elimination even of this residual unease: a context in which system imperatives so dominate social life that any means of legitimation other than the recognition of economic or administrative value is inconceivable. The flexible society would have arrived. If this were to be the case, then our argument that action oriented to mutual understanding is possible even in systemic contexts would fall. Or rather, it would simply be pointless, as it would be impossible to accede to a non-systemic perspective from which the global value status of the system could be assessed. There would be no difference between formal and substantive rationality.

Whether or not we concede that this kind of social development might eventually be possible, the current crisis of corporate legitimacy is strong evidence that forms of legitimation that rely on consensus formation in language have not been entirely superseded. The critique of capitalism proposed by the anti-globalization movement is precisely a normative critique that relies on establishing the gap between corporate behaviour and the moral and political-ethical norms that 'belong' to wider society. The crisis of the welfare state and the rise of neoliberalism may, ironically, have had a de-fragmenting effect in the sense that a global or totalizing understanding of the scope and effect of capitalism is now within easier reach.

Nonetheless, even if we accept that open competition between system and social integration is a coherent possibility, it could still be argued that when participants in action adopt a strategic attitude, their interpretation of the action situation involves a lighter interpretive commitment than that made by actors who adopt a communicative attitude. In other words, the strategic attitude is the position to which actors inevitably 'default' because of the lack of logical support for rational motivation that defines media-steered contexts. However, in practice, the adoption of a strategic attitude involves an interpretive commitment which is as rationally unsustainable as that involved in acting communicatively. Consider the following points about the exchange relationship:

1) There is a political-ethical standard with respect to the fair distribution of goods that actors would accept as valid in informal action contexts.

2) Each party to the exchange knows rather more about the material situation of other market actors than the minimum necessary to conduct a strategic negotiation as we defined it above. This information is in most cases enough to be able to assess the fairness of the existing distribution of goods as between the parties.

3) Where it is apparent that this distribution is *not* fair, then if the actor nevertheless acts strategically in the sense of pressing home an empirical bargaining advantage, he makes a normative choice that requires the support of good reasons.

4) Of necessity, those reasons must involve some global interpretation of the economic system *as it is* as the best available way to ensure the fair distribution of commodities in the context of the preservation of other liberties, the innovating power of capitalism etc. While actors may recognise that the situation is not as they would ideally wish it to be, they recognize that the changes required to mitigate the unfair distribution of the costs of the economic system are such as to threaten the advantages that it brings.

Cut down to its essentials, the argument in the final point is simply that the distribution of goods cannot be improved without damage to the economic system. But surely this is at least as profound an interpretive commitment as that of the communicative actor, who believes that system functioning will *not* be damaged by non-strategic action? More to the point, the two positions are logically equivalent in the sense that neither can be guaranteed before the outcomes of action are known. They both involve the circularity that makes the choice of attitude dependent on knowing the outcome of that choice. In short, it appears not only that actors in systemic contexts can adopt a communicative attitude, but that in so doing they are making no more of an interpretive commitment than those actors whose attitude is strategic. In either case, participants have to interpret the nature of social systems *in advance* of action, based on an external observation of system inputs and outcomes.

The Sacred System

This leaves us in some difficulty, as it suggests that in developed modern societies, social actors will simply be hopelessly confused about what to do. However, if we bring to bear the idea of a worldview in the sense of a pre-interpretation of a lifeworld in which the normative and the objective are in some sense fused, then we can suggest that even under conditions of developed modernity it is possible for political-ethical claims whose validity is, in the final analysis, not criticizable to carry a binding force comparable to that arising from the recognition of redeemable validity claims.

Habermas does not appear to consider the possibility of worldviews in which restrictions on communication are due to something other than the existence of rationally-impenetrable sacred doctrines underpinning the legitimation of social and legal authority. Yet, there seems to be no reason why partially fused cultural spheres of validity have to be manifest in this way. Part of the problem, perhaps, is simply the difficulty of conceiving something which is simultaneously non-sacred or non-mythical, and rationally impenetrable. What we want to suggest, however, is that the system itself, and more particularly the market economy and the capitalist enterprise, can be understood in this way. The defining characteristic of pre-modern worldviews is that at some point validity is confused or confounded with empirical efficacy, and internal relations of meaning are confused with external relations between objects. Our discussion of social interaction in systemic contexts shows that this is precisely what occurs in market exchange and private authority relationships.

Exchange: Social Relationships and the Characteristics of Commodities

We saw above that where a market for a commodity exists, it is only by reference to the market price that a fair exchange value can be defined. We saw that this is also the case where substantive norms are assumed to be absent: participants are unable to assess the strategic optimality of an exchange-value except by reference to the standard of the market. So, regardless of whether we say that the exchange-value agreed upon in some exchange is fair in a substantive sense, or whether we say merely that it is acceptable to both parties in the light of their strategic objectives, what we are saying is that the exchange value settled upon is coherent with the current market value of the commodity. The term 'coherence' is important here. It is not the case that a fair or optimal exchange value is identical to the market value. Rather, as we argued above, it is a value that stands in a rational relation to the market value after having taken into account the material circumstances of the participants and the characteristics of the actual goods exchanged. Since each agreed exchange-value affects the market value, we can say that the market value expresses or encodes both the material circumstances of market actors and the physical characteristics of commodities. The economic system, then, is truly a mirror of society. More than simply a system of relationships between things, it is also a system of relationships between people in the sense of expressing relative material well-being in terms of the possibilities for the satisfaction both of universal basic needs and individual wants and desires.

This inextricable intertwining of the material and the social means that interpretations of the economic system are at root uncriticizable. The argument is essentially that the economy is based on strategic rational action and expresses nothing more than the scarcity and substitutability of commodities together with the individual preferences of actors; but this could be objected to on the grounds that since fair exchange is possible – some would argue even plausible – and the outcomes of the economic system are reasonably just, then that system must itself be the result of normatively valid interactions. To the counterargument that the outcomes of the system are unjust could be opposed the view that the preferences of individuals and the physical nature of commodities represent fixed inputs which restrict the possibilities for action within the system, and that the outcomes are thus as just as it is possible for them to be. This argument cannot be resolved. It could be carried on ad infinitum, even in the absence of any dispute about the historical/empirical evidence on which these conflicting opinions are based, or indeed about the basic processes through which individual social interactions give rise to autonomous social systems.

Authority: Political-Ethical Order and Effective Social Action

In the case of a private authority relationship, the resolution of interactions depends on the participants' understanding of the de facto validity of a political-ethical order, which will be more or less closely related to the formal, written rules of the organization, depending how it is interpreted in practice. As in the case of market relationships, it makes no difference whether this externally-observed order is conceived of as substantively based or merely as an empirical fact. On the one hand, the de facto valid political-ethical order implies the functional characteristics of the organizational system. An assessment of the potential effectiveness of compliance with an instruction as a contribution to the realization of collective goals obviously cannot be made without an understanding of these characteristics. On the other hand, a strategic assessment of the likelihood that subordinates will obey a particular order – or, from the perspective of the subordinate, what risk of expulsion from membership is carried by resisting that order – cannot be made without an appreciation of the established patterns of validity within the organization. Hence, all organization actors, regardless of their attitude, have to have recourse to considerations of political-ethical validity in order to determine the empirical effectiveness of certain courses of action as a contribution to the realization of their goals.

Systemic Worldviews

We want to propose, then, that modernity can be characterized by the existence of 'systemic worldviews'. These are global interpretations of social systems in which beliefs about the functional characteristics of systems are fused with opinions about the value status of those systems to produce an action-orienting outlook. Once such a worldview has been adopted, the logical circularity we first identified in Chapter 3 is resolved for the immediate purposes of action and the pragmatic discourse in which it is planned. A systemic worldview provides actors with a way of 'breaking in' to the circle of inference that relates the four different types of cultural knowledge about systems that can form part of the lifeworld context of actors: theoretical knowledge that defines the laws and principles of a system and the technical conditions that have to be assumed in order for that system to function as predicted; empirical assessments of whether these technical conditions actually obtain; moral and political-ethical knowledge about the outcomes that systems ought to have; and empirical assessments of whether these outcomes are attained in practice.

Systemic worldviews have two components or aspects that pertain to the meaning of social relationships and the functional characteristics of systems. They pre-specify how social relationships in formally organized contexts will be understood in such a way as to partially determine the normatively appropriate response to an offer of communication (from the internal or action perspective) or to enable the prediction of the likelihood that an interaction will have a particular outcome (from the external or system perspective). Systemic worldviews predict not just how interactions are likely to be resolved in practice, but how they *ought* to be resolved. The possibility of assigning a certain probability to an interaction outcome arises from an assessment of the degree to which participants will see participating in the action that leads to that outcome as the right thing to do. At the same time, participants' perceptions of the rightness of a relationship depend in part on their ability to predict its consequences. Hence, systemic worldviews involve both pre-judgements about the meaning and validity of exchange or authority relationships and theoretical conceptualizations of the system that relate actions to outcomes. These relationship paradigms and structural models cannot be separated. They are two aspects of a single phenomenon.

Ideology, Truth and Dissonance

As with pre-modern worldviews, systemic worldviews imply the existence of restrictions on communication, but in the latter case these restrictions are not due to the existence of a rationally impenetrable sacred order that provides the ultimate motivation for social action. Rather, it is the application of juridical rationality to the resolution of interactions that is at the root of the phenomenon. Once a particular systemic worldview has been adopted, neither competing theories nor dissonant empirical evidence are of any consequence in pragmatic decision-making. Worldviews are rationally self-sufficient systems of thought, from the perspective of which behaviour and ideas that are incompatible with the theoretical perspective or the established interpretation of the empirical evidence can be dismissed as ill-intentioned, erroneous or irrelevant. In the early 19th century, the argument that factory wages should be increased – because, for example, workers were barely managing to avoid starvation – could be dismissed because of the sacred duty of a master to consider the moral tutelage of the working classes: the tendency of the working classes to moral weakness meant that paying more than a subsistence wage would put temptation in their way and deprive them of opportunities for redemption through work. In the absence of the prevalent religious-metaphysical worldview this argument is simply nonsense. However, from the perspective of the corporate theory of society – a good example of a systemic worldview – a similar argument could be dismissed on the grounds that wages are, and should be, set by the market. Once it has been accepted that neoclassical economic laws and principles are correct, and that the technical conditions for fair exchange obtain in practice, then external intervention to increase wages will represent a distortion that is likely to have an effect on the performance of the economic system as a whole. The application of a politicocultural standard of fairness according to which wages are judged to be too low is at best an irrelevance and at worst an unwarranted attempt to disrupt the proper functioning of the system that is likely to have negative repercussions for society as a whole. From within the perspective of the corporate theory of society, the only relevant standard of fairness is that of market outcomes.

An obvious question that arises with respect to worldviews is their relationship to empirical truth. Habermas is in no doubt that the mediatization of lifeworlds characteristic of early modern societies was sustained by ideologically effective worldviews in which the legitimacy of economic and political power was justified 'against all appearances of barbaric injustice' (Habermas, 1987, p.189). However, as we saw above, neither is he in any doubt that the historical phase of ideologies is over and that we are now in the era of open colonization.

It seems likely that Habermas would argue that systemic worldviews as we have defined them here are ideological on the grounds that they give rise to systematic restrictions on communication. At the same time, it would be difficult to argue a priori that the adoption of a particular systemic worldview necessarily means that the lifeworld of participants in action is characterized by 'objectively false consciousness'. Even if it could be shown that participants are unaware of the functional consequences of certain value/action orientations – and in our view this is surely an empirical issue – it still may not be the case that these consequences are incoherent with the action orientations which are their cause.

What we are suggesting is that systemic restrictions on communication can exist even where it is not the case that a 'compromise between internal validity claims and external survival imperatives can be achieved only at the cost of institutionalizing and internalizing value orientations not in keeping with the actual functions of the corresponding action orientations' (Habermas, 1987, p.233). Obviously, this is not to say that the situation cannot be as Habermas suggests. Rather, whether or not a systemic worldview is ideological in the sense of involving some kind of objectively false belief is once again an empirical question – theoretically unsatisfying though this position may be. The transparency of the systemic relationship paradigms characteristic of modernity does not lie in the fact that there is no totalizing worldview behind them, but rather in the awareness of participants that worldviews different to the one adopted are available. The influence of the system on the lifeworld is indeed discernible, but participants in action are in principle able to make a judgment as to whether this is or is not a good thing. In short, it is possible to *choose* a systemic worldview. From the normative perspective, what matters is whether participants in action have the opportunity to make such a choice.

We certainly need not find ourselves at odds with Habermas's definition of a worldview in arguing this line. When he first introduces the concept it is in the context of a disagreement with Peter Winch over whether it makes any sense to compare or 'rate' one worldview in comparison with another. As we mentioned above, Habermas argues that although worldviews are neither true nor false in themselves, they nonetheless '*make possible* utterances that admit of truth'. On this reading, worldviews are potentially not entirely 'immune' to dissonant experiences. For all that worldviews influence the interpretation of historical evidence about social behaviour, being repeatedly faced with statistical or other evidence which is incoherent with a worldview will tend to lead to its replacement with another.

We can say, then, that the four types of knowledge that together form a worldview must be both coherent and cognitively adequate if the worldview is not to be put into question. If the distribution of commodities in a market economy is generally considered to be fair, then by reverse inference it can be argued that market prices must also be fair and that the conditions of access to the market, availability of information, and so on are being met. Likewise, if the instructions of office-holders are seen to represent effective means of achieving legitimate goals, then it likely also to be accepted that the managerial interpretation of the formal specification of effectiveness institutionalized in the legal system is in fact accurate. The reverse, of course, is also true. A distribution of commodities which is considered to be *un*fair implies that market prices do not reflect the interests of all participants. Bureaucratic machinery for goal-achievement which is deemed to be ineffective implies that the legal specification of effectiveness is inadequate and/or that office-holders are incompetent or ill-intentioned. Of course, it always remains possible to interpret systems as neither fair nor unfair, neither effective nor ineffective.

Types of Systemic Worldview

Social systems can be interpreted from the perspective of three different types of worldview. First, a system can be interpreted as meaningless or norm-free. We saw in Chapter 4 how this is possible and what it implies for social interaction. Second, a system can be interpreted as a transmission belt for valid norms. We saw in Chapter 5 that this is also a coherent possibility, but that in principle it implies that participants in action will adopt the same strategic approach as those who consider the system to be meaningless. Third, a system can be interpreted as transmitting invalid norms. It is understood to embody political-ethical values that are not legitimizable from the perspective of all participants. As we will see, participants who adopt this worldview can either bargain aggressively, engage in conflict or respond to offers of communication in a way that aims to correct the illegitimacy of the system.

Meaningless systems Where a worldview paints a system as meaningless, it takes on the same status as physical necessity. It is thought to be external to and separate from immediate decisions about coordinated action. The satisfaction of the imperatives of the system is a means to an end rather than an end in itself. The 'ought' of systemic action is entirely hypothetical. The vendor of a commodity who is obliged to sell at a loss because the market has moved to her disadvantage may not be happy, but her attitude is likely to be one of resignation rather than resentment. She will not seek to blame another individual or group for her misfortune. Similarly, actors in organizations will have a pragmatic attitude to 'working with the grain of the system'. At the politicocultural level, attitudes to systems are also likely to be pragmatic, stressing the need to avoid the 'politicization' of economic, administrative or organizational action. In terms of concrete modes of action coordination, the important thing is success. Any administrative or organizational configuration that permits the satisfaction of system imperatives is a good one. In the same way, any kind of non-conflictual relationship within the system – bargained, cooperative or something in between – is acceptable.

Positive systems From the perspective of a worldview that sees a system as positive in itself, conformity with system imperatives is an end rather than a means and needs no further justification. System imperatives are an integral part of the normative justification of action. Working with the grain of the system is not simply likely to be effective, it is effective *because* it is the right thing to do. Similarly, if (say) wages are set at the level the labour market can bear, then by definition they are fair wages. Although the positive system worldview does not differ from the meaningless system worldview in terms of its technical approach to determining the imperatives and parameters of system action, the worldviews diverge with respect to attitudes to action coordination. If systems are given a positive value status, then from the political-ethical standpoint, not conforming with system imperatives is a *culpable* failure. To resist or challenge the authority of an office-holder in an organization, for example, is to put oneself in opposition to the organizational community as a whole. The only acceptable attitude is cooperation.

Negative systems The third possible type of systemic worldview is that which accords the system a negative value status. From this perspective, system imperatives are coercive. Actors will comply only for the empirical reasons of material necessity or the avoidance of sanctions. Since system imperatives arise because of the (culpable) actions of other actors, the negative system worldview necessarily implies the existence of an opposing politicocultural reference community – a 'them' whose interests conflict with those of 'us', and who have the social power to pursue those interests at the expense of other groups. From the perspective of this type of worldview, there are three rational responses to the coercive system. First, participants may engage in conflict, whether via 'cheating', sabotage, public protest or some other means of direct or indirect opposition to 'them'. Second, participants may attempt to organize themselves so as to form a countervailing social power with the aim of reaching a bargained accommodation with 'them', thereby defusing the coercive aspects of the system. Finally, and perhaps least likely, participants may attempt a communicative response, engaging in the kinds of behaviour we discussed in Chapter 5 when considering whether the attitude of actors makes a difference to system outcomes. In effect, participants can try to 'correct' the illegitimacy of the system by applying a substantive politicocultural standard of fairness or effectiveness to the resolution of interactions. Whether or not this is successful naturally depends on whether both parties to an interaction are, or can be persuaded to become, oriented to mutual understanding.

Characteristics of Systemic Worldviews

We need to be clear about three characteristics of systemic worldviews. First, while the logic of formal pragmatics is binary or deterministic – a claim is either valid or it is not – the logic of statistical association is probabilistic. This opens the possibility that there can be degrees of certainty or uncertainty about systemic worldviews. This in turn implies that the distinction we have drawn between positive, negative and meaningless worldviews should be regarded as referring to the extremes of a range of interpretations rather than to three mutually exclusive types.

Second, systemic worldviews condition the interpretation of the historical evidence that forms the subject matter of social learning processes. Those who assume that the market has an inherent tendency to produce fair outcomes will treat empirical evidence about the distribution of commodities very differently to those who assume that the tendency is the opposite.

Third, as we have just seen, systemic worldviews are insusceptible in themselves to judgments of truth or falsity. We should regard them, then, as the outcome of social learning processes that can only ever reach a provisional conclusion. Before we can discuss these learning processes – which we could call the production and reproduction of systemic worldviews – we need to give some further brief consideration both to the structure of communication in systemic contexts and to the role of structural models of systemic functioning in such communication.

Systemic Relationship Paradigms, Rationality and the Behaviour of Actors

As we have seen, it is possible to approach social action in systemic contexts with either a strategic or a communicative attitude. The meaning of a systemic relationship to an actor is crucial in the determination of which mode is adopted as it directly affects the interpretation of offers and instructions, i.e. the validity claims a hearer understands a speaker to be raising, and hence the way in which speaker and hearer understand their relationship. On an aggregate level, they affect the outcome of actions and thus the functional characteristics of systems.

A layer of complexity is added, however, by the fact that the speech acts of speakers are open to interpretation in a way they are not in informal social contexts. Hearers need to take a view on whether speakers share their worldview, and hence to decide the likelihood that both participants understand their relationship in the same way, that is, that they are both operating with the same systemic relationship paradigm. In systemic contexts, then, speakers can both *intend* to raise and (separately) be *understood by hearers* to be raising claims using one of two different 'registers' that correspond to a formal or substantive meaning of the relationship between speaker and hearer. If a claim is taken to be merely formal (meaningless) it is understood that the appropriate response is strategic: a flat 'yes' or 'no' depending solely on the success of the speaker's claim about profitability or sovereignty. The speaker is understood to be attempting to motivate the hearer by premising the case for compliance on the empirical consequences for the strictly individual interest of the hearer. If on the other hand a claim is taken to be substantive, the appropriate response is communicative: a 'yes' driven by rational normative commitment, or a 'no' accompanied by queries or reasons which emerge from *the same* normative commitment to distributive fairness or the realization of collective goals. In this case the speaker is taken to be arguing the case for compliance on the basis of its contribution to the pursuit of some legitimizable collective or general interest.

The great potential advantage to a speaker of raising claims about the inherent legitimacy of social systems is that where these claims succeed, the quality of the hearer's compliance is altogether better than where claims do not go beyond the nominal. On the other hand, the scope for disagreement is considerably widened by the addition of these extra claims. The risk appears even greater if one recalls

Habermas's crucial point that in systemic contexts there is no need to raise claims in what we have called the substantive register. Even if substantive claims fail, the formal claims may well still be valid. Thus the incentive to engage in processes of consensus formation in language in order to resolve any disagreement is that much less powerful since the speaker will usually have the option of resorting to purely empirical motivation. That it is guaranteed to be impossible to reach a logically secure consensus obviously exacerbates the situation.

One final element of complexity is added by the fact that the same nominal claim can be made and interpreted in both ways. There is a possibility that a speaker's intended register is mistaken by a hearer, or that a speaker may make a strategic attempt to have his hearer mistake the register in which the claim is made – to believe that a merely formal claim is substantive – in order to take advantage of the better quality of compliance that arises where substantive claims are redeemable. Suspicion that this kind of fraud is being attempted is likely to give rise to conflict or bargaining.

The Production and Reproduction of Systemic Worldviews

The multiple feedback processes that connect systemic worldviews, the behaviour of actors and the historical evidence on the outcomes of action are illustrated in Figure 6.1. The diagram, drawn from the perspective of the hearer considering a proposed interaction, shows how systemic worldviews both influence and are influenced by the outcomes of social interaction in systemic contexts. The lifeworlds of hearers contain knowledge about the outcomes of action in the past – derived both from the direct experience of actors and from other sources of cultural knowledge such as family, education and the media – and systemic worldviews premised on this knowledge. The relationship paradigms derived from these worldviews determine in the first instance the register in which communication is understood. Depending on the systemic relationship paradigm adopted by a hearer, the communicative intent of a speaker will be interpreted and the register of the speech act located somewhere on the continuum from substantive to formal. In the light of this presumed intention, the redeemability of validity claims is assessed and appropriate action follows: either a strategic or a communicative response. Once complete, each interaction, and any consequences believed to be connected to it, become part of the evidence on which systemic worldviews are premised, serving either to confirm or to put in question the existing assumptions of participants.

Conclusion

What we hope to have shown in the critique and reconstruction of Habermas's work proposed over the last three chapters is that system and lifeworld are not independent but *inter*dependent. Both the functional characteristics of economic and political-administrative systems and the meaning of the social relationships conducted within

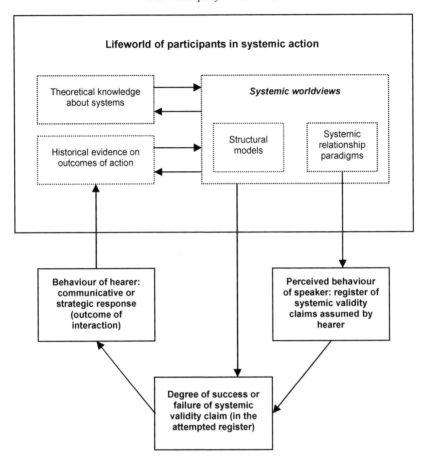

Figure 6.1 The production and reproduction of systemic worldviews

those systems ultimately depend on a systemic worldview: a global or totalizing interpretation of society in which pragmatic and political-ethical judgements are inextricably bound up with one another. The political-ethical order that defines a social system both implies and is implied by the aggregate outcome of the interactions taking place within it. To use the terms we introduced in this chapter, systemic relationship paradigms and structural models of systems are mutually dependent.

Within this general framework, we have argued that there are three 'ideal types' of interpretation of each system. From one of these perspectives, systems are thought to be meaningless. From the other two, they are thought to be meaningful. A priori, none of these interpretations has greater explanatory power than any other. All are compatible with the existence of autonomous social systems and provide adequate explanations of the resolution of interactions from the perspective of the participant. Nevertheless, although systemic worldviews cannot be true or false in themselves, they do permit the inference of statements about the social world that can be empirically tested. These statements can be pragmatic, involving claims about the relation between action and outcome, or political-ethical, involving claims about the success of a system in meeting the criteria of the fair distribution of material goods or the effective realization of legitimate collective goals. Perhaps most importantly, they can also be simultaneously both pragmatic and normative. For example, some claim might be made about the extent to which certain sociocultural standards of fairness and effectiveness are attainable given the existing functional characteristics of the system. We have argued that no claim of this sort requires any greater a priori interpretive or theoretical commitment than any other. For this reason, the resolution of conflict about social action depends on the evaluation of claims in the light of the empirical evidence. But since evidence can only be interpreted from the perspective of a pre-existing worldview, policy decision-making is ultimately a political-ethical question. It depends on *choosing* to understand society in a particular way. Like any political-ethical question, answers will depend on the values and interests whose validity can be established within the relevant politicocultural reference community. It is not the case that there is a single optimal solution coherent with the empirical evidence. Hence, for example, as both Altman's and Lazonick's work demonstrates (see Chapter 2), supposedly pragmatic interventions in business and economics will in fact tend to reflect the interests of managers because it is this group that has the empirical social power to determine the values and interests that are pursued in any given context.

At the same time as we have to concede that there is no normative 'view from nowhere', we can still argue that the standard against which the fairness of the distribution of commodities and the effectiveness of goal-achievement must be measured is necessarily a substantive one. It is not relative only to the satisfaction of system imperatives but to the material well-being of every member of society. The argument of the anti-globalization movement, for example, is that with respect to this objective standard, our existing national and international economic and political systems are patently failing. The distribution of wealth is grossly unfair, the goals of political and industrial organization are not legitimizable, and the methods and techniques of the managers of global capitalism are incompatible with the mutual respect that ought to characterize any form of social interaction.

Finally, we want to point out two important theoretical implications of our recasting of the relationship between system and lifeworld. The first is that there is no difference in principle between the models of system functioning arising, as Habermas himself has it, from the 'counterintuitive knowledge of the social sciences developing since the eighteenth century' (1987, p.173) and the models used by social actors in their everyday lives. Indeed, to argue that these methods are counterintuitive in the modern world is entirely mistaken. The use of statistical approximation and probabilistic logic to navigate the social worlds of economic and political organization is a defining characteristic of modernity. Other than the degree of precision and rigour, the only difference between a social scientific and lay use of structural models is that while social scientists for the most part adopt an entirely external viewpoint, social actors retain a perspective on action which is always at least partially internal. They retain an ability to step back from the formally organized context and to understand the situation from the viewpoint of morality, politics and ethics. This strongly supports our earlier argument that any adequate social theory will take systems and social action approaches equally seriously, regardless of the nature of the context.

The second implication is that the characteristics of social systems are not constant. The 'laws' of economics and the other empirical social sciences that are based on the probabilistic evidence of statistical association are, although in some cases very stable over both space and time, ultimately mutable. This is not simply a consequence of the advance of knowledge, for example the increasing sophistication of quantitative research techniques. Rather, it is because the meanings of the social relationships in which participants in action in systemic contexts find themselves are not constant. Systemic worldviews are the outcome of social learning processes, including in particular those processes in which the identity of a community is clarified and that thereby produce the value decisions that reflect the changing 'politicocultural self-understanding of an historical community' (Habermas, 1996, p.160). It follows that one role of social theory is to clarify the normative assumptions that underpin pragmatic/theoretical propositions about society, highlighting the latent political-ethical content of the structural models already in use, and drawing out the implications of different systemic relationship paradigms for coordinated social action in pursuit of particular interests and values. An important means to this end is the kind of research programme that aims to identify erroneous social-theoretical assumptions underpinning policy decision-making and to relate these errors to the pursuit of partial interests and values. The revived Institutional Economics and Critical Management Studies are two such research programmes.

Chapter 7

Systemic Worldviews in Practice: Corporate Legitimacy and the Employment Relationship

In this chapter, we want to make our discussion rather less abstract by focusing specifically on the corporate action context. Up to now, we have considered only those situations in which the money medium *or* the power medium is implicated in the determination of the outcomes of action. This has involved the conceptually important but empirically unrealistic abstraction of private organization membership from any economic context. It will have been obvious to the reader, however, that by far the most common form of private organization membership is employment. The capitalist business corporation quite clearly qualifies as a voluntary politicocultural reference community (PRC) with a legally enforceable normative order. In accepting membership of a corporation, actors consciously agree to participate in relationships of authority and accept that sanctions may be applied if they do not comply with valid instructions. At the same time, there is a strong element of exchange in the employment relationship. On the one hand, a significant element – for many, the *only* significant element – of an employee's private interest in organization membership is the wage or salary. On the other, the corporation's interest in providing this payment is the receipt of the employee's contribution to production. It would appear to be logical, then, to argue that social interaction in the context of the employment relationship is simultaneously steered by the money and power media.

That this is the case has frequently been proposed. There are many approaches to the study of employment, in particular labour process and other Marxian approaches, that emphasize the equal or greater importance of the economic context as compared to the social and legal aspects of the relationship. Perhaps more interesting, however, is the effect of the social organization of work on the market economy, an area of analysis that is the speciality of institutional economics. Institutional economists argue that neoclassical economic theory is inadequate to the explanation of concrete historical forms of economic behaviour because it emphasizes monetary exchange at the expense of other, equally important forms of social interaction. The most important of these are the interactions that take place within the corporation. Commons, for example, argued that market exchange is only one of three forms of 'transaction' in which ownership is legally transferred (Kaufman, 2004, pp.104-9). The other two, the rationing transaction (the exchange of property rights commanded by a legal superior) and the managerial transaction (the exchange of the worker's property rights over her labour power with the employer) require the presence of an institutional structure that goes well beyond the simple law of contract. The concepts of the rationing transaction – in effect, managerial plans and strategies – and the managerial transaction – the social organization of the labour process – allow the construction of a rather more realistic approach to economics in which the existence of positive transaction costs is recognized. As Kaufman argues, the 'non-neoclassical assumptions of bounded rationality, imperfect information, incomplete markets and costly enforcement of contracts' permit the conceptualization of the economy as a 'mix of markets and organizations, including large hierarchical firms with an employment relationship' (2004, p.105).

The idea that certain systemic social relationships might simultaneously be steered by two media is coherent with institutional economics. To put it in terms of systems theory, we can say that the bargaining transaction represents the money medium, and the rationing and managerial transactions represent the power medium. The interaction of the three types of transaction – or of the money and power media – produces the structural model of the corporation in its market environment that is used to predict the outcome of actions. What we can add to the picture drawn by institutional economics is the perspective of system actors. From this perspective, steering imperatives are experienced as the conduct of transactions: as the ensemble of managerial plans and strategies, the social organization of labour designed to put them into practice, and the interpretation of the market imperatives to which corporate action is designed to respond. In other words, they are experienced as the political-ethical order of the corporation. The employee's participation in the fulfilment of this order can be equated with the employment relationship. The legitimacy of the political-ethical order of the corporation, and hence the legitimacy of corporate action, is therefore indistinguishable from the legitimacy of the employment relationship.

The Employment Relationship in the *Theory of Communicative Action*

For Habermas, the role of employee is one of the social roles that, from the perspective of the lifeworld, 'crystallize' around the 'interchange relations' between the economic and political-administrative systems and the lifeworld (1987, pp.318-23). There are four such roles: employee, client of the state, consumer and citizen. Employee and consumer are the 'economic' roles, while client of the state and citizen are the 'political' roles. Since the political roles relate only to compulsory PRCs, in what follows we will devote our attention exclusively to the economic roles.

The concept of a social role found in TCA is not dissimilar to the idea of systemic relationship paradigms, proposed in Chapter 6. Social roles are collections of action and value orientations that condition the response of individuals to various forms of communication. However, Habermas draws a distinction between the roles of employee and consumer that cannot be sustained in the context of the arguments put forward in the previous chapter. He argues that whereas the role of employee is *dependent* on the organization, that of consumer, although defined *with reference to* the economic system, is not dependent on it. Actors who assume the role of employee have 'detach[ed] themselves from lifeworld contexts and adapt[ed] themselves to formally organized domains of action' (Habermas, 1987, p.321). They have left their private way of life behind. The role of consumer, on the other hand, refers to 'prior self-formative processes in which preferences, value orientations, attitudes, and so forth have taken shape' (ibid.). However, we have argued that in private organizational contexts, the pre-existing preferences of individuals shape their behaviour in a way that is precisely analogous to the influence of the utility preferences of consumers on the determination of the outcome of exchange interactions. This argument has two main implications. First, it is not straightforwardly the case that legally valid instructions will meet with compliance, even where actors have assumed the role of employee. Rather, it depends on the particular interpretation or understanding of that role adopted by each actor. This understanding will reflect 'prior self-formative processes' similar to those that Habermas argues are of relevance to the role of consumer. Second, since the attitudes, values and preferences of employees are always implicated in the functioning of organizational systems, we cannot accept Habermas's argument that the monetarization and bureaucratization of innerorganizational relationships are subject to 'boundaries of normality' beyond which (and *only* beyond which) these processes have sociopathological consequences. We must therefore also question the possibility that organization members can have action orientations characterized by the fact that 'all their actions fall under… the premises of a legally regulated domain of action' (ibid., p.310). As we saw above, employees do not necessarily simply adapt themselves to organizational rule systems, instead becoming involved in a negotiation over the scope of sovereignty of office-holders, as a consequence of which the outcomes of action reflect the individual and collective preferences of employees as well as the formal normative order of the organization. Hence, action within organizations is itself a self-formative process, the results of which will be reflected in the identities of individual organization members and translated into cultural knowledge. To this extent, system imperatives will have an effect – and not just a constraining or limiting effect – on the symbolic reproduction of the lifeworld. Exactly how employees will conceive their role, however, and whether these meanings objectively involve self-deception or more profound pathologies, are surely empirical questions.

Conceiving Employment as a Dual-Media-Steered Relationship

In any case, in the *Theory of Communicative Action* it is suggested that the employment relationship is governed by both the money and power media (Habermas, 1987, p.320, Figure 39). The systemic output factor of wages involves the money medium, while the input factor of labour involves the power medium. Habermas's claim is that the receipt of wages gives rise to a generalized willingness to obey legal instructions. The immediate response of an employee to a manager's instruction will therefore depend solely on the conformity of that instruction with the letter of the contract of employment. The element of exchange is not immediately relevant. However, we want to argue that the resolution of each interaction in the context of the employment relationship is simultaneously dependent on both media.

We suggested above that, contrary to Habermas's claims, participants in action in organizational contexts do not detach themselves from lifeworld contexts, and that their action orientations cannot be straightforwardly characterized in terms of a generalized willingness to obey legal instructions. For this reason, the analysis of action in private organizational settings requires an appreciation of what actors consider their individual interest in membership to be. Where membership is characterized by actors making some organization-specific contribution and being compensated for it in the form of wages or salaries (ibid., p.321), at least part of that interest will be money (indeed it may be the actor's *only* interest in membership). Thus, it is part of the normative order of the organization that members are financially compensated for their contribution. In terms of reciprocal obligation, an individual member owes compliance with the instructions of office-holders to all the other members of the organization (including herself), and they owe her a wage or salary. The crucial point that Habermas does not take into account – largely because he does not give proper consideration to the non-generalizable status of the goals of the private organization – is that, just as is the case with the reciprocal obligations of exchange, the rights and duties of the employment relationship must be in some kind of balance that is profitable for both parties. Since employee and organization commit themselves to a relationship extending over a period of time rather than just for the momentary duration of an exchange, the normative order of the private employing organization will necessarily include the notion of maintaining a particular equivalence between employee contribution and reward which at least maintains the same average profitability for both parties for the length of the contract of membership. We can make this claim on the grounds that neither employee nor organization could rationally agree to a contract of membership whose profitability is wholly unforeseeable. Thus, whether an employee complies with an instruction depends not just on its effectiveness in the sense of a contribution to the realization of certain outcomes at the level of the organization, but on the maintenance of the agreed equivalence between contribution and reward. It depends on the realization of certain outcomes at the level of the employee. The outcome of interactions within the employment relationship therefore appears to depend simultaneously on power (collective goals) and money (individual goals).

Systemic Worldviews and the Completion of the Employment Contract

We argued above that systemic interactions, regardless of whether they are approached with a communicative or strategic attitude, cannot be resolved in the absence of a contextualizing social structure, be this an economic market or a political-administrative bureaucracy. The employment contract is a perfect example of a systemic relationship in the sense that it possesses this kind of formal incompleteness. Although the employee has by definition 'agreed to obey certain instructions with respect to his work, to submit to some kind of discipline' (Flanders, 1975, p.99), this obviously does not give the employer the right to demand that the employee comply with just any instruction. Beyond the explicit contractual specification of the rights and duties of employee and employer, there remains to be defined the greater part of the employment relationship. As Wilhelm Baldamus put it,

> Though [the employment contract] stipulates precise wage payments for the employer, nothing definite is ever said about effort or efficiency; nor anything about the components of effort, the acceptable intensity of impairment, the intolerable degree of tedium or weariness. Instead it merely mentions hours of work, type of job, occupational status and similar external conditions. At the most there are vague and concealed references to an implied level of effort... (cited in Townley, 1993, p.524).

In fact, although Baldamus argues that the contract is incomplete only with respect to the obligations of the employee, neither side of the bargain is precisely specified. Employees can and in many cases do benefit from organization membership in more than simply financial terms. The latent benefits to the employee in terms of job satisfaction, self-fulfilment, social status, and so forth also remain unspecified.

Despite this incompleteness – whether from the perspective of employer or employee – we can nonetheless see in the employment contract the attempt to specify both the work-wage equivalence and a definition of effectiveness relating to a particular employee's role in goal achievement. If we were to describe the minimum required characteristics of a contract of employment, these would include a description of the type of work, of the hours of work, and of the wage or salary to be paid. There is an obvious sense, then, in which the employment relationship assumes a broad quantitative equivalence between abstract labour and money. The concept of a legal minimum wage, for example, suggests that at the simplest level, this equivalence can be stated in terms of the minimum permissible exchange value of one hour of labour, whatever that labour involves. Nonetheless, in the majority of cases, the *type* of work that is to be undertaken is of central importance in the definition of its value. A particular level of compensation can generally only be agreed with reference to a definition of what the employee's qualitative obligations are to be. If these obligations change, then this may invalidate the previously agreed level of compensation. At the same time, the contractual definition of work arguably also represents a minimal formal specification of effectiveness, defining the basic circumstances in which a manager is sovereign and is able to take binding decisions. For example, an employee taken on as a professional accountant but set to work cleaning windows would almost certainly be within her rights to refuse to comply on the grounds that it would be so implausible to claim that cleaning was an effective use of her abilities that the manager who issued the instruction can be assumed to have been acting from some ulterior, unlawful motive. A similar claim would be unlikely to be sustainable if the same accountant were to be asked temporarily to take on some financial record-keeping duties in the unforeseen absence of a more junior colleague. In this case, a plausible argument that this was an effective means to the realization of the organization's goals in the circumstances could almost certainly be made.

If we apply the process of resolution of media-steered interactions we proposed above to the employment relationship – that is, the comparison of the action situation with a model – we can divide the contractual regulation of the relationship into two parts roughly along the lines suggested by Baldamus, which is to say into the objective and social aspects which are specifically and more or less unambiguously defined, and those which are subject to interpretation. Thus on the one hand we have objective matters such as those related to the temporal confines of organization membership (the working day, holiday entitlement, flexitime), or to levels of pay (hourly rates, overtime); and social/normative matters such as the identification of office-holders entitled to issue instructions, or requirements for certain types of conformity such as the wearing of uniforms. These are not generally matters where contractual compliance or non-compliance on the part of employee or employer is difficult to determine – although this is not, of course, to suggest that there may not be difficulties of interpretation in certain circumstances. The validity of the contractual norms in question is not dependent on the individual situations of the other members of the PRC. Beyond these basic parameters, however, we move into those contexts where the assessment of validity depends on the adoption of a worldview. It is these contexts to which management and industrial relations writers in the Foucauldian tradition tend to refer as the 'space to be governed' in between the few precise terms of the contract and what is owed to the employer in practice. As we suggested in Chapter 4, however, the idea of power/knowledge is surely an inadequate theoretical explanation for the government of this space, discounting as it does the possibility that the system may represent an empirical force with which employers and employees both have to contend but about whose characteristics agreement is in principle possible. In this chapter, we present an alternative explanation of how the 'space between promise and performance' is governed.

A Typology of Enterprise Worldviews

We noted above that contractual definitions of work can be understood in both a quantitative and a qualitative sense. If we understand employment as a power relationship, then the *quantitative* equivalence of labour and wages as outlined in the contract represents the specification of the effectiveness of an interaction from the perspective of the individual employee. If we understand it as an exchange relationship, then the *qualitative* specification of the work to be performed represents the organization's end of the bargain, its entitlement under the contract. Thus we cannot in fact define employment as one thing or the other. If we are to be able to understand it in abstraction from either perspective, we must allow that social interactions in the context of the employment relationship are simultaneously steered by both power and money. The worldviews appropriate to the understanding of the employment relationship, then, and to the construction of structural models of the employing enterprise in its economic context – let us call them 'enterprise worldviews' – will involve assumptions about both types of media-steering.[1]

---

[1] While it would be logical to use the term 'corporate worldviews', the contemporary sense of the term 'corporate' in this context implies a managerial perspective. Since we intend to refer to these worldviews in a generic sense, without wishing to suggest that the perspective we have in mind is that of any particular group, we will instead use the less loaded qualifier, 'enterprise'.

Enterprise worldviews are characterized by the interaction of views about money and views about power. Views about money take the form of opinions about the value status of economic imperatives. These can be seen as providing politically and ethically legitimate direction to decisions about action, as normatively neutral survival imperatives, or as embodiments of the partial interests of the owners of capital. Views about power take the form of opinions about the value status of the de facto political-ethical order of the corporation; that is, the degree to which what is actually done in the corporation reflects the authentic collective interest of its members. Opinions can range from a belief that the order of the corporation is entirely valid in itself, through the view that it is simply what is required in order that the individual aims and interests of members be satisfied, to the belief that it reflects the interests only of certain members, privileging these at the expense of those of the others.

The interaction between the dimensions of money and power gives rise to the nine ideal types of enterprise worldview which we want to propose, and which are set out in Table 7.1 below. Each of the worldviews represents a way of thinking about and understanding the capitalist business corporation. We will briefly attempt to describe each of these worldviews from the perspective of the actor in a social system, before going on to discuss the corresponding paradigms of the employment relationship and structural models of the corporation in its institutional context.

Table 7.1 Enterprise worldviews

Market System	Organizational System		
	Positive	**Meaningless**	**Negative**
Positive	Legitimate Community	Legitimate Bureaucracy	Ethical Conflict
Meaningless	Market Community	Market Bureaucracy	Localized Conflict
Negative	Pluralist Community	Bureaucratic Pluralism	Class Conflict

Positive Organizational Systems

The three worldviews in which the organizational system has a positive value status are united by their common assumption that the corporation is a politicocultural reference community founded on substantive aims and values. The relationships that exist within corporations, for all that they would not exist in the absence of the corporate context, have an intrinsic value. We might say that they are the analogue in the economic sphere of legitimate political institutions. Indeed, we can draw some direct parallels between these worldviews and the paradigms of democracy that Habermas proposes in BFN. The 'legitimate community' worldview corresponds to what Habermas calls the 'discourse' model of democracy, the 'market community' worldview to the 'republican' model, and the 'pluralist community' worldview to the 'liberal' model.

The Enterprise as a Legitimate Community

Habermas summarizes the discourse conception of politics as follows:

> Democratic procedure, which establishes a network of pragmatic considerations, compromises, and discourses of self-understanding and of justice, grounds the presumption that reasonable or fair results are obtained insofar as the flow of relevant information and its proper handling have not been obstructed. According to this view, practical reason no longer resides in universal human rights, or in the ethical substance of a specific community, but in the rules of discourse and forms of argumentation that borrow their normative content from the validity basis of action oriented to reaching understanding. In the final analysis, this normative content arises from the structure of linguistic communication and the communicative mode of sociation (1996, p.296).

The legitimate community worldview is comparable to the discourse conception of politics because it too assumes the primacy of discourse. It represents the closest possible assimilation of corporate action to legitimate social action. The ultimate market goals of that action, the intermediate plans and strategies of the corporation and the social relationships by which those plans are realized are all deemed to have a positive value status. Perhaps the most distinctive feature of this worldview is the idea that the corporation is connected to society via a legitimate market. Since market relationships are legitimate relationships, the corporation and its members do not form an isolated group acting only on its own behalf, but instead are active participants in the social process of material reproduction. The corporation exists both to satisfy the interests of its members and to contribute to the fair distribution of commodities across society as a whole. If it can be assumed that such a fair distribution is achieved, or that it represents a genuine overarching goal, then the actions of the corporation are not simply permissible, but are legitimate in a highly generalizable political-ethical sense. While participation in some particular corporation may not be obligatory in itself, the actions of those who do choose to participate are socially useful and to that extent laudable.

From this perspective, and leaving aside any objectively technical or scientific aspects, the role of management is one of political leadership and representation. The actions of the corporation, like those of any market actor, will have an effect on the legitimacy of the market. As we have seen, if it is assumed that the conditions for perfect competition do not obtain in practice, then market actors are likely to be faced with a range of choices of action in response to market imperatives. The valid choice is that which preserves or improves the fairness of the market as a whole. However, these choices are not simply given. Rather, they depend on politicocultural interpretations of the economic system. These interpretations cannot be technical in the sense that medical or engineering knowledge is technical. They are inherently normative both in the sense that they rely on assumptions about the validity of aims and values in society as a whole, and in the sense that they embody the aims and values of the members of the corporate community. Where the enterprise is conceived as a legitimate community, to pretend that some kind of purely technical approach to management could uncover this normative knowledge of the organizational and market systems in such a way that it would be beyond dispute will appear rather far-fetched. This is not to say that certain individuals will not be capable of 'reading' a group; of grasping its self-identity in a way that the group's members recognize as accurate. As we argued above, it makes perfect sense to suppose that actors could come to trust an individual to articulate 'who they are' as members of a corporation and of society, and hence to trust in that individual's recommendations for action. Nonetheless, whether or not individual managers have this ability is entirely an empirical question and it can be assumed neither that any such individuals will exist, nor that their capacity for leadership is transferable between different social groups, nor that this capacity can permanently be trusted. In the same way that it would be unwise to assume that it will always be possible to find a 'philosopher king' who is able to articulate the general will of a political community better than the members of that community could articulate it themselves, from the perspective of the legitimate community worldview only the procedural guarantee of *deliberative democratic* forms of management – together with the analogous procedural guarantee of free trade – can provide an appropriate degree of assurance that corporate action will be legitimate.

From the perspective of the legitimate community worldview, there is no permanent preconceived idea of what that ideal employment system will look like. Instead, it will be the outcome of co-operation; of ongoing processes of consensus formation in language. The role of formal regulation is therefore extremely limited. Indeed one might even say that an effective employment system is best achieved by dissolving hierarchical administrative systems in favour of flexible systems of self-management. Thus, decisions about what the enterprise is to do can be focused on its responses to economic imperatives, but the identification both of what these imperatives are and the range of effective responses that are normatively acceptable will be a matter for all members of the enterprise to agree on the basis of open discussion and dialogue.

The Enterprise as Market Community

Habermas's republican conception of politics and democracy would have it that 'democratic will-formation takes the form of ethicopolitical self-understanding; here deliberation can rely on the substantive support of a culturally established background consensus shared by the citizenry' (1996, p.296). The ethicopolitical self-understanding of the 'market community' places effective market action at the head of the social ordering of cultural values. From this perspective, there is no distinction between a strategy for market action that is technically effective and one that is politically and ethically legitimate. The 'culturally established background consensus' of the community that pre-defines legitimate coordinated action simply 'refers' to whatever aims and values make for effective action in the market. In practice, this reference is to managerial expertise.

Managerial expertise can be equated with technical effectiveness because of the objectivist conception of the economy that is characteristic of the market community worldview. The economy is seen as a non-normative phenomenon that has to be dealt with in the same way as physical necessity. From this perspective, to say we are coerced by the economic system only makes as much sense as saying that our bodies force us to eat or that the rain forces us to take shelter. At the same time, neither does it make any sense to say that the 'ought' in 'we ought to eat' or 'we ought to take shelter' is anything other than hypothetical. The interpretation of what the market demands from the corporation is therefore conceived as a technical process and management as a profession whose members aim only to make the most scientifically effective interventions. Hence, the formal-legal specification of the scope of managerial competence coincides with the managerial definition of market effectiveness.

The objectivist understanding of the economy also means that the corporation is conceived as unconnected to wider society. The fact that the market also involves other individuals is of little importance. They and their situations remain anonymous and impersonal. Taking action in the market is not an activity that connects one to others in anything other than the most superficial sense. For this reason, the goals of the corporation cannot be generalized beyond its boundaries. It is an isolated group of actors whose values and interests, like those of the market, remain entirely non-generalizable from the societal perspective.

In this context, then, 'democratic will-formation' does not necessarily require what we would recognize as democratic processes. Since the commitment of participants to the order of the organization is essentially hypothetical, since the option of 'exit' always remains open, and since managerial decisions are assumed to be effective, it can straightforwardly be assumed that community members actively consent to the authority of managers, whatever this should involve. They will have a positive normative commitment to managerial direction. In a word, the members of the market community are flexible. The other side of this employee commitment, however, is an open and liberal style of management. Flexibility is incompatible with a 'Theory X' approach to management (Pugh and Hickson, 1989, pp.156-61). From within the market community worldview, rigid, one-way authority relationships, the close pre-specification of employee effort, and surveillance-oriented supervision are all entirely inappropriate.

The Enterprise as a Pluralist Community

Habermas defines the liberal conception of politics and democracy as follows:

> According to the liberal view, the democratic process is effected exclusively in the form of compromises among interests. Rules of compromise formation are supposed to secure the fairness of results through universal and equal suffrage, the representative composition of parliamentary bodies, the rules of decision making, rules of order and so on. Such rules are ultimately justified in terms of basic rights (1996, p.296).

From the perspective of the pluralist community worldview, the economic system cannot be represented as politically neutral or fair in itself. Rather, it embodies the values and interests of a limited group in society: the owners of capital and their agents in management. Just as the existence of competing interests in society does not mean that legitimate forms of political organization are impossible, this does not mean that the order of the corporation cannot be valid. It simply means that validity must be the outcome of bargained compromises.

In BFN, Habermas discusses bargaining at some length, providing a definition of the process which is coherent with the industrial relations pluralism we discussed in Chapter 1:

> Bargaining processes are tailored for situations in which social power relations cannot be neutralized in the way rational discourses presuppose. The compromises achieved by such bargaining contain a negotiated agreement (*Vereinbarung*) that balances conflicting interests. Whereas a rationally-motivated consensus (*Einverständnis*) rests on reasons that convince all the parties *in the same way*, a compromise can be accepted by the different parties each for its own *different* reasons (1996, pp.165-6; emphasis in original).

Those who adopt the pluralist community worldview see the demands of the market, articulated by employers or managers, as value-laden. They are pragmatic recommendations drawn up with the aim of realizing the values and interests of capital. As such, they may well be highly effective, but they will not be universally valid. As Flanders put it, 'Managerial initiative, even when it is intelligent and far-sighted, is taken to suit the aims of management and these do not necessarily coincide with the aims of unions and the people they represent' (1975, p.23). This having been said, it remains the case that the aims and values of management are perfectly legitimate in the sense of being socially permissible. Employers and the owners of capital are entitled to proper representation of their interests in the goals of the enterprise just as workers are. While it is not rational for workers to co-operate with employers (and vice versa) regardless of what the other wants to do, it is certainly rational to seek to strike a bargain in which each side gets as close to what it wants as is compatible with the same outcome for all; in other words, a bargain which is fair.

Since the validity of any bargain is defined in relation to this substantive standard, it cannot be said that a fair bargain is necessarily the best bargain possible for one side or the other on the basis of the empirical balance of power. The demands of the market have to be respected because they represent the legitimate interests of one group in society without the co-operation of which other groups could not pursue their own interests. The respect due, however, is limited by the need to accord equal respect to the interests of other groups. Once again, this kind of balance cannot be specified in concrete terms, but it is possible to draw up procedural parameters for negotiation that ensure that outcomes will be fair:

> The procedures intended to secure the fairness of possible compromises regulate, among other things, the right to participation, the choice of delegates, and hence the composition of delegations. If necessary they extend to such matters as the moderation and length of negotiation; they also stipulate the kinds of issues and contributions, the admissibility of sanctions, and so forth. These and similar questions are regulated with a view to ensuring that all the relevant interests are given equal consideration and all parties are furnished with equal power... Compromise procedures are intended to avert the danger that asymmetrical power relations and unequally distributed threat potentials could prejudice the outcome of bargaining (Habermas, 1996, p.177).

In the context of this kind of procedure, the business plans and strategies of the corporation are the concern of management alone, just as the aims and values of workers are no concern of management. What *is* of joint concern is the labour process, in which workers make the contribution for which they are compensated, and in which employers receive the value of the workers' labour power. The legitimacy of managerial authority depends not on the validity of the aims and values of management, but on the validity of the compromise between these and the aims and values of employees. Where managerial instructions are coherent with a fair negotiated order, then they will be recognized as valid.

The conception of the economic system as a social structure that embodies interests beyond the organization means that the validity of the negotiated arrangements eventually agreed can be generalized beyond the organization. If the interests of employees are conceived in a solidaristic way, that is as a 'subset' of a workers' interest on a national or even international scale, then an organizational order based on fair compromise has a political-ethical validity at a high level. For those who have chosen to be involved, the rights and duties of the organizational order represent not just mutual obligations, but obligations to society as a whole.

Meaningless Organizational Systems

Where systems of corporate organization are interpreted as meaningless, then they are understood as having no legitimizable content beyond that borrowed from the goals they seek to realize. The relationships that exist within them have no intrinsic value, but the absence of such value is not experienced as a culpable failure. The organizational system is therefore a purely pragmatic mode of action coordination that can be specified from a technical perspective. It is assumed that the design of effective systems is a matter of the application of expert knowledge. For this reason, democratic forms of organization are seen as inappropriate.

The Enterprise as a Legitimate Bureaucracy

From the perspective of the 'legitimate bureaucracy' worldview – in many ways assimilable to the classical Weberian model of political-administrative bureaucracy – economic success is seen as a positive social value, a benefit to society in general. However, the imperatives of the market are conceived broadly, in such a way as to be more or less self-evident. Much more important are the technical means by which these ends are achieved. This, rather than the interpretation of the market, is the focus of the expertise of management. The aim is to design and operate the most efficient and rational organization that is possible – to find something like Taylor's 'one best way' of organizing production. Corporate roles are conceived impersonally, in isolation from the capacities of individuals.

At the same time, the positive value status of the market means that conformity with the technical-bureaucratic requirements of organization is invested with a political-ethical value in such a way that the corporation appears as a carrier of the values of the society in which it operates. The particular role of each employee may have no intrinsic value, but the fact of being a cog in the machine is nonetheless laudable, something to be proud of. The corporation, with its extensive formal regulation and the culture that fixes an interpretation of these rules, is the focus of its employees' collective identity. The politicocultural self-understanding of the corporation is dominated by the technical needs of the organizational system: what is good for the corporation is good for its members.

The corporation's role as a carrier of social values also means that it is likely to be accorded a de facto role in national economic governance. While corporations may not feature in the legal structure of democracy, consultation with business leaders in advance of policy-making is entirely coherent with the idea that the economy is a legitimate social phenomenon.

The Enterprise as a Market Bureaucracy

The 'market bureaucracy' worldview represents the most anomic possible conception of the corporation: the meaningless corporate structure in pursuit of meaningless market goals. From this perspective, management is an entirely technical process encompassing both the interpretation of market imperatives and their translation into corporate action via organization structures and modes of production. Participation in the corporation is wholly strategic and hence individuals will see duties as something to be minimized and rights as something to be maximized. The corporation is likely to be characterized by rigid authority relationships, limitation of employee effort, and surveillance-oriented management.

The objectivist conception of both the economic and organizational systems means that members of the corporation will not consider themselves to be 'connected' to society via their participation in collective action. The two systems are not conceived as providing any normative linkage between actors. While normal social relations may persist outside the corporate context, within it actors are entirely isolated.

The Bureaucratic Pluralist Enterprise

The key characteristic of the 'bureaucratic pluralism' worldview is the belief that to act according to the demands of the economic system is to act in the interest of a certain social group of which employees are not members. Nevertheless, since employees, whether individually or collectively, can do nothing to change this situation, they are forced by their material circumstances to work within that economic system. It is therefore rational for employees to co-operate with employers – in the sense of working towards the fulfilment of market demands – if this co-operation is rewarded in such a way that their material needs are met. Similarly, employers can do little to change the politically or socially sanctioned ability of employees to resist their authority, whether this resistance takes the form of organized collective action or more individualized conflictual practices. Hence, it is rational for them to accept the power of workers as long as it is possible to maintain an adequate return on the investment in labour. The definition of adequacy here is tactical or pragmatic: an adequate reward or return on investment is the largest which is practically (politically) possible given the balance of power between capital and labour. Employees will carefully measure and restrict their input to ensure that the employer gains nothing for which she has not paid. For their part, employers will carefully monitor the behaviour of employees to ensure that their contribution is precisely as has been agreed.

On this view, both the demands of the economic system and the essentially non-economic individual or collective goals of workers or trade unions are reflected in the negotiated order that governs the enterprise. Perhaps most importantly, since market imperatives merely represent the intentions of a particular group, the viability of enterprises need not be damaged by the apparent non-optimality of enterprise action under these circumstances. All that is required is an adjustment of capital's expectations to the unavoidable social reality of worker power. Optimal corporate performance – from all perspectives – depends on the adoption of the most technically effective systems of collective bargaining.

Negative Organizational Systems

The unique feature of the negative organizational system worldviews is that participants believe that the normative order of the corporation privileges the aims and values of certain of its members over those of the others. These worldviews can therefore be characterized principally by the absence of any assumption that trust and understanding between the different members of the corporation will naturally arise. The relationships that exist are premised on the belief that willing cooperation within the corporation is more or less impossible.

Conflict is more likely to occur when participants perceive the organizational system as having a negative value status than when they perceive the economic system as negative. No matter how large an organization is, it remains considerably smaller and easier to grasp that the economy. It is thus easier to personalize conflicts of interest, blaming the lack of balance in the corporate order on an internal, identifiable 'them', almost inevitably management from the employees' perspective or employees – especially if organized in a trade union – from the managerial perspective.

Negative organizational systems can exist only because of the material need of participants. From the employee perspective, the sanction attached to non-compliance with management authority is exclusion from the corporation and hence from the material benefits of membership. From the management perspective, failing to secure the compliance of employees with instructions will mean the failure to achieve corporate objectives. Mutual dependence is thus the only reason the employment relationship persists.

The Corporation as a Site of Ethical Conflict

Where the market economic system is viewed positively, but the corporate system is seen to be illegitimate – that is, the way in which action is coordinated is not thought to be rationally defensible – then the corporation will experience political-ethical or even moral conflict. Participants will tend to blame the failure of the corporation to construct a universally acceptable order on the other participants. Employees may blame corporate failure on managers, for issuing instructions that do not accurately capture the collective interest of the corporation's members. Managers – who will consider that their instructions *do* properly reflect the collective interest – may in turn blame employees for refusing to comply, thereby unreasonably putting their individual interests ahead of those of the corporation. In both cases, the blame has a moral character. The blamed participants are seen to be selfishly preventing the corporation from effectively pursuing market goals, an activity of great value to society.

At the same time, the positive value status of the market may lead actors to remain within the corporation despite its internal problems. The members of the organization will not persist with their conflictual relationships simply because of their individual material need, but because of the needs of the local community or society in general. While negotiated forms of organization may be seen as fundamentally forced, they will nonetheless be perceived as better than abandoning the corporation altogether.

The Corporation as a Site of Localized Conflict

The distinction between the 'moral conflict' and 'localized conflict' enterprise worldviews turns on the perception of the market. Whereas in the former case it is seen as social phenomenon, in the latter it is thought of as something objective. For this reason, the failure of participants in action to agree on modes of organization will not be considered an injury to society, but a matter of bad faith, ignorance or incompetence on the part of existing members of the corporation. The conflict within the corporation is therefore unrelated to any features of wider society. Members will persist with their participation in action only for as long as their individual situations mean that their interest in membership remains positive.

The Corporation as a Site of Class Conflict

Where the enterprise is conceived as the site of class conflict, participants' actions will be designed to pursue the partial values and interests of reference communities beyond the corporation. From the perspective of this worldview, the corporation is permanently and irrevocably divided into an 'us' and a 'them'. Division within the corporation reflects the conflicting economic interests of capital and labour in wider society. An agreed definition of effective organization is simply impossible, as it makes no sense to argue that interests can be aligned even temporarily. Depending on whether one adopts an employee or managerial perspective, either the corporation exploits the material need of the workers, or the workers exploit the initiative and organization of the corporation. Each side coerces the other. The organizations of each side – employers' associations and trade unions – take on the aspect of conspiracies plotting to prevent the other from receiving its proper entitlements. Maintaining the corporation in a minimally viable functional state is the best that can be hoped for.

The Employment Relationship from the Perspective of the Enterprise Worldviews

In the previous chapter, we described systemic relationship paradigms as 'formulae' that partially determine the outcome of social interactions in systemic contexts. Each paradigm of the employment relationship will partially determine the outcome of interactions between employees and managers. They represent an actor's predisposition to understand offers of communication in a particular way; a prejudgement both of the relevance and value status of certain elements of the action situation and of their relationship to each other. The global interpretation of the whole represented by the enterprise worldview means that for actors in corporate contexts, certain claims about the validity status of the economic and corporate systems are 'always already' redeemable or not redeemable. Regardless of the actual intentions of their interlocutor, participants in action will interpret offers of communication *as if* it had been established that these claims were valid (or not valid). Where participants share a worldview, the immediate resolution of social interactions is simply a matter of establishing the coherence of an offer of communication with the de facto order of the corporation – that is, ensuring the validity of the third of the three claims that characterize the structure of communication in voluntary politicocultural reference communities (see above, p.71). To this extent, the basic structure of communication is consistent across all of the possible paradigms.

Two things vary from type to type. First, there is the nature of the normative order itself, that is, the logic or grounding of managerial sovereignty; and second, the way in which the inevitably under-specified employment contract is interpreted in the case of ambiguity or conflicting interpretations. The characteristics of each paradigm are summarized in Table 7.2, below. The three positive organizational system worldviews support paradigms of the employment relationship that can all be described as conceptions of *citizenship* in the organizational community. The order of the corporation is in the interest of the employee in the sense that the employment relationship is intrinsically legitimate. The meaningless organizational system worldviews support paradigms in which the employment relationship is conceived as bureaucratic *membership*. The order of the corporation is in the interest of the employee in the sense that, in the light of the needs, preferences, political-ethical value orientations and attitudes of the employee, the obligations of membership are outweighed by its benefits. From the perspective of the negative organizational systems, the employment relationship is thought to be characterized by illegitimate subordination of workers. The order of the corporation could not rationally be chosen by employees, but they have no choice but to participate because there is no alternative means to satisfy their individual material need or that of their community or class. However, their participation will involve neither cooperation nor passive acceptance. The employment relationship is conceived as *resistance to management*.

The case of the manager issuing a direct instruction to an employee is not, of course, the only type of social interaction that occurs within the context of the employment relationship. There are different types of managerial communication – giving or seeking information, canvassing opinion, giving or asking for advice, and so forth – as well as communication directed to managers by employees. The direct counterpart to a managerial instruction, for example, is an employee's claim to receive her contractual entitlements. However, for simplicity's sake, the brief accounts of the different paradigms of the employment relationship which follow are drawn from the perspective of the employee reacting to an instruction.

Table 7.2 Characteristics of paradigms of the employment relationship

	Positive Organizational System			Meaningless Organizational System			Negative Organizational System		
	Legitimate Citizenship	Market Citizenship	Pluralist Citizenship	Legitimate Membership	Market Membership	Pluralist Membership	Ethical Resistance	Localized Resistance	Class-Based Resistance
Value of Employment	Intrinsically positive			Extrinsically positive				Negative	
Grounding of Managerial Sovereignty	Deliberative consensus	Managerial expertise	Fair compromise	Substantively valid rules	Formally valid rules	Negotiated rules	Collective material need	Individual material need	Class material need
Resolution of Conflict or Ambiguity	Discourse	Consultation	Integrative collective bargaining	Reference to hierarchy	Individual strategic negotiation	Adversarial collective bargaining	Application of sanctions		

Legitimate Citizenship

From the perspective of the 'legitimate citizenship' paradigm of the employment relationship, normatively authorized instructions will embody the collective interest of all the members of the corporation. The manager who issues an instruction or presents some plan is understood to be making claims about both the fairness and the effectiveness of the coordinated social action involved. Her proposals will be founded on an interpretation of the market and the corporation that is intended to capture the self-understanding of the corporate community. This self-understanding will have been developed in processes of consensus formation involving all the members of the corporation. Where employees agree that this interpretation is accurate, and that the proposals for coordinated action follow logically from it, then they will comply. This agreement may arise either from an advance of trust – where there are good reasons to trust in the technical or ethical-political competence of the manager in question – or from the simple recognition that what the manager is suggesting is valid. If employees do not agree, they will enter into moral, political-ethical and pragmatic discourses in order to resolve the issue. It will be understood that in the absence of any resolution, no obligation to comply can exist.

Market Citizenship

The normative authorization of managerial instructions from the perspective of the 'market citizenship' paradigm of the employment relationship is a question of the technical efficacy of the instruction. A command will deserve compliance to the extent that it contributes to the realization of the goals of the corporation, and employees will assume that managers are sincere in their claim that some plan or instruction is technically effective in this way. The employee makes the same advance of trust that would be made by the passer-by helping a doctor at the scene of an accident (see above, p.93). There is no pre-specification of what is and what it not an effective intervention to which the manager's instruction is compared. For this reason there is no possibility of ambiguities of interpretation. Beyond some minimum standard of plausibility rooted in cultural knowledge about work and employment – even the most flexible worker is unlikely to accept that extending the working day to sixteen hours is the best way to deal with a recruitment crisis – compliance with managerial instructions will be equated with effective coordinated action.

Despite their generalized willingness to comply, employees remain oriented to mutual understanding. They will therefore question instructions that, for whatever reason, seem unlikely to be effective. Since managers are also oriented to mutual understanding, in the face of such queries they will seek to enter into technical discourse to explain or clarify the issue. Managers will be open to any alternative propositions that are more effective, and will be willing to revise plans in the face of new information. Nonetheless, it remains their right to determine what the corporation ultimately requires from its employees. This cannot be negotiated. It may be the case that plans and strategies that are technically effective from the corporate perspective may impose costs on the employee that tip the balance against organization membership. In this case, the only option for the individual employee is to resign.

Pluralist Citizenship

In the context of the 'pluralist citizenship' paradigm of employment, managerial instructions are perceived as normatively authorized to the extent that they are coherent with the negotiated order of the corporation. In seeking to resolve any eventual problems of interpretation, managers and employees will be oriented to mutual understanding. What this means in practice is that it will not be automatically assumed that the problem arises from a conflict of interest. As Habermas puts it, bargaining 'becomes permissible and necessary when only particular – and no generalizable – interests are involved, something that ... can be tested only in moral discourses' (1996, p.167).

In cases where there are difficulties that genuinely cannot be resolved at the point at which they arise, the matter will be referred to joint worker-management representative structures at the appropriate level. If a manager issues an instruction about which there is some dispute or difficulty, then it is not appropriate for the employee to engage in an individual strategic negotiation of the scope of the manager's sovereignty with a view to establishing a mutually acceptable interpretation of the employment contract. The employee is connected to other employees via the society-wide workers' politicocultural reference community, and hence she has a duty to act from the perspective of the workers' interest rather than her own individual interest.

The belief that the characteristics of a system cannot be taken as *already* representing a valid order is characteristic of positive systemic worldviews. From this perspective, approaching the negotiation of an organizational order with a purely strategic attitude runs the risk of giving rise to outcomes that do not represent *fair* compromises. If one party's appreciation of the other's situation is founded on an extrapolation from aggregate historical information, but if that information reflects the functional characteristics of organizational systems that do not arise from fair compromises, then the result will be a distorted or inaccurate picture of that situation. This in turn will affect the range of settlements that participants will be willing to accept. The definition of a fair compromise, therefore, has to be based on an understanding of the other's situation *from their perspective*. This implies that the appropriate mode of bargaining is that which Walton and McKersie (1965) described as 'integrative' bargaining.

Legitimate Membership

The 'legitimate membership' paradigm predisposes those who adopt it to recognize as the substance of a managerial instruction a claim about the coherence of the instruction with the formal bureaucratic order of the corporation. Employees 'always already' accept that if an instruction is formally valid then it demands compliance in a quasi-categorical sense, because of the connection that is assumed between the rules of the organization and the effective pursuit of the socially valid imperatives of the market. The employment relationship is equated with 'carrying out the order of the organization' in a very direct sense. Any ambiguity or disagreement about the coherence of an instruction with the formal regulation of the organization will be referred to the next level of the bureaucratic hierarchy for resolution.

Bureaucratic Membership

The 'bureaucratic membership' paradigm is perhaps the most straightforward in the sense that the employment relationship is understood as a matter of compliance with managerial instructions to the minimum degree compatible with retaining membership in the corporation. The employee's interest in membership is seen as purely strategic and individual – simply a matter of necessity, without political significance – and hence the only rational course is to minimize the costs of membership. The minimum contribution likely to be possible is calculated via an assessment of historical patterns of compliance in the corporation. The rational structure of the decision to comply will follow that set out in the right-hand column of Table 4.1.

Pluralist Membership

As with the pluralist citizenship paradigm, the resolution of interactions from within the 'pluralist membership' paradigm depends on the conformity of management instructions with the negotiated order of the corporation. The latter is distinguishable from the former, however, by its emphasis on the strategic resolution of ambiguities of interpretation. The strategic interests in question are not those of the worker qua individual, but the collective interests of workers in general. Just as the individual strategic actor attempts to bridge the gap between rule and action by assessing the empirical probability of 'getting away with' a certain level of compliance, organized workers will try to establish what interpretation of a formally negotiated order is the best possible given the balance of power between themselves and management, and the outcomes of bargaining on other occasions. Since the organizational system is interpreted as meaningless and hence objective, the idea of a *fair* compromise makes little sense. Negotiation aims to secure the compromises that are empirically possible. In contrast to the pluralist citizenship paradigm, then, a distributive, competitive or adversarial approach to bargaining will appear to be the most appropriate.

Ethical Resistance

Those who understand the employment relationship as 'ethical resistance' are likely to believe that the management of the corporation is guilty of conduct that is morally or ethically wrong, or that it is clearly incompetent. The order of the corporation is either illegitimate and hence by definition ineffective, or ineffective and hence by definition illegitimate. Employees therefore have an ethical *duty* to resist the authority of management – insofar as this is possible given the sanctions managers have at their disposal – in the attempt to secure the more effective pursuit of the economic aims and values of the corporation and the society in which it operates. This duty of resistance will be tempered by the political-ethical imperative of maintaining the corporation in operation for the sake of those who depend on it. The decision to comply or not comply with an instruction depends on a negotiation in which the empirical power of management is weighed against the ethical values and interests of workers and the wider community that is dependent on the corporation.

Localized Resistance

The conception of the employment relationship as 'localized resistance' differs from the two other conflictual paradigms in the sense that management action is perceived neither as being related to conflict in wider society, nor as representing an injury to anyone other than the corporation's employees. Organized worker opposition, where it exists, will be directed only towards the corporation itself and will not be seen as part of a more generalized political struggle. Employment per se will not be conceived as an illegitimate social relationship, and conflict in the workplace is likely to be viewed as resolvable, at least in principle. While it will be seen as legitimate for workers to adopt an attitude of active resistance to managerial instructions should they so choose, this will be grounded on the concrete actions of managers within the corporation. The normal attitude of employees, however, is likely to be one of minimal compliance in order to secure the material benefits of membership in the corporation. Any tactics and strategies employees can use to maximize their returns and minimize their obligations, including cheating and fraud, will appear to be ethically and politically permissible. The option of 'exit' will be exercised where at all possible.

Class-Based Resistance

Where employment is conceived as 'class-based resistance', the relationship is at its most conflictual. Both the economic system and the structures of the corporation are perceived as illegitimate. From the perspective of the employee, the employer has no right to demand even those elements of contractual compliance that are entirely unambiguous. The notion of freedom of contract is an ideological fiction. The employee is merely compelled by her material need to enter into an entirely illegitimate relationship of subordination and will experience each instruction as a threat. For this reason, employees will not simply behave in the same way as those who have adopted the bureaucratic membership paradigm. Rather, responses will arise from the logic of active, principled opposition to management. From the perspective of this paradigm, the subordination to capital which is characteristic of wage labour will be interpreted as extending to employees as a class rather than being a localized phenomenon. Where worker organization exists, its ultimate rationale is likely to be the end of the economic and corporate systems as they currently exist. Soldaristic forms of industrial action – action which is not taken in pursuit of some grievance arising in the workplace – will be commonplace.

Enterprise Worldviews and Structural Models of the Employment System

In Chapter 6, we suggested that the method of the social sciences is not in fact counterintuitive, as Habermas suggests, but that the construction, use, evaluation and amendment of conceptual models based on the external observation of social systems is something common to all participants in social action. This is to say that ordinary actors possess an intuitive understanding of the systems within which they act, based on the worldview through which they interpret their lifeworld context. The range of structural models suggested below, then, simultaneously represents a typology of abstract academic conceptualizations of the enterprise and of possibilities for the interpretation of the enterprise in practice.

We should emphasize that the structural counterpart of a paradigm of the employment relationship is not simply a model of the corporation, but of the 'employment system': the corporation in its economic and institutional context. The term 'employment system' is not intended to carry any great theoretical weight, however. We do not wish to suggest that it represents something separate from the money and power systems. Rather it is simply a convenient means of referring to the structures in which the two systems that steer the employment relationship coincide. In principle, then, the term encompasses a large part of the institutional apparatus of capitalism, but we mean to refer more particularly to the labour market, employment law, the institutions of industrial relations and, of course, the pattern of internal regulation in enterprises. These components will appear to be more or less important depending on the structural model adopted.

A priori, we cannot say that any one structural model is more appropriate or accurate than any other. Given what we have already argued about the variability of systemic characteristics in the context of different approaches to social relationships within the system, it should be clear that the choice of a structural model for use in the social scientific analysis of systems depends on a proper understanding of the meanings of systemic relationships to those who participate in them. Arriving at such an understanding is not a straightforward process. There are two difficulties in particular that have to be taken into account.

The first is that, even aside from the variation in types of paradigm, every individual's understanding of the employment relationship is her own. As we argued above, the conception of the social role of employee is influenced by 'self-formative processes' that are by definition unique to each individual. Hence, it is impossible to have direct knowledge of all of the paradigms of the employment relationship that the many millions of participants in the employment system bring to the enterprises in which they work. The broad pattern of relationship paradigms must instead be inferred from whatever structural model best explains observed regularities in behaviour in the context of the systems that already exist. However, as Weber argued, these regularities are in themselves meaningless. Their interpretation is only possible on the basis of pre-existing assumptions about the relationships whose aggregated outcomes are the phenomena under observation.[2] The construction of structural models therefore depends on assumptions about the meaning of relationships that cannot be systematically supported with evidence directly derived from the life-experience of participants in social interaction. The less uniform and the less stable the pattern of adherence to paradigms among these participants, the more likely it will be that the

---

[2] We are assuming here that psychological or other types of determinism are not being practised, i.e., that the connection between action and outcome is conventional rather than necessary.

external observation of conjunctions or regularities – interpreted in the light of a single worldview, and this not necessarily the dominant one – will give rise to an inaccurate specification of the functional characteristics of the system in question.

The second problem is that worldviews change, both in the light of the experience of action within the system, and because of influences from outside it. In Chapter 6 we proposed a basic model for the production and reproduction of systemic worldviews that showed how the resolution of social interactions in systemic contexts feeds into the construction of structural models of systems, and how the observation of the functional characteristics of those systems in turn affects the resolution of social interactions. We also argued that this feedback process is open to influences from the wider lifeworld context. To put it more simply, change in worldviews can be prompted either by evidence about the system-level outcomes of action (for example the success or failure of particular managerial strategies or types of trade union action) or by developments in lifeworld contexts (for example changes in the acceptable types of subordination or standards of living).

Structural Models of the Employment System from the Perspective of the Enterprise Worldviews

This having been said, the essential stability of employment systems is such that it remains plausible to argue that certain broad patterns of adherence to paradigms of the employment relationship must exist. Depending what these patterns are thought to be, different structural approaches will appear to be more or less appropriate. The 'other side' of the attribution of a positive, meaningless or negative value status to systemic relationships is the conception of the system as loosely steered, tightly steered or dysfunctional. A loosely steered system is one in which system imperatives give a general direction to action, but where processes of consensus formation in language remain important. Compliance with system imperatives is a positive choice based on the continual assessment and reassessment of the substantive rationality of system outcomes. Non-compliance is regarded as a rational means to correct any system distortion that has arisen because the technical conditions for perfect system functioning do not obtain in practice. A tightly steered system is one in which close compliance with system imperatives is regarded as the only rational possibility. The technical conditions for perfect system functioning are thought to obtain, and hence system outcomes are legitimate – or at least, not illegitimate. A dysfunctional system is one in which system imperatives are regarded as illegitimate. Compliance is constrained or coerced. The system will be characterized by periodic crises and it is unlikely to remain stable in the long run. Dysfunctional systems could also be described as loosely steered, although obviously the derogation from system imperatives occurs for different reasons.

The interaction of the money and power systems, however, means that a range of different results is possible. There are three possibilities. First, a functional system, whether loosely or tightly steered, can stabilize a dysfunctional system. Second, a loosely steered functional system can 'lend' its positive value status to a tightly steered one, just as a dysfunctional system can lend its negative value status. Finally, where both systems are dysfunctional, they can nonetheless be mutually stabilizing. The brief descriptions of the structural models that follow are intended to give the reader a broad idea of the types of externalist approach to understanding action situations that are possible, and to show how these relate to the systemic worldviews. We do not pretend that they do justice to the range of academic and informal types of approach that are possible within each area. The structural models and the perceptions of the money and power systems to which they relate are summarized in Table 7.3.

Table 7.3 Structural models of the employment system

Market System	Organizational System		
	Positive	Meaningless	Negative
Positive	Historical and institutional economics	Classical bureaucracy	Community power struggle
Meaningless	'Soft' business school	'Hard' business school	Internal power struggle
Negative	Liberal pluralism	Industrial relations system	Class struggle

Institutional/Historical Economic Models

Where both the organizational and economic systems have a positive value status, structural models of an employment system will have the complex character of social-historical analysis. The accuracy of the prediction of the consequences of action will depend above all on an appreciation of the arguments for action that are likely to be convincing in the corporate context. A hermeneutic appreciation of the ethical and politicocultural self-understanding of the corporation and the society in which it operates will be combined with realistic economic and organizational models that take account of the social topography of valid aims, values and interests.

'Soft' Business School Models

The combination of an economic system that is seen as meaningless with an organizational system that is accorded a positive value status implies structural models that relate legitimizable relationships within the corporation to the successful pursuit of objectively-conceived economic goals. Positive outcomes in terms of market performance are explained by the existence of politicocultural value systems that legitimize technically effective patterns of behaviour. The validity of the organizational system is indistinguishable from its effectiveness in achieving market goals. Hence, market goals 'borrow' the positive validity status of the organizational system. In this sense, the market penetrates into the interior of the corporation and organization-specific imperatives disappear from view. However, since the market lacks any kind of inherent legitimacy, the positive value-status of the organizational system has to be 'artificially' maintained. The task of professional managers is to ensure that employees will regard as valid whatever behaviour is technically effective.

This is achieved by the active 'management' of corporate culture and values. Thus, the employment system is grasped via a combination of 'hard', objectivistic models of the market and 'softer' psychological, sociological or ethnographic models of human interaction.

Liberal Pluralist Models

The model of the employment system implied by the interaction of a negatively-viewed economic system and a positive organizational system is similar to the Madisonian model of pluralist politics. The organizational system exists to resolve the inevitable conflicts of interest that arise in the economic system, which would otherwise be dysfunctional. The connection between action and outcome depends on the instutionalized mechanisms of negotiation and conflict resolution both within and beyond the corporation. These in turn will vary depending on substantive social and cultural expectations of what an employment relationship which is fair to both employer and employee entails in terms of organizational forms and structures, levels of pay and terms and conditions, job design, and so forth. Accurate models of the employment system will involve an appreciation of the possible organizational configurations that are compatible with sociocultural conceptions of fairness while at the same time representing an appropriate response to the economic imperatives facing the corporation.

Classical Bureaucratic Models

A positively-conceived economic system will infuse otherwise meaningless organizational structures with purpose. The generalizable aims and values of the market endow bureaucratic regulation with legitimacy, replacing the non-generalizable interests of individuals, the pursuit of which would otherwise be the only motivation for action. Detailed economic imperatives disappear from view, hidden behind the formal regulation of the corporation, which is assumed to embody an accurate definition of technical effectiveness and, hence, to enshrine the corporation's aims and values. Successful outcomes will depend directly on the effectiveness and efficiency of the bureaucratic regulation in place. Structural models of the employment system are dominated by conceptions of administrative efficiency and regulatory good practice.

'Hard' Business School Models

Where both the economic and organizational systems are interpreted as meaningless, the employment system will be conceived as tightly steered but highly complex. The attitudes and action orientations of individual participants will be categorized as epiphenomenal. Outcomes of action in the employment system will be regarded as depending on the interaction of multiple economic and organizational variables: financial and non-financial incentives, organization structures and processes, product and labour market structures, government economic and industrial policies, technology, and potentially many more.

Industrial Relations System Models

The interaction of an economic system with a negative value status and a meaningless organizational system will give rise to an employment system conceived as a system of industrial relations. The organizational system exists to resolve conflict in the economic system, but in so doing, brings that conflict into the corporation. The negotiated rules that specify the formal order of the corporation are premised on the assumption that the employment relationship is about the resolution of conflict. Models of the employment system will centre on hypothesized causal relationships between institutional processes for conflict resolution – industrial relations machinery, trade unions and employers' organizations, labour law, etc. – and economic outcomes at the level of the corporation and the economy: productivity levels, earnings growth, inflation, the balance of trade and so on.

Community Power Struggle Models

Just as a positive organizational system can stabilize an economic system with a negative value status, the imperatives of a valid economic system can stabilize a negatively-perceived organizational system. Employees will tolerate illegitimate forms of subordination as long as in so doing their material well-being and that of the community is assured. However, the forms of subordination that are tolerable, and therefore the probability of active resistance to management, will depend both on the politicocultural self-understanding of the community and on the (perceived) possibility of reforming the governance of the corporation while maintaining its economic viability. Models of the employment system will combine economic and business analysis with hermeneutic interpretations of the ethical and political perspectives of employees and the community in which they live in order to assess the likelihood of system stability, successful governance reform or deterioration into open conflict.

Internal Power Struggle Models

When a negatively-perceived organizational system interacts with a meaningless economic system, the result is an employment system in which individual material need stabilizes a corporate order that workers would otherwise abandon. At the same time, the market imperatives that structure the internal organization of the corporation take on an oppressive aspect. The key variables in the prediction of the outcomes of action are the corporation's market environment on the one hand, and on the other, individual subjective perceptions of subordination and the possibility of resistance.

Class Struggle Models

If both the economic system and the organization itself have a negative value status, then corporation and economy are likely to be perceived as mutually supporting. The illegitimate order of the corporation exists to ensure that the illegitimate social distribution of wealth and power can be maintained. At the same time, the illegitimate distribution of wealth means that employees have no choice but to tolerate their illegitimate subordination in the corporation. Models of the employment system will focus on the tension between economic and organizational steering imperatives and employee resistance. The principal question is whether, and if so how and when employee resistance will give rise to system crises. Important variables will be the degree of class consciousness and organization, the nature of the labour process, and the stage of development of capitalist economic organization.

Conclusion

In this penultimate chapter we have argued that the interaction of interpretations of economic and organizational systems gives rise to enterprise worldviews. Since there are three possible interpretations of each system, there are nine possible enterprise worldviews, within which nine paradigms of the employment relationship correspond to nine structural models of the employment system. Each enterprise worldview represents an internally coherent portrait of the corporation in its market context that gives a direction to action by permitting actors to grasp the pragmatic and normative significance of corporate organization. From the external perspective, no one worldview can be said to be more 'true' than another since all are logically possible explanations of social behaviour that are adequate both at the action and system levels. There is no a priori theoretical reason to choose to adopt one enterprise worldview over another.

This having been said, it remains the case that there may be both pragmatic and normative reasons to prefer a particular worldview. As we argued in Chapter 6, although worldviews are not in themselves susceptible to judgements of truth or falsity, they allow the inference of statements that are. For this reason, worldviews can be compared according to the criterion of cognitive adequacy. We saw in Chapter 2, for example, how the corporate theory of society – which we would suggest falls into the category of 'market community' worldviews – has been roundly criticized precisely because many of the claims that its exponents make about the world are simply not compatible with the empirical evidence.

As we have emphasized throughout this book, empirical statements about social systems are necessarily also statements about the de facto validity of norms, values and conventions. Hence, to argue that a systemic worldview is cognitively inadequate in an empirical sense is also to argue that it represents an inaccurate picture of the politicocultural self-understanding of participants in action. The other side of this particular coin is the fact that the adoption of structural models of the employment system and paradigms of the employment relationship that are coherent with a legitimizable interpretation of 'who we are' is likely to permit the inference of cognitively adequate statements about corporations that can feed into the pragmatic discourses in which coordinated social action is planned. Successful coordinated action will in turn tend to reinforce the legitimacy of the self-understanding on which it is premised. In our final chapter, we will consider in some more detail the practical and political implications of this normative approach to social and economic theory.

Chapter 8

Repoliticizing Management

According to the definition of legitimacy that we have proposed, most corporate action is not legitimate. This would explain why signs of a legitimacy crisis are currently manifest in the social and cultural spheres (Parker, 2003). Despite this, it seems unlikely that the employment system will collapse any time soon. Most people, most of the time remain willing to participate in economic and organizational systems as consumers and employees. The political and ethical unease that is the result of participating in social systems that are not grounded in valid norms is clearly insufficient to destabilize national and international structures of production, distribution and exchange from the inside.

It ought not to be surprising, then, that the ideological leadership of the current wave of anti-capitalist protest is located outside the mainstream of industrial and consumer society. Whereas protests against capitalism have historically come from within the system – articulated by organized workers – the strongest contemporary dissenting voices come from outside it: from groups who are 'excluded', whether economically, socially, politically or geographically, and from non-government organizations (NGOs) which are not dependent on any particular political, economic or corporate structures. Thus at the forefront of the protest movement we find organizations of the unemployed, groups that support 'anti-consumerist' or ecologically-aware lifestyles, political parties of the far left, workers' and peasants' movements from the developing world, as well as NGOs involved in aid, development, fair trade and other anti-poverty activities.

While the kind of grand historical and cultural analysis that would properly illuminate this situation is beyond the scope of this book – and beyond the talents of its author – we might at least tentatively observe that the great social cleavage of the 19th and 20th centuries, that between the owners of capital and those obliged to sell their labour to survive, has been replaced by a division between global capitalism's 'insiders' and 'outsiders'. While it is increasingly common to refer to this new cleavage as that separating the global North and South, this spatial terminology is not only geographically dubious, but also fails to capture the presence of socio-economic exclusion and opposition to the system in 'the North', as well as support for it in 'the South'.

We can define global capitalism's insiders as those who adhere to the corporate theory of society, which we have also described as the market community worldview. Logically, then, the outsiders are those who do not accept the validity of this worldview; who argue that another world is possible. Exactly what this other world might look like is less easy to establish. One thing at least that has become clear over the past thirty years is that the answer to Slichter's question – 'how to prevent our ideals, our scales of values, from being too much affected by the standards of the market-place' – is not to be found in either of the two historically significant alternatives to the corporate theory of society: the Soviet-style planned economy and the social democratic welfare state. Neither abandoning economic markets altogether, nor conceiving them as the embodiment of society's economic interest, against which it is necessary to apply the counterweight of a social interest articulated by organized workers, have proven to be durable solutions. Insiders and outsiders appear to agree that production for profit and international trade are generally seen as the only viable, long-term routes out of poverty. Global capitalism may be the problem, but it also seems to be the solution.

One might reasonably ask, then, whether the problem of the corporate legitimacy deficit is really that serious. There are two perspectives from which this question needs to be addressed. On the one hand, we can try to assess how likely it is that the legitimacy crisis will develop into an internal system crisis in the future, that is, whether some kind of corrective action will be forced upon us because the employment system has ceased to fulfil its essential functions. On the other, we can consider whether the magnitude of the concrete social and environmental problems caused by global capitalism is such as to demand that we take action, regardless of the presence or absence of system crises. If we can assume that this is indeed the case, the overall issue becomes the capacity of the employment system to react to problems that arise outside it.

Internal System Crises: The Lessons of the 1970s and 1980s

The partisans of the corporate theory of society – governments, mainstream political parties and the experts of the economic-industrial-advisory complex – have stood firm in their adherence to it, despite the arguments of anti-globalization and environmental campaigners. In truth, there has been no pressing need for a change of perspective because the current crisis of corporate legitimacy is not an internal system crisis. As Habermas recently put it, the majority of those who work in politics 'manifestly recognize themselves in Luhmann's description of the political system, which is to say a mechanism for providing the strategic responses best adapted to the environment of voters' choices' (2005, my translation). Other things being equal, until that environment demands stabilizing action, it is unlikely that there will be any fundamental change in the policy perspective.

We can state the conditions for the existence of such an internal system crisis in the terms we have been using to talk about systemic worldviews. An internal crisis will arise when the different types of knowledge that make up the components of a worldview no longer possess some minimum degree of mutual coherence. We can illustrate this process with reference to the events of the twentieth century's third major crisis of corporate legitimacy, as these were played out in the United Kingdom.

In Britain in the 1960s, there was a broad economic and industrial relations policy consensus that we can locate somewhere between the pluralist community and bureaucratic pluralism worldviews, probably rather closer to the latter. Thinking about management and employment was dominated by the assumption that there was an inevitable conflict of economic interest between capital and labour, but that this conflict could be resolved in practice as long as the terms of the employment relationship – the organizational order – were negotiated between management and trade unions. System equilibrium or homeostasis was conceived as an appropriate balance between the economic imperatives carried or transmitted by the market and the social imperatives carried by organized labour. It was widely assumed that full employment and real year-on-year increases in standards of living were compatible with a competitive and profitable economy.

At some point during the second half of the 1950s, signs that suggested this equilibrium was not being achieved had started to appear. Perhaps the most concrete of these signs was the poor performance of the British economy relative to its competitors, especially the Federal Republic of Germany (Davies and Freedland, 1993, p.137). A perception arose that, between them, employers and trade unions were failing to put in place the industrial modernization that was required to maintain the capacity of British industry to compete in world markets.[1] Over the course of the 1960s and 1970s, government policy on economics, business and industrial relations focused on the design of interventions to encourage or even to force the system into the socio-economic equilibrium it was proving so difficult to arrive at spontaneously. While these interventions initially arose from a pluralist worldview that was evidently shared by all the main players in politics and industry, in the late 1960s the policy consensus began to fragment. This fragmentation was manifest in the appearance of arguments that, instead of blaming the failure of policy interventions on their technical inadequacy, accused one or other side of industry of misunderstanding its proper role or of putting the realization of partial interests ahead of an achievable compromise. During the 1970s, the evidence that neither the social imperatives of labour nor the economic imperatives of capital were being met continued to accumulate. It seemed increasingly clear that the socio-economic balance that ought to have been possible could not be achieved. Opinions polarized. The path proposed by contemporary 'insider' experts, in effect the adoption of the pluralist community worldview, was laughably implausible because it assumed that a high level of trust between management and workers could be achieved. The trade unions and the left wing of the Labour Party moved towards a class conflict worldview. They argued that it had been demonstrated over the previous two decades that employers and managers were incapable of accepting the legitimate aspirations of workers and of organizing production so that they could be met. Their alternative proposal was a complex system of economic planning and workers' vetoes over management decision-making. The Conservative Party set off in the direction of market bureaucracy, arguing that in the final analysis the imperatives of the economy were more important than the immediate interests of employees and that if employees and unions were not prepared to accept

---

[1] It is interesting to note in the light of Martin Parker's comments on the current crisis of corporate legitimacy (see above, p.9) that the later 1950s was also characterized by cultural manifestations of discontent with the system, for example the Boulting brothers 1959 movie 'I'm Alright Jack' in which both intransigent trade union officers and incompetent managers are ruthlessly satirized.

that then too bad. They were encouraged in this journey by neoclassical economic theory, which had arrived from the USA in the early 1970s. Aside from its undoubted political convenience – a respectable theory that deems the economic interests of some of a political party's most important supporters to be the only ones that count is not to be passed up lightly – neoclassical economics was rather more appealing from what Habermas calls the 'quasiaesthetic and truth-independent standpoints of coherence, depth, economy [and] completeness' (1987, p.58). Beside the technically complex and bureaucratic mode of government intervention that had been dominant since the 1960s, the prescriptions of free market economics were simple and elegant. They made for a straightforward political message, unified policy and a clear break with the failures of the past. The public was convinced, and in 1979 Margaret Thatcher's Conservative Party won the general election. After it had become clear that a return to high levels of unionization was unlikely, the harder-edged market bureaucracy worldview largely gave way to the market community perspective. The Labour Party abandoned its quasi-marxist policies of the early 1980s, distanced itself from the trade union movement – association with which was no longer thought to be an electoral asset – and the corporate theory of society gradually emerged as the new policy consensus.

The most important thing to note about this series of events is that the shift in the policy consensus was prompted by the unequivocal cognitive inadequacy of the pluralist worldview. To use Habermas's terms, in the pluralist language system, too few true statements about how to achieve economic success were possible. The theoretically possible outcomes were not being achieved in practice, and that this was the case could not be missed or glossed over. Almost as important was the existence of a plausible alternative location for policy. The 'New Right' offered a worldview that not only appeared to have the potential to produce effective policies but whose post-patrician, anti-system populism had a definite cultural resonance.

The Magnetism of the Meaningless Market

It is at least arguable that the resolution of the system crisis of the 1970s is still valid; that all that is required to resolve the current crisis of corporate legitimacy is some fine-tuning of the existing system via piecemeal reform. Indeed, this is the message of virtually every mainstream political party in the democratic-capitalist world, regardless of their supposed orientation on the traditional left-right spectrum. In the aftermath of the race to the centre that has characterized national politics in recent years, particularly in Europe, distinguishing any genuine difference between socialist and conservative party approaches to economic and business policy is virtually impossible. The almost universal assumption seems to be that the existing system may have some problems, but that it is fundamentally justifiable and requires no major modification. We might even go so far as to say that the corporate theory of society is the working social theory of government all across the developed world. The market community worldview appears to be the dominant perspective among those who make the rules of economic and political life.

We need to be cautious about drawing any conclusions from this apparent unanimity on the issue of change, however. The breadth of agreement in politics and business about how to organize economy and society is certainly less a reflection of widespread *positive* commitment to the dominant socio-economic model than of widespread difficulty in conceiving a viable alternative. This difficulty in turn makes it very hard to calculate the balance of advantage between modest and radical reform. Even in the face of urgent political and ethical problems, it would be a brave politician or manager who would attempt a resolution whose cost could not be calculated in advance. At the same time, the level of unease with global capitalism is sufficient to make a strong normative stand in support of its structures politically hazardous. To say that we will carry on with the existing system because it is just and worthy of support implies an acceptance of responsibility for all of its outcomes, negative as well as positive. Rather easier to defend in the face of disquiet about system outcomes is the argument that the system is as it is and that there is little or nothing we can do to change it.

This externalist argument has its action-level counterpart. As we argued in Chapter 6, the inherent interpretive commitment involved in deeming social relationships meaningless is no less than that involved in deeming them meaningful. However, in practice, the argument that the system is nobody's responsibility and that it cannot be changed provides a resolution of the unease of system participants which, while less effective in principle than reforms that would permit a genuine legitimation of the system, has the enormous advantage of not requiring radical social and economic change – change that is likely to alter the existing distribution of relative advantage in an unpredictable way.

The market community worldview is politically attractive not simply because the conception of the economy as a quasi-natural, non-normative force helps to resolve ethical difficulties, but also because it holds out the possibility of legitimate social relationships in the workplace without infringing the existing prerogatives of management. The conception of management as a technical profession – made possible precisely because of the objectivistic conception of the economy – allows the resolution of the contradiction between the presumption that social action should be democratically coordinated and the absence of democratic processes in the governance of the workplace. Just as accepting the authority of a doctor at the scene of an accident does not violate the rational autonomy of the passer-by, from the perspective of the market community worldview, accepting the authority of management does not violate the rational autonomy of employees.

Is Another Internal System Crisis Possible?

Given the degree to which the market community worldview explains and justifies existing economic relationships and prerogatives, and the absence of a competing vision, it seems highly unlikely that there will be any significant policy innovation unless there are urgent problems that need to be addressed. However, it also seems unlikely that an internal system crisis such as that which caused the urgent problems of the 1970s will occur again in the foreseeable future. There are a number of reasons to believe that this is the case. First, from the perspective of the market community worldview, the corporation has no goals other than market goals. The kinds of aims and values that could be qualified as 'non-economic' can be pursued only subject to their not conflicting with economic objectives. Neither can they be conceived as goals that have any validity beyond the boundaries of the corporation. Solidarity is confined within the organization. Thus the steering imperatives of the power medium cannot conflict with those of the money medium. This in itself does not rule out the possibility of an internal system crisis, but it certainly makes it easier to avoid.

The second reason is that corporations and governments have become very good at responding to economic imperatives. The degree of stability of the world macro-economy is arguably unprecedented. Even events that would historically be classed as catastrophic economic shocks now seem to have relatively little impact.[2] This improvement in the capacity for economic management is partly a question of old-fashioned learning, but may also owe something to the 'embodiment' of economic knowledge that we mentioned in Chapter 2. The greater the degree to which economic decision-making is based on computer models that all use essentially the same mathematical algorithms, the more closely economic behaviour will conform to these models, and the greater the possibility that rational expectations will be in line with actual outcomes.

The third reason that an internal system crisis is unlikely is that the problems that have given rise to the current crisis of corporate legitimacy are external to the system. The damaging environmental and community impact of production and consumption; the social and cultural impact of advertising and marketing campaigns; the degradation of the democratic process as a result of corporate political lobbying; the ineffectiveness of consumer protection; poor labour standards; unfair trade or the exploitative conduct of relationships with suppliers: none of these political-ethical transgressions will have an effect on corporate action unless (i) they are so serious as to lead to violations of existing legislation, or (ii) the 'reputational damage' that corporations suffer as a result of being held responsible for them is translated into consumer boycotts or other directly economic forms of action. Between action that could arguably be deemed blameworthy and action that has legal or economic consequences sufficient to alter corporate behaviour, there is a very wide area in which valid values and interests, and even moral norms, can be ignored with impunity because they have no impact on 'the bottom line'.

There is perhaps a fourth reason, and we say 'perhaps' because it is not strictly speaking anything to do with the system itself. We can assume that the measures taken to avoid a system crisis will be proportional to what is perceived to be at stake should such a crisis occur. The Thatcher government in the UK, for example, simply abandoned any attempt to shore up the pluralist employment system because it was sufficiently confident that there was a viable alternative to put in its place. From the perspective of the market community and market bureaucracy worldviews, there were many plausible steps that could be taken to resolve the economic crisis that had not yet

---

[2] Perhaps the most striking example is the rise in the price of crude oil from just over $30 per barrel at the beginning of 2004 to almost $60 per barrel eighteen months later.

been tried because they were not available from pluralist perspectives. At present, however, only one of the nine possible worldviews is 'untried' and hence the source of genuinely innovative policy solutions. We can discount the class conflict worldview as it implies the abandonment of markets altogether. The other two conflictual worldviews are obviously not likely to provide politically saleable policy solutions. The pluralist worldviews have been too recently discredited, and the bureaucratic community worldview, which we might characterize as the traditional IBM model, is equally out of favour. If we also discount the currently-dominant corporate theory of society (the market community worldview), and the similar but harder-edged market bureaucracy worldview, then we are left only with the legitimate community worldview as a source of untried policy solutions. The principal innovation that this worldview implies is, of course, industrial and economic democracy. At present, there are no mainstream political parties in the developed world that would support such a policy. Needless to say, neither are there any major corporations that would be willing to accord their employees democratic rights that would interfere with management's existing prerogatives. Thus, there is a very strong incentive for those who are in a position to take the measures required to ensure that a system crisis is not allowed to arise.

Dealing With Problems External to the System

To borrow Altman's phraseology, managers who have accepted the systemic logic of the position accorded them by the corporate theory of society will not 'incorporate into their objective function' the cost of the social, cultural and environmental externalities of corporate action. For this reason, although the problems caused by the employment system will not provoke a system crisis, neither can they be solved via systemic mechanisms. Nevertheless, it would be folly to assume that simply because these problems do not appear on the corporate radar they can safely be ignored, even in the short term. Two solutions are commonly proposed: legal regulation and voluntary self-regulation.

As we noted earlier, Habermas argues that if 'normatively substantive messages' can be translated into an appropriate legal code, then they become comprehensible and hence effective in systemic contexts. Certainly, legislation that aims to prevent certain types of externality can be an effective tool in some circumstances, but there is clearly a limit to what can be achieved via formal regulation. Corporations may take a minimalist or strategic attitude to compliance, particularly where penalties are merely financial. There are also areas in which legislation is almost impossible to design. How, for example, does one legally define cultural degradation? Perhaps most important, the multinational status of the world's largest corporations means that effective regulation has either to be enacted on the international level, or has to be coordinated across nation states. However, as Habermas himself has recently pointed out (2005) with respect to the European Union, international political opinion- and will-formation is extremely difficult to achieve. In the absence of a political project, and even in the relatively rare cases where a problem can be defined so that it is universally recognised as such, international regulation almost inevitably becomes a question of what is expedient rather than what is just or effective.

Voluntary self-regulation via CSR policies and programmes ought in principle to involve corporations consciously accepting that their decisions about action will take non-system norms and values into account. Yet, from the perspective of the two market worldviews, the idea that this might make a difference to decision-making simply makes no sense. These worldviews do not support the idea that there can be a difference between system imperatives and what ought to be done in a substantive normative sense. This perhaps explains why, for the corporate advocates of voluntary self-regulation, the 'ought' in 'corporations ought to be socially responsible' is hypothetical: from the perspective of the corporate theory of society, the only possible case for voluntary CSR initiatives is a *business* case.

We have arrived, then, at a situation in which 'the debate has become locked in a clash between 'reformists' and 'regulators' – those who believe that progressive reform can be achieved through winning the business-case for CSR against those who believe that companies will not improve their ethical performance across the board until new regulatory systems are in place' (New Economics Foundation, 2005). Neither of these positions is adequate. Although legal regulation is a tool that cannot be dispensed with, it is suitable only in the case of 'broad brush' measures. There is a very high risk that more complex normative messages will be inaccurately translated into systemic incentives. As for the reformist solution, if we assume that the corporate theory of society remains the dominant worldview, then it is simply not a solution. As long as the case for CSR is thought to be a business case, there is no possibility of any significant change in corporate behaviour.

Legitimate Corporate Action: Bringing Non-Market Aims Back Into the Picture

Simple logic suggests that the corporate theory of society cannot be 'cognitively adequate' if the social and environmental damage caused by capitalism is as serious as the anti-globalization campaigners suggest. It cannot be true that most corporate actions, most of the time, are just and worthy of support if the result is, for example, obesity in the developed world and malnutrition elsewhere; or climate change that threatens most seriously the way of life of those who have least part in causing it. However, the reverse is also true: if corporate actions *are* legitimate, then social and environmental externalities cannot be sufficiently serious to pose a real threat. Hence, the dominance of the market community worldview has a significant cognitive impact that prejudices the ability of actors to evaluate the case against capitalism. The presumption of legitimacy that arises from the ubiquity of social institutions and practices that are products of the corporate theory of society will promote scepticism about the scale of the problems caused by, but external to, the employment system.

To the extent that non-system problems are perceptible at all from the perspective of the market worldviews, and to the extent that they are seen to be the result of capitalist economic organization, they will appear to be no-one's *responsibility*. Yet, the market is made up of the decisions of human beings and in the final analysis its imperatives are contingent, not necessary. To believe that economic actors cannot and should not be held responsible for their actions is to abandon any possibility of change. It is evident, then, that the problems caused by the employment system cannot be addressed effectively while the market community and market bureaucracy worldviews remain dominant.

The principal argument we have made in this book is that there is a coherent alternative to the objectivistic conception of the market in the shape of the 'legitimate community' enterprise worldview. We have argued that, under ideal circumstances, social systems can transmit valid norms, principles and values. Both the organizational system and the economic system can have a positive value status. Where this is the case, compliance with system imperatives cannot lead to problems outside the system since, by definition, systemic action is substantively legitimate – valid beyond the system as well as within it. However, we have also argued that the circumstances under which systemic action takes place are rarely if ever ideal, and that non-ideal circumstances can be recognized by actors who are oriented to mutual understanding. Actors can subsequently respond to system imperatives in such a way as to compensate for the distortion to the system caused by unfair exchanges and ineffective authority relationships. In so doing, they contribute to the functional maintenance of the system as well as to the prevention of external problems.

From the perspective of the legitimate community worldview, the employment system is not the only relevant environment for decision-making, but merely an imperfect tool that exists to realize a political-ethical vision. That the system is imperfect need not be an insurmountable problem as long as this vision is used as a regulatory ideal for action in the market and within corporations. The concept of CSR makes considerably more sense in this context because the market is conceived as politically and ethically fallible. Thus, the suggestion that there may be a difference between what the market or the employment system demands and what ought to be done appears entirely plausible. Rather than adopting a purely strategic approach, the socially responsible corporation will ground decisions about action on a *normatively regulated interpretation* of systemic imperatives. In this way, any potential social, cultural or environmental problems related to corporate action will fall within the normal terms of reference for decision-making.

Envisaging an Ethical Capitalism

It is not easy to imagine how such a legitimate, ethical capitalism would operate, but a good indication of what might be possible is to be found in the work of institutional, ecological and other heterodox economists. A comprehensive overview is beyond the scope of this book, but we can at least give a brief example of the kind of expanded system analysis that is typical of these fields. In a recent paper discussing the concept of the steady state economy, Philip Lawn (2005) argues that orthodox economics entirely neglects the physical aspects of the economic process. The conventional circular flow model represents the macroeconomy as an isolated system with no inflows of resources or outflows of wastes. 'In this model, the exchange value embodied in human-made goods flows from firms to households and is called the Gross Domestic Product (GDP). An equal value flows back to firms from households

and is called the national income'. The exclusion of physical transformation processes
from this model means that 'it is erroneously believed that what is true of the abstract
system that measures the exchange value of physical goods is also true of physical
goods themselves (i.e. physical goods have the ability to circulate independently of the
natural environment)' (p.211). Thus, the biophysical limits of economic growth – the
ability of the Earth to support resource extraction and to process waste – are
completely ignored. Similarly, economic welfare is measured purely in terms of the
exchange value of consumption goods. Lawn argues that the conventional model of
the macroeconomy should be substituted with what he calls a linear throughput model
in which 'psychic welfare' and the net cost of the utilization of natural resources are
integral factors. This move would focus attention on two crucial questions that are
generally ignored: 'How big can the macroeconomy grow before the throughput of
matter-energy required to maintain it can no longer be ecologically sustained?' (p.214)
and 'How big should the macroeconomic subsystem grow before economic welfare
begins to decline and growth itself becomes uneconomic?' (pp.214-5). Asking these
sorts of questions has led to the development of alternative indices of economic
progress such as the Index of Sustainable Economic Welfare (ISEW).[3] Proposed as a
'green' alternative to GDP, the ISEW demonstrates that between 1950 and 1995,
sustainable welfare in the major western economies increased along with GDP up to
the 1970s or early 1980s, at which point it began a downward trend even though GDP
continued to grow (p.219). As Lawn puts it, this result represents 'a strong suggestion
that the macroeconomies of many developed nations have grown beyond their optimal
scale' (p.218).

   Lawn also provides a highly plausible rebuttal of the argument that putting limits
on economic growth will prevent the market economy from delivering the social and
political benefits that are its *raison d'être*. The argument is too lengthy to rehearse in
its entirety, but its essence is that the critics' mistake is to assume that a steady state
economy is a static system in which the composition of output is fixed. There is,
however, no reason at all why the existence of a constant physical quantity of human-
made capital should prevent us from 'improving both the quality of goods we produce
and the manner in which we organize ourselves in the course of producing them…
This allows for a more rapid rate of profit growth and the expansion of investment
opportunities' (p.223).

   What Lawn's paper demonstrates is that by including non-financial variables in the
structural model of the economic system, an entirely different interpretation of system
imperatives can emerge even though the fundamental aspects of the capitalist
economy – production for profit, and the pricing and distribution of goods via free

---

[3] The ISEW is a monetary index that is derived by weighting private consumption expenditure
according to a range of other indicators that are proxies for the general state of social welfare.
Expenditure is weighted upwards or downwards in line with an index of distributional equality,
and then inflated or discounted to take account of, for example, the services yielded by transport
networks, the services provided by volunteer work, public expenditure on health and education,
the cost of noise pollution, the cost of crime, the cost of family breakdown, the cost of ozone
depletion, the cost of logged old-growth forest and so forth (Lawn, 2005, p.218).

markets – are retained. While the work of heterodox economics seems to be confined principally to questions of macroeconomics, there is no reason why the kinds of social and environmental priorities reflected in the ISEW could not also inform corporate decisions about production and investment. The role of management would thus be refocused away from the maximization of purely financial performance indicators like profits, price-earnings ratios or market share, towards the pursuit of coherent sets of substantively valid aims and values.

Of course, even if this were to occur, there would still be no guarantee that social and environmental problems would be adequately addressed. The members of corporations are human, and they can and will make honest mistakes, whether in the course of their opinion- and will-formation or in translating that will into action. Unfortunately, we must also allow that they might lie, cheat or steal, whether for individual or collective advantage. Nevertheless, what they cannot do is to push the blame for their actions onto the market. From the perspective of the legitimate community worldview, the employment system is not an external constraint on action. It does not absolve corporate actors from taking responsibility for *all* of the results of their decisions. The discourse principle implies that corporations have an obligation to take into account the repercussions of their actions not just within the system but also beyond it. Thus, the adoption of the legitimate community worldview would mean that corporate action was self-policing. It would be subject to the same internal normative control system that prevents most individuals most of the time from violating valid legal and informal norms of behaviour, even in cases where no sanction would follow.

The Political and Structural Conditions for Corporate Legitimacy: Free Markets and Workplace Democracy

As we have seen, systemic worldviews are circles of inference in which the different components both imply and are implied by each other. From the perspective of the market community worldview, the defining assumptions of the meaningless economic system and the positively-valued organizational system imply that the achievement of socially responsible or legitimate corporate action requires nothing more than careful attention to market imperatives and a degree of mutual respect in the workplace. CSR initiatives make sense only as post hoc explanations of how corporate action is already legitimate. Hence, if social and environmental performance is successfully and permanently to replace market performance as the dominant value of the corporation, it is not enough simply to add CSR to the existing list of corporate priorities. Rather, it has to be implemented as part of an entirely different approach to corporate action, supported by the structural components of the legitimate community worldview that it implies and by which it is implied. Since action in the employment system is steered by both money and power, the most important structural conditions for CSR or corporate legitimacy are fair market prices and effective structures of authority.

In this book, we have tried to construct working definitions of fairness and effectiveness using Habermas's concepts and categories. Our goal has been to show that his arguments are applicable in the sphere of corporate action. For our purposes, perhaps the most important of these arguments is that there is a necessary connection between the rule of law and deliberative or discursive forms of democracy:

> the permission for legal coercion must be traced back to the expectation of legitimacy connected with the decisions of the legislature. The positivity of law is bound up with the promise that democratic processes of lawmaking justify the presumption that enacted norms are rationally acceptable... Enacted law cannot secure the bases of its legitimacy simply through legality, which leaves attitudes and motives up to the addressees... without religious or metaphysical support, the coercive law tailored for the self-interested use of individual rights can preserve its socially integrating force only insofar as the addressees of legal norms may at the same time understand themselves, taken as a whole, as the rational *authors* of those norms (Habermas, 1996, p.33; emphasis in original).

For Habermas, the process of rational authorship cannot be other than a deliberative democratic one, since if the point is to arrive at valid consensuses, the logical principles of formal pragmatics dictate that 'reasonable or fair results are obtained insofar as the flow of relevant information and its proper handling have not been obstructed' (1996, p.296). *Any* restriction on the right or capacity of individuals to have their voice heard will represent such an obstruction. Hence, the answer to Weber's 'what should we do?' 'no longer resides in universal human rights, or in the ethical substance of a specific community, but in the rules of discourse and forms of argumentation that borrow their normative content from the validity basis of action oriented to reaching understanding' (ibid.).

Free Markets

The agreement of an exchange-value is clearly not a deliberative process, but Habermas accepts that negotiated compromises do not 'snap the discursive chain of rational will-formation' as long as 'the procedural conditions under which actual compromises enjoy the presumption of fairness [can] be justified in moral discourses' (1996, pp.166-7). We have argued that in the economic sphere, the procedural conditions that ensure fair compromises are coterminous with the technical conditions for perfect competition. A fair distribution of commodities cannot be defined in any absolute or enduring substantive sense, but depends for its realization on the strategic action of participants in the context of an institutional structure constructed so as to ensure that the technical economic conditions for perfect competition apply. The market is built up from, and ought accurately to reflect, the material values and interests of market actors. The legal structures that regulate the conduct of exchanges exist to guarantee the accuracy of that reflection. From the perspective of the individual economic actor, fair markets indicate the range of possibilities for aligning his strategic interests with those of all the other participants. In this sense, market action cannot be conceived as the result of coercion based on material need. A fair market resolves the apparent contradiction between private and public autonomy in the economic sphere because it guarantees that the outcome of any individual's strategic action will not represent a net cost to any other.

However, there is an important qualification to be made to this argument, which reflects Habermas's insistence that the procedural conditions for fairness have to be substantively justifiable. If it can be shown that the economic system is not producing fair outcomes, then corrective action will have to be taken. It can never blindly be assumed that the conditions for perfect competition are met in practice, no matter how sophisticated and refined the regulatory structures that exist to ensure that they are. Markets exist to ensure the fair distribution of commodities, but fairness cannot be defined with reference to the market system itself. It is, rather, a judgement that can only be made with reference to the politicocultural self-understanding of the community in which economic action takes place.

If we can assume that the contemporary distribution of commodities does not in fact meet any reasonable criteria of fairness, then corrective action should come high up the political agenda. In principle, free trade prevents excessive profits and ensures that the distribution of commodities is fair. However, the fair distribution of commodities is only a possible outcome if market prices are fair to begin with. But market prices will be fair only if the distribution of commodities is fair. To break into this circle, it is arguably not enough for the participants in exchange themselves to take action. For the vast majority of consumer goods, there is no explicit negotiation of price and no possibility of agreeing different prices for the same goods depending on the relative situation of buyer and seller. A rather more practical solution is for measures to be taken directly to limit differences in wealth and income.

Although the medium of exchange is money, the relative material needs, preferences and values of market actors can be measured only via the intangible concept of marginal utility. The more money an actor possesses, the greater weight his preferences carry in an exchange. The marginal utility of money itself to that actor decreases, and thus the amount of money he will be prepared to pay to satisfy his needs and desires increases. In the context of wide variations in income and wealth, then, money is an imperfect medium since the 'rate of exchange' between needs and preferences and money is not constant.

This is not to say that fair exchanges will only arise if buyer and vendor have *exactly* the same amount of money. What it does mean is that it is important to ensure that income differentials both within and between societies are kept within reasonable limits. In practice, this implies two things. First, wage differentials should periodically be subject to review to ensure that they remain in a reasonable relationship with substantive definitions of fairness.[4] Second, some provision should be made for intervention to ensure that the distribution of scarce but essential goods is fair. The ability of the wealthier individuals in a society to drive the price of scarce goods to levels that exclude the less wealthy from any possibility of buying them can present a serious social problem. This depends on the goods in question, of course. While there is no pressing need to ensure that the price of diamonds remains within the reach of the less wealthy, the prohibitively high price of inner-city housing, caused by nothing more than the buying power of the better off, clearly requires some kind of action. On the global level, the huge income differentials between states and the consequent

---

[4] We suggested above that the direct application of a cultural standard of fairness in price determination will tend to correct any deviation from that standard consequent on imperfect bargaining conditions.

differentials in the price of labour and the purchasing power of consumers mean that opportunities for enormously excessive profit-making by a range of intermediaries are opened up. International trade can only be fair if poorer countries receive the full benefit of their low labour costs.

Workplace Democracy and Trade Unionism

Since the real value of the power medium is the realization of valid collective goals – goals that are in the interest of all of the members of a collectivity – it is rather easier to see how administrative hierarchies can be related to the concept of 'rational authorship'. As Habermas puts it,

> Whereas no agreement among the parties to an exchange is required for them to make a judgment of interests, the question of what lies in the general interest calls for a consensus among the members of a collectivity, no matter whether this consensus is secured in advance by tradition or has first to be brought about by democratic processes of bargaining and reaching understanding. In the latter case, *the connection to consensus formation in language*, backed only by potential reasons, is clear (1987, pp.271-2; emphasis in original).

It is certainly true that in the private organizational context there remains an irreducible core of subjective choice in the decision to comply or not to comply with authority. Nevertheless, the effective realization of the corporation's goals depends not just on the coherence of organization membership with each member's individual aims, values and interests, but on the political-ethical validity of corporate goals and the organizational means by which they are realized. The employment relationship can be thought of as a negotiation between the collective and individual personalities of the employee. The role of the manager is to represent the collective interest of all of the members of the corporation, including the employee himself. Looked at in this way, the rational autonomy of the employee cannot be sustained solely on the basis of his ability to exercise the option of 'exit' – although the possibility of mobility remains vitally important for the existence of fair labour markets. It also requires that the managerial definition of the collective interest is valid. In this respect, we have argued that a technical definition of the validity of an organizational order is not possible. Whereas the validity of the market as a reference point for action can be defined using the technical criteria of perfect competition, no such neat criteria are available for the power system. No science of 'organizational dynamics' can exist that is comparable to economics in its generality and predictive power. The discourse principle therefore has to be applied directly: a valid collective interest can only be defined on the basis of deliberative or discursive forms of democracy. Legitimate employment relationships, and therefore legitimate corporate action, can only exist where management is democratically accountable to all of the members of the corporation.

Just as the procedural guarantee of free trade implies that there should be a limit on disparities in income and wealth, the procedural guarantee of workplace democracy implies that there should be a limit on disparities in the ability of organizational actors to put and have heard the case for or against the collective adoption of certain aims and values, or the case that proposed actions are or are not coherent with norms already adopted. In this respect, managers are at a significant advantage, but this gap could be considerably narrowed simply by taking advantage of the established ability of trade unions to conduct research, construct arguments and train employees to represent themselves and others in debate.

More broadly, the trade union movement has a vital role to play in achieving and supporting democracy in the workplace. Unions are still the largest and best-organized voluntary social/political associations that exist in democratic societies. Perhaps more importantly, they are uniquely placed to influence corporate action since they are the only groups capable of placing limits on that action from within – of preventing socially damaging action from ever taking place. It has long been clear, especially to the unions themselves, that there is little point trying to prevent certain actions at the stage of implementation. Intervention is obviously most effective at the stage at which decisions are taken. External regulation, aside from being politically unfashionable, is clearly less effective than internal.

However, in the context of workplace democracy in which the basic unit of collective identification is the corporation itself, the traditional role of trade unions is put into question. We want to suggest that rather than representing the economic interests of workers, whether conceived as a class or as simply as a group within a particular corporation, the role of unions should be to articulate the non-systemic, social, political and environmental interests of wider society.

The question that immediately arises is whether the trade union movement is sufficiently in touch with wider society to act as its spokesperson. Forty or fifty years ago it may have been possible to argue that the labour movement was reasonably representative of the working class, and thus that it was likely to articulate a set of aims and values which would be recognized as valid by a majority of the population. Today this is clearly not the case. What was once a fairly monolithic 'Left' has fragmented into a large number of political action groups and associations, many of which would identify themselves with the anti-globalization movement rather than with traditional forms of radicalism. While the degree of popular support these groups can claim is difficult to establish, their very existence suggests that they are representative of social and political aims which have not been adequately voiced by the mainstream political parties of the left or the trade union movement.

What this implies is that unions should be acting as the focus of social action coalitions rather than behaving as interest associations. This does not mean that they cannot or should not define and articulate their own social and political aims, or that these aims may not in fact represent a general social interest. Unions have always been more than simply interest associations; to such an extent, indeed, that their behaviour in many political contexts cannot be explained in terms of narrow self-interest.[5]

---

[5] Flanders argued that unions were certainly interest associations, but that union action was also a 'sword of justice'. Similarly, Terry Cradden has argued that the behaviour of the trade union movement in Northern Ireland is simply incomprehensible unless it is recognized that union officers and members have a commitment to certain normative goals, in this case anti-sectarianism, which overrides union self-interest as traditionally understood (Cradden, 1993).

Nonetheless, there is a need for trade unions to be aware of the limits of their capacity to represent the social interest on their own and therefore to extend the opportunities presented by their position within the corporation to other social and political groups.[6]

Conclusion

In Chapter 1, we defined as responsible, and hence legitimate, any corporate action that embodies an acceptable balance between the demands of material reproduction and the political-ethical values of the society or societies in which that action takes place and in which its effects are felt. Attempting a thought experiment in the style of Rawls's 'original position' (Rawls, 1973), we might venture that it seems implausible that any modern society would accept that widespread poverty, environmental degradation and workers' subjection to arbitrary authority is an acceptable price to pay to preserve the freedom of global capitalism's most privileged insiders to drive overpowered cars, buy clothes cheaply and consume so much food that obesity is a serious public health problem.

Clearly, there is no society in which this Faustian bargain has consciously been struck. However, there are many in which both capitalism and its damaging effects are thought to be unavoidable and hence no-one's responsibility. This is not simply an ideological fiction. What we have argued in this book is that the currently dominant market community worldview, which we have also called the corporate theory of society, is such that the social and environmental problems caused by global capitalism are excluded from the corporate agenda. As Habermas would put it, there is a systematic distortion of communication that prevents these non-systemic problems from being articulated in a way that *demands* corporate action in response. Quite simply, there is no possibility that any rational assessment of the legitimacy of corporate action can take place within corporations. The objectivistic conception of economic markets leaves decision-makers with no option but to exclude questions of political and ethical validity from their definition of the environment for corporate action. At the same time, the corporate theory of society would have it that managerial decisions are fully legitimate so long as they are taken in reaction to market imperatives. From the perspective of the market community worldview, the argument that corporations are anything but a force for good appears ridiculous.

While the pluralist worldviews beloved of trade union movements across the world were in the end shown to be cognitively inadequate, they at least had the virtue of guaranteeing that certain non-market goals were placed on the corporate agenda. By conceiving the social power of organized labour as an autonomous part of the system environment, pluralism made the satisfaction of workers' demands as important an

---

[6] Most of the existing cases in which groups other than unions have been involved in bargaining or deliberation alongside corporate interests have occurred in the course of national level policy-making (see Baccaro, 2002). However, as Thomas Kochan recently pointed out in an address to the ILO, it is increasingly the case that successful industrial action involves local coalitions of support as well as just workers and unions (Kochan, 2003).

imperative for management as the satisfaction of the demands of the market. From the action perspective, the justification for trade unionism and collective bargaining was not founded on any kind of 'business case' but on rights to representation and participation derived from the most basic and incontrovertible principles of natural justice.

Unfortunately, the substance of these rights has been lost along with the particular historical form of their implementation. The former is certainly the more serious loss. Indeed, in isolation from the democratic principles on which they were founded, the concrete practical aspects of pluralist approaches to management and industrial relations arguably did more harm than good. An important part of the inadequacy of the pluralist worldviews is the assumption that the employment relationship must always be based on bargained compromises. From the pluralist perspective, there is no possibility of discovering aims, values and interests that are common to all the members of a corporation. There is no single political-ethical self-understanding of the corporation that can be shared by all involved. Rather, there are workers, there are employers and there are bargains between the two. This assumption is ultimately corrosive of relationships within the corporation and damaging to its effectiveness. We also have to recognize the failure of the unions to take proper account of the interests of large classes of workers, most notably women and workers from ethnic minorities, as well as their reluctance to put onto the corporate agenda the kinds of social and environmental problems we discussed above. Although in the 1960s and 1970s much was made of the role of the trade unions in extending democracy into the economic sphere, the scope of collective bargaining – and the interests represented within it – were and remain very narrow.

The assumption that conflict is endemic within corporations only makes sense in the context of the belief that the market exclusively embodies the aims, values and interests of the owners of capital and their agents in management. The great victory of neoliberalism has been to banish this belief in favour of the assumption of the market's normative neutrality, autonomy and objectivity. From this perspective, the legitimacy of corporate action is a function of its technical effectiveness, and technical effectiveness is a function of managerial expertise. The current crisis of managerial and corporate legitimacy provides an opportunity to take a step which is at once backwards and forwards: it is backwards in the sense that legitimate corporate action will once again be defined as that which takes non-market aims and values into account. It is forwards in the sense that these aims and values will be universal rather than those of a working class that arguably no longer exists. We need to believe that the economic system is potentially a positive force for good in itself. What we hope to have shown is that the only obstacle to achieving this is the way we currently interpret the world. If markets are to be a legitimate means to achieve legitimate ends, then they must embody aims, values and interests that every participant agrees are just and worthy of support. Since economic action is what creates and sustains markets, then it too must embody these aims, values and interests. Legitimate corporate action is therefore a reflection of what we think is valid, which is no different from saying that it is a reflection of who we are. Thus, in a very precise sense, the determination of what corporate action is to be is a *political* task. The sooner we recognize that every area of management involves political and ethical choices, and the sooner corporate decision-making structures reflect the right of every member of the corporation to participate on an equal footing in the making of these choices and to hold managers accountable for actions taken in their pursuit, the sooner corporate action will be genuinely legitimate.

Bibliography

Ackroyd, S. (2000), 'Connecting Organisations and Societies: A Realist Analysis of Structures', in S. Ackroyd and S. Fleetwood (eds), *Realist Perspectives on Management and Organisations*, Routledge, London.

Altman, M. (2002), 'Economic Theory and the Challenge of Innovative Work Practices', *Economic and Industrial Democracy*, **23**(2), pp. 271-90.

Andrini, S. (2000), *Max Weber's Sociology of Law as a Turning point of his Methodological Approach*, unpublished paper delivered at the European University Institute, 14 January 2000.

Atkinson, J. (1984), *Manning for Uncertainty – Some Emerging UK Work Patterns*, Institute of Manpower Studies, University of Sussex, Brighton.

Avio, K. (2004), 'A Modest Proposal for Institutional Economics', *Journal of Economic Issues*, **38**(3), pp. 715-45.

Baccaro, L. (2002), *Civil Society Meets the State: A Model of Associational Democracy*, Discussion Paper 138/2002, International Labour Office, Geneva.

Barley, S. and Tolbert, P. (1997), 'Institutionalisation and Structuration: Studying the Links between Action and Institution', *Organization Studies*, **18**(1), pp. 93-117.

Bendell, J. (2004), 'Barricades and Boardrooms: A Contemporary History of the Corporate Accountability Movement', Paper No 13, Technology, Business and Society Programme, UNRISD, Geneva.

Bourdieu, P. (1994), 'Structures, *Habitus* and Practices', in *The Polity Reader in Social Theory*, Polity, Cambridge.

Brecher, J. (1972), *Strike!* Straight Arrow Books, San Francisco.

Burns, T. and Stalker, G. (1961), *The Management of Innovation*, Tavistock Publications, London.

Burrell, G. (1994), 'Modernism, Postmodernism and Organizational Analysis 4: The Contribution of Jürgen Habermas', *Organization Studies*, **15**(1), pp. 1-45.

Burrell, G. and Morgan, G. (1985), *Sociological Paradigms and Organisational Analysis*, Gower, Aldershot.

Cannon, B. (2002), 'The Politics of Demoralization', paper presented at the conference *Demoralization: Morality, Authority and Power*, Cardiff University, 5-6 April 2002.

Centre for Policy Studies (1975), *Why Britain Needs a Social Market Economy*, CPS, London.

Courpasson, D. and Dany, F. (2003), 'Indifference or Obedience? Business Firms as Democratic Hybrids', *Organization Studies*, **24**(8), pp. 1231-60.

Cradden, C. (2004), *Beyond Pluralism: Reconciling the British Industrial Relations Tradition and Habermas's Theory of Communicative Action*, unpublished PhD thesis, European University Institute, Florence.

Cradden, T. (1993), 'Trade Unionism, Social Justice and Religious Discrimination in Northern Ireland', *Industrial and Labor Relations Review*, **46**(3), pp. 480-99.

Crouch, C. (1977), *Class Conflict and the Industrial Relations Crisis: Compromise and Corporatism in the Policies of the British State*, Heinemann Educational, London.

Davies, P. and Freedland, M. (1993), *Labour Legislation and Public Policy*, Clarendon, Oxford.

Du Gay, P., Salaman, J. and Rees, B. (1996), 'The Conduct of Management and the Management of Conduct: Contemporary Managerial Discourse and the Constitution of the 'Competent' Manager', *Journal of Management Studies*, **33**(3), pp. 263-82.

Dunlop, J. (1958), *Industrial Relations Systems*, Holt, New York NY.

Eagleton, T. (1991), *Ideology: An Introduction*, Verso, London.
Fevre, R. (2003), 'Economy and Morality: The End of Economic Sociology', *Proceedings of the European Sociological Association Conference 2003*, European Sociological Association.
Flanders, A. (1975), *Management and Unions*, Faber and Faber, London.
Fox, A. (1966), *Industrial Sociology and Industrial Relations*, HMSO, London.
Fox, A. (1974), *Beyond Contract: Work, Power and Trust Relations*, Faber and Faber, London.
Giddens, A. (1984), *The Constitution of Society: Outline of the Theory of Structuration*, Polity, Cambridge.
Guest, D. (1987), 'HRM and Industrial Relations', *Journal of Management Studies*, **24**(5), pp. 503-22.
Guest, D. (1999), 'Human Resource Management: The Workers' Verdict', *Human Resource Management Journal*, **9**(3), pp. 5-25.
Habermas, J. (1984), *The Theory of Communicative Action Volume 1: Reason and the Rationalization of Society* (trans. T. McCarthy), Polity, Cambridge.
Habermas, J. (1987), *The Theory of Communicative Action Volume 2: Lifeworld and System — A Critique of Functionalist Reason* (trans. T. McCarthy), Polity, Cambridge.
Habermas, J. (1996), *Between Facts and Norms* (trans. W. Rehg), MIT Press, Cambridge MA.
Habermas, J. (1998), *On the Pragmatics of Communication* (ed. M. Cooke), MIT Press, Cambridge MA.
Habermas J. (2005), 'UE: Nouvel Essor ou Paralysie?', *Libération*, 8 June 2005.
Hamilton, P. (1999), 'Persuasion and Industrial Relations: A Case of Argument in a Joint Consultative Committee', *Industrial Relations Journal*, **30**(2), pp. 166-77.
Harvard Business Review (1997), 'Looking Ahead: Implications of the Present', *Harvard Business Review*, **75**(5), pp. 18-19.
Hendry, C. and Pettigrew, A. (1986), 'The Practice of Strategic Human Resource Mangagement', *Personnel Review*, **15**(5), pp. 3-8.
Hirschman, A. (1970), *Exit, Voice and Loyalty: Responses to Decline in Firms, Organizations, and States*, Harvard University Press, Cambridge MA.
Hobsbawm, E. (1962), *The Age of Revolution*, Weidenfeld and Nicolson, London.
Howe, G., Howell, D., Joseph, K. and Prior, J. (1977), *The Right Approach to the Economy: Outline of an Economic Strategy for the Next Conservative Government*, Conservative Central Office, London.
International Labour Organization (1919), *Constitution of the International Labour Organization*, International Labour Office, Geneva.
International Labour Organization Committee of Experts (1989), *Observations 1989*, International Labour Office, Geneva.
Kaufman, B. (2004), *The Global Evolution of Industrial Relations: Events, Ideas and the IIRA*, International Labour Office, Geneva.
Kerr, C. (1964), *Labour and Management in Industrial Society*, Doubleday, Garden City NY.
Kochan, T. (2003), *Efficiency and Equity: The ILO's Role in Building 21st Century Work and Employment Institutions*, paper presented to the Governing Body of the International Labour Organization, March 2003.
Lawrence, P. and Lorsch, J. (1967), *Organization and Environment: Managing Differentiation and Integration*, Division of Research, Graduate School of Business Administration, Harvard University, Boston MA.
Lazonick, W. (2003), 'The Theory of the Market Economy and the Social Foundations of Innovative Enterprise', *Economic and Industrial Democracy*, **24**(1), pp. 9-44.
Legge, K. (1995), *Human Resource Management: Rhetorics and Realities*, Macmillan, London.
Lounsbury, M. and Ventresca, M. (2003), 'The New Structuralism in Organization Theory', *Organization*, **10**(3), pp. 457-80.

Mackay, L. and Torrington, D. (1986), *The Changing Nature of Personnel Management*, IPM, London.

McKinlay, A. and Starkey, K. (1998), *Foucault, Management and Organization Theory: From Panopticon to Technologies of Self*, Sage, London.

Mouzelis, N. (1997), 'Social and System Integration: Lockwood, Habermas, Giddens', *Sociology*, **31**(1), pp. 111-19.

New Economics Foundation (2005), *Transforming Markets*, http://www.neweconomics.org/gen/trans_markets_top.aspx, accessed June 2005.

Newton, T. (1998), 'Theorizing Subjectivity in Organizations: The Failure of Foucauldian Studies?', *Organization Studies*, **19**(3), pp. 415-48.

Newton, T. (1999) 'Power, Subjectivity and British Industrial and Organisational Sociology: The Relevance of the Work of Norbert Elias', *Sociology* **33**(2), pp. 411-40.

O'Reilly, C. and Anderson, J. (1982), 'Personnel/Human Resources Management in the United States: Some Evidence of Change', *IBAR – Irish Business and Administrative Research*, **1**(2), pp. 3-12.

Outhwaite, W. (1994), *Habermas: A Critical Introduction*, Polity, Cambridge.

Parker, M. (2003), 'Ethics, Politics and Organizing', *Organization*, **10**(2), pp. 187-203.

Piore, M. and Sabel, C. (1984), *The Second Industrial Divide: Possibilities for Prosperity*, Basic Books, New York NY.

Pugh, D. and Hickson, D. (1989), *Writers on Organizations*, 4th edn, Penguin, Harmondsworth.

Purcell, J. (1995), 'Corporate Strategy and Its Link with Human Resource Management Strategy', in J. Storey (ed.), *Human Resource Management: A Critical Text*, Routledge, London.

Rawls, J. (1973), *A Theory of Justice*, Oxford University Press, Oxford.

Reed, M. (1997), 'In Praise of Duality and Dualism: Rethinking Agency and Structure in Organizational Analysis', *Organization Studies*, **18**(1), pp. 21-43.

Rorty, R. (1979), *Philosophy and the Mirror of Nature*, Princeton University Press, Princeton NJ.

Rose, M. (1978), *Industrial Behaviour*, Penguin, Harmondsworth.

Sayer, A. (2004), 'Moral Economy', Department of Sociology, Lancaster University, http://www.comp.lancs.ac.uk/sociology/papers/sayer-moral-economy.pdf, accessed April 2005.

Scherer, A. and Palazzo, G. (forthcoming), 'Towards a Political Conception of Corporate Responsibility – Business and Society Seen from a Habermasian Perspective', *Academy of Management Review*.

Sewell, G. and Wilkinson, B. (1992), ''Someone to Watch Over Me': Surveillance, Discipline and the Just-in-Time Labour Process', *Sociology*, **26**(2), pp. 271-89.

Shalev, M. (1992), 'The Resurgence of Labour Quiescence', in M. Regino (ed.), *The Future of Labour Movements*, Sage, London.

Steiner, P. (2001), 'The Sociology of Economic Knowledge', *European Journal of Social Theory*, **4**(4), pp. 443-58.

Stone, N. (1997), 'The Practical Value of Ideas', *Harvard Business Review*, **75**(5), pp. 14-16.

Storey, J. (1992), *Developments in the Management of Human Resources*, Blackwell, Oxford.

Storey, J. (1995), 'Human Resource Management: Still Marching On, or Marching Out?' in J. Storey (ed.), *Human Resource Management: A Critical Text*, Routledge, London.

Tarnas, R. (1996), *The Passion of the Western Mind*, Pimlico, London.

Thompson, J. (1994), 'Ideology and Modern Culture', in *The Polity Reader in Social Theory*, Polity, Cambridge.

Townley, B. (1993), 'Foucault, Power/knowledge and its Relevance for Human Resource Management', *Academy of Management Review*, **18**(3), pp. 518-46.

Trades Union Congress–Labour Party Liaison Committee (1982), *Economic Planning and Industrial Democracy*, Labour Party, London.

Walton, R. and McKersie, R. (1965), *A Behavioral Theory of Labor Negotiations*, McGraw-Hill, New York NY.

Weber, M. (1978), *Economy and Society: An Outline of Interpretive Sociology* (eds G. Roth and C. Wittich), University of California Press, Berkeley CA.

Weber, M. (1992), *The Protestant Ethic and the Spirit of Capitalism* (trans. T. Parsons), London, Routledge.

Zafirovski, M. (1999), 'Unification of Sociological Theory by the Rational Choice Model: Conceiving the Relationship Between Economics and Sociology', *Sociology*, **33**(3), pp. 495-514.

Index

Note: page numbers in italics refer to figures or tables

www.ingramcontent.com/pod-product-compliance
Ingram Content Group UK Ltd.
Pitfield, Milton Keynes, MK11 3LW, UK
UKHW020351010325
455677UK00021B/399